THE ROOTS OF
FOOTBALL HOOLIGANISM

AF

THE ROOTS OF FOOTBALL HOOLIGANISM

An Historical and Sociological Study

ERIC DUNNING
PATRICK MURPHY
JOHN WILLIAMS

University of Leicester

WITHDRAWN

London and New York

First published in 1988 by
Routledge & Kegan Paul Ltd

Reprinted 1989, 1990, 1992
by Routledge
11 New Fetter Lane, London EC4P 4EE
29 West 35th Street, New York, NY 10001

Set in 10 point Melior Roman
by Columns of Reading
and printed in Great Britain
by T.J. Press (Padstow) Ltd,
Padstow, Cornwall

British Library Cataloguing in Publication Data

Dunning, Eric, 1936–
    The roots of football hooliganism: an historical and sociological
    study.
    1. Great Britain. Association football supporters. Anti-social behaviour.
    Social aspects
    I. Title II. Murphy, Patrick, *1943*– III. Williams, John, *1954*–
    306.'483

    ISBN 0-415-03677-1

Contents

Foreword by Lord Aberdare, Chairman, the   vii
    Football Trust
Preface   ix
Introduction: Football hooliganism as a social   1
    phenomenon

1 Understanding football hooliganism: a critical   13
   review of some theories
2 The football fever (1)   32
3 The football fever (2)   54
4 Football hooliganism and the working class before   74
   the First World War
5 'An improving people?'   91
6 'Incorporation' and English football crowds   108
   between the wars
7 'Soccer marches to war'   132
8 From the teds and the skins to the ICF   157
9 The social roots of aggressive masculinity   184
Conclusion   Towards a developmental theory of   217
          football hooliganism
Postscript   Heysel and after   246
          Notes and references   250
          Index   268

Foreword by the Rt Hon
Lord Aberdare, KBE, GCStJ
Chairman of the Football Trust

Football hooliganism is, like education, one of those subjects on which most people consider themselves experts. We all know how to solve the problem, if only *they* (the government, the football authorities, magistrates, parents) would listen. Of course we know how it started, and when, and its causes. Why bother with clever analysis carried out by sociologists?

When Eric Dunning, Patrick Murphy and John Williams started their programmes of research into football crowd violence on behalf of the Football Trust, I heard sceptical comments from several eminent people in the football world. 'Academics never tell us anything we don't know', 'There's nothing new in their reports', and similar remarks greeted their early work. But as time has gone by, their experience and expertise have grown, and the Leicester University Team are now rightly regarded as the country's foremost academic research team in this field.

The Football Trust (and thus its sole funders, the Spotting-the-Ball competition of pools companies Littlewoods, Vernons and Zetters) has contributed substantial sums to Leicester's sociology department for its work in football. For 1985–7 the programme was funded jointly by the Department of the Environment and ourselves. For the next three years from 1987 we have made a contribution of £100,000 to the university, and we look forward to receiving further high-quality reports on the game's problems and the issues they raise.

The principal supporter on the Trust for commissioning

academic research was our first deputy chairman, Sir Norman Chester. Having twice been asked to conduct enquiries into football (once by the government and once by the Football League), Sir Norman was particularly conscious of the lack of research data. It is therefore most fitting that the unit at Leicester University has been officially named 'The Sir Norman Chester Football Research Centre'. He would have liked that, and he would have welcomed the publication of this book. I commend *The Roots of Football Hooliganism* to all students and followers of the game, and privately I dedicate it to Norman Chester's memory.

Preface

This is the second book on football hooliganism based on research we have been conducting since 1978. The first, *Hooligans Abroad: the Behaviour and Control of English Fans in Continental Europe*, was published in 1984.

Although it was published first, *Hooligans Abroad* was actually based on material gathered in the second phase of our project. *The Roots of Football Hooliganism* begins to report the findings of what we consider to be our major research. More particularly, it is an historical study which traces variations in the reported incidence of soccer-crowd disorderliness and football hooliganism from the beginnings of the professional game in the 1870s and 1880s to the present day. Our current research is for *Football Hooliganism: What is to be Done?*, a book on football hooliganism and social policy.

We have tried in the present study to write as far as possible in a manner and style that will make the book accessible to a general readership and not just specialist sociologists. However, since we are attempting here to address the issue of *explanation* systematically and at some length, it has been necessary for us to consider a number of theoretical issues explicitly and in detail. More particularly, in Chapter 1 we look critically at the main popular and academic explanations of football hooliganism that have so far been proposed. In Chapter 9 we subject a number of theories of male aggressiveness to critical scrutiny and construct our own, sociological, alternative. Finally, in the conclusion, we contrast our approach to football hooliganism and working-class youth to that of the Marxist 'subculturalists', and locate our findings and conclusions in the context of Elias's theory of 'civilizing processes'.

In writing *The Roots of Football Hooliganism* we have been helped enormously by a number of friends and colleagues. Joe Maguire deserves special mention for the data from West Midlands newspapers that he gathered when working on his PhD under the supervision of Eric Dunning. Ilya Neustadt, Ivan Waddington and Tim Newburn read through many of our initial drafts, providing numerous helpful comments and critical suggestions. Special thanks are also due to Aubrey Stephenson of the Leicestershire Library Services, to the Central Photographic Unit at Leicester University for their assistance in recording our historical data, and to members of the Leicestershire Probation Service for their help during the early stages of the project. Ian Stuttard of Thames TV provided a number of important insights in the later stages of the book's preparation. Responsibilities for typing were shared by Margaret Milsom, Eve Burns and Val Pheby, without whose patience and good humour no final manuscript would have emerged! Finally, we should like to express our gratitude not only to the Football Trust and the Department of the Environment for their continuing funding but more especially to the Economic and Social Research Council, for whom the research on which this book is based was originally conducted between 1979 and 1982.

Football hooliganism as a social phenomenon

The need for an historical approach

The fundamental thesis of this study is that football hooliganism is a social phenomenon which is deeply rooted in two main ways. It is deeply rooted first because, contrary to popular belief, forms of it have been a frequent accompaniment of association football in this country ever since the 1870s and 1880s, the period when the game emerged in a recognizably modern form. The incidence has varied considerably over time, but our finding is that there has never been a period in the history of modern soccer when spectator disorderliness on a greater or lesser scale has been entirely absent from Britain. The second way in which football hooliganism is deeply rooted relates to the strength of commitment of those who, nowadays at least, engage in it most persistently. For them, it is part of a way of life and they cling to it despite all the preventative measures that the football authorities and the government have tried.

It is with a review of the principal reasons why we adopted an historical approach in our research that we shall begin these introductory remarks on football hooliganism as a social phenomenon. The fact that we approached the problem historically stems, in part, from the sociological perspective to which we adhere, namely the 'sociogenetic' or 'figurational-developmental' approach advanced by Norbert Elias.[1] This lays stress on the need to study long-term processes and recommends in this connection a synthesis of sociology and history. We also wanted to relate the problem of football hooliganism to Elias's theory of 'civilizing processes'. However, our historical approach to football hooliganism had another source as well. We knew prior to embarking on our research that spectator disorderliness had occurred at football matches in this country before the First World War. We were also highly suspicious of the currently popular view that the inter-war years and the years immediately following the Second World War were periods in which the soccer terraces of Britain were totally peaceful places attended solely by good-humoured and well-behaved crowds. Such a view smacks of romanticism, and romanticized versions of the past are always sociologically suspect.[2] However, at that stage our knowledge was rudimentary and we wanted to know more.

Knowledge of the history of football hooliganism is not simply valuable for the light it throws on the past; it is also vital to an adequate understanding of the present-day phenomenon. More particularly, historical analysis is crucial in order to provide a comparative frame of reference which can highlight what, if any, the distinctive features of the contemporary phenomenon really are. It will also shed light on whether, as seems to be widely believed at present, we are living in an age of excessive and escalating violence in and around our football stadia and elsewhere. Furthermore, such an analysis is crucial in order to follow the build-up of football hooliganism to its current dimensions. And finally, an historical analysis is vital in order to ensure that an appropriate conceptual apparatus is employed in constructing an explanation. Many aspects of present-day football hooliganism are different from earlier forms. That is what one would expect given the social changes that have occurred in this country since the 1880s. However, as we shall show, there are common aspects, too, and we want to avoid the mistake of explaining a long-standing social phenomenon with deep historical roots solely by reference to social processes in the recent past.

The roots of contemporary football hooliganism

Let us now turn to the second way in which football
hooliganism is deeply rooted. In a report on football hooliganism published jointly by the Sports Council and the Social
Science Research Council (SSRC) in 1978, the authors
concluded that 'an element of fashion pervades the behaviour
and that like other youth fashions . . . hooliganism may
gradually subside'. Alternatively, they suggested, media
interest, which plays an important part in focusing public
concern upon the problem, may shift elsewhere.[3] Events since
this was written, however, suggest that the authors of the Joint
Report were optimistic, not only regarding football hooliganism
as a form of behaviour but also as a focus for media interest and
public concern. In fact, although things on the soccer front
were relatively quiet between the end of the First World War
and the mid-1950s – as we shall show, that was less true of
Scotland than it was of England – by 1978 football hooliganism had been a firmly established part of the British football
scene for some twenty years or more. Since that time,
moreover, although the annual incidence has waxed and
waned, it has continued to be a focus for public anxiety and
media concern. This anxiety and concern reached a crescendo
with the events at the European Cup Final in Brussels in May
1985.

To say that the football hooliganism of today is deeply
rooted is not to deny that an element of fashion pervades it.
The forms of dress favoured by young football fans over the
last couple of decades provide an example. They have tended
to reflect the changes in youth styles that have occurred more
generally in those years. In that period, the songs and chants
of goal-terrace fans have undergone changes too. So, in some
respects, have the contexts in which football hooligan
encounters take place. In the mid-1960s, football stadia
themselves were the major locations; however, from the late
1960s onwards such encounters took place increasingly
outside them. Indeed, after the mid-1970s, English football
hooligans ceased to ply their trade solely in the domestic
context and became involved more and more in hooligan
activities abroad. Having said this, however, such aspects of

the phenomenon are arguably surface manifestations of something deeper and more enduring, namely the occurrence of violence, vandalism and disorder in and around football stadia or involving travelling fans. Football, of course, is not the only context in which hooligan behaviour occurs but it is a remarkably persistent one. In short, the differences between the phases of youthful misbehaviour that have been evident in a football context since the 1950s and in fact for considerably longer, are probably less significant than either the common characteristics they share or the more slowly-evolving under-lying structures that generate them. It is with these underlying structures that we are principally concerned.

Two further aspects of football hooliganism as we have known it since the 1950s are worthy of special note; namely the levels of public and official anxiety expressed about it, and the escalating demands for 'tougher' action. They, too, show how deeply-rooted a social phenomenon it is. The anxiety over football hooliganism, of course, is understandable. So, to an extent, are the demands for tougher action. Football hooliganism can, in extreme cases, cost lives. Not infrequently, it leads to considerable damage to property inside and outside football stadia. It is also sometimes a threat to football fans and ordinary citizens who are not themselves directly involved. Moreover, it has been one factor in the long-term decline of football-match attendances. However, it is impor-tant to stress in this connection that, despite their escalating 'toughness', few, if any, of the remedial measures tried so far have succeeded in coming to grips with hooliganism. As a result, the anxiety continues.

Indeed, the currently available evidence suggests that, far from curbing the problem, some measures may have contri-buted to its escalation; that is, the public anxiety recurrently generated by widely-publicized football hooligan incidents and the reflex imposition by the authorities of harsher punishments and more stringent controls appear themselves to be part of the total problem, in the sense that they may reinforce it. Although it has helped in many ways to make grounds safer for orderly supporters, the practice of segrega-ting and 'penning' rival fans is a possible case in point. It was widely introduced following the recommendations of the Lang

Report in 1969, but there is reason to believe that, by allocating young rival fans to separate sections of terracing, it may have played a part in enhancing their solidarity and in giving them a sense of proprietorship over the goal-end areas of grounds.[4] Similarly, both segregation and the introduction of more intensive policing *inside* football stadia probably played a part in driving the phenomenon on to the streets outside; that is, into situations where, on the whole, it is more difficult to control. Furthermore, whilst it is probably the case that harsher penalties for football-related offences have deterred some fans from attending matches – such fans, of course, may continue to engage in hooligan behaviour in *non-football* contexts – policies of this kind have clearly failed to eradicate the problem.[5] Finally, the introduction of more sophisticated strategies by the police appears to have contributed to an increase in the sophistication of the tactics and organization of the hooligans; that is, the authorities and the hooligans appear, to a degree, to be locked into a process of mutual reinforcement.

The fact that football hooliganism is more deeply rooted than is often supposed suggests that the current understanding of its 'causes' is deficient. The present study is an attempt to probe these causes – the past and present social roots of football hooliganism – more deeply than has been done so far. More particularly, it is an enquiry into:

1 the social circumstances inside and, more importantly, outside the game within which such behaviour is recurrently generated; and

2 the reasons why its frequency and seriousness vary over time.

But let us enquire into its present-day manifestations a little more deeply.

The present-day manifestations of football hooliganism

As a form of behaviour, the disorderliness that attracts the label 'football hooliganism' is complex and many-sided. In popular usage the label embraces swearing and behaviour which, in other contexts, might be excused as simple 'high spirits' or 'horseplay'. In fact, many of the fans arrested in a football context have only engaged in such minor misdemeanours. In the more serious manifestations, however, the label refers to pitch invasions that appear to be deliberately engineered in order to halt the match and, perhaps most seriously of all, to large-scale fracas between opposing fan-groups and fights with the police that are often violent and destructive. It is with this latter form of the phenomenon that we are principally concerned. More specifically, as we shall show, the evidence suggests that, although many fans are *drawn* into hooligan incidents — fans who did not set out for the match with hooligan intent — the hard core — those who engage most persistently in hooligan behaviour in a football context — view fighting and aggressive behaviour as an integral part of 'going to the match'.

Football-hooligan confrontations take a number of different forms and they can take place in a variety of contexts besides the football ground itself. They can, for example, take the form of hand-to-hand fighting between just two rival supporters or between two small groups of them. Alternatively, they can involve up to several hundred fans on either side. In the most serious incidents weapons are sometimes used. Football-hooligan confrontations can also take the form of aerial bombardments using as ammunition missiles that range from innocuous items to dangerous, even potentially lethal, ones such as darts, metal discs, coins (sometimes with their edges sharpened), broken seats, bricks, slabs of concrete, ball bearings, fireworks, smoke bombs, and, as has happened on one or two occasions, crude incendiary devices.

Missile throwing can take place inside or outside the ground. As a consequence of the policy of segregating rival fans, large-scale fights on the terraces became relatively rare during the 1970s and early 1980s. Small groups of fans, however, still frequently managed to infiltrate the territories of their rivals in order to create a disturbance. Participating in a successful 'invasion' — 'taking' somebody else's 'end' — is a source of great kudos in football-hooligan circles. Since the introduction of segregation, however, the fighting more usually takes place either in the unsegregated seated sections of grounds or before the match, for example in and around town-centre pubs. It also takes place after the match, when the police are trying to keep the rival fans apart and to get the main body of away supporters to the railway or bus station without serious incident. It is then that the largest-scale confrontations tend to occur. These often start with a 'run', that is, with a rush of up to two or three hundred young male fans who charge along the street looking for opposing fans or for a breach in the police defences that will enable them to make contact with their rivals. The 'hard core' hooligans, however – those who are most committed in their desire to engage groups of opposing supporters – often operate apart from the main body and use elaborate tactics in their attempts to outflank the police. If they are successful, what usually takes place is a series of skirmishes scattered over a relatively large area involving young males from either side punching, kicking and chasing each other, dodging in and out of moving traffic and, occasionally, attacking vehicles carrying rival supporters. Confrontations can also take place when groups of rival fans en route to or travelling away from different matches meet accidentally. On occasions, too, football hooligans on their way to or coming back from a game stop off in a different town and fight with local youths who have not been to a football match themselves. In addition, fights also sometimes occur within particular fan-groups, the participants in such cases being drawn, for example, from differing housing estates in the same locality.

This description of some of the main parameters of present-day football hooliganism – before the First World War it seems more usually to have taken the form of attacks on match officials and players of the visiting team – is consistent with the central point we made earlier, namely that the youths and young men involved in the most serious incidents tend to view fighting and confrontations with opposing supporters as an integral part of attending a football match. The songs and chants which form a conspicuous feature of inter-fan-group rivalry, especially inside the stadium, point in the same direction. Although some of the 'hardest' lads regard singing and chanting as 'soft' or 'lacking style' and tend not to get involved in it, during a match the bulk of the rival fan-groups direct their attention as much, and sometimes more, to one another as they do to the match itself, chanting and gesticulating *en masse* as expressions of their opposition. Their songs and chants are in part related to the match but they also have as a recurrent theme challenges to fight, threats of violence towards the opposing fans and boasts about past victories. Each fan-group has its own repertoire of songs and chants, although many of these are local variations on a stock of common themes. Central in this connection is the fact that their lyrics are punctuated with words like 'hate', 'die', 'fight', 'kick', 'surrender', all of which convey images of battle and conquest.[6] Apart from violence, symbolic demasculinization of the rival fans is another recurrent terrace theme; for example, the reference to them and/or the team they support as 'wankers', a charge accompanied by a mass gestural representation of the male masturbatory act. Yet another recurring theme is denigration of the community of the opposing fans.

The media treatment of football hooliganism

Although we have been heavily dependent in our research on the press as a source of information, the media treatment of football hooliganism creates specific difficulties as far as sociological analysis is concerned. This issue is worth singling out, not only on account of the part it plays in focusing public concern upon the problem, but also because, along with the government, the police, the courts, the football authorities, the football clubs and, of course the football hooligans themselves, it constitutes an active ingredient in the phenomenon of football hooliganism considered as a social totality. In particular, press coverage appears to have played a part in both de-escalating the problem of football hooliganism in the inter-war years and in escalating it from the 1960s onwards. In short, whilst it cannot be said that newspapers and the other mass media 'create' problems of this kind, neither are they neutral agents which simply report events.

A common feature of media coverage of hooliganism today is the description of the fans involved as 'animals', 'savages', 'mindless morons', 'lunatics' and 'thugs'; that is, in terms of a rhetoric which dehumanizes them, raises doubts about their sanity or casts them entirely beyond the pale. However, the pre-emptive diagnoses of football hooligans as 'mindless', 'savage' or 'sub-human' – analyses of the sort that are implicit in the majority of popular journalistic responses – actually contribute to perpetuating the problem; that is, they express in an exaggerated manner the social distance that exists between 'ordinary citizens' and 'hooligan fans', and thus help to reinforce the prejudices that each group holds about the other. At the same time, they rule out any possibility of understanding the behaviour of the persons involved and what it is that leads them to act as they do. The crucial point, of course, is that such an understanding is the only possible basis for constructing and implementing rational measures; that is, measures which, because they are derived from observation and analysis and are not solely or mainly an expression of political and other forms of prejudice, will actually stand a chance of resolving the problem.

Understanding is similarly ruled out by another feature typical of the present-day media coverage of football hooliganism – the frequent invocation of a 'conspiracy' involving the National Front. Extreme right-wing groups have for some time been trying, with varying degrees of success, to recruit football hooligans to their cause. However, simple reference to a conspiracy on their part is not a satisfactory explanation. This is because football hooliganism existed for a considerable time before such neo-fascist groups became involved and because one has to explain why football hooligans have come to have characteristics which make them appeal to the extreme right as a likely source of recruits. In its simplicity, reference to an extreme right-wing conspiracy may give intellectual and emotional satisfaction and suggest an easy course of action – 'Ban the National Front' or 'Prevent them from recruiting in a soccer context' – but, to the extent that it is a way of deflecting attention away from the *social roots* of football hooliganism, it makes it seem unnecessary to seek answers to the complex questions that are raised in this connection.

As we have said, media practice in the reporting of problems such as football hooliganism also creates specific difficulties for sociological analysis. This is because media reports help to shape the attitudes and perceptions of politicians and the general public, many of whom have never been to or even near a football ground themselves or who have never encountered football hooliganism directly. More particularly, to the extent that it fixes an understanding of a phenomenon in people's minds, and because of the political implications that it frequently explicitly or implicitly conveys, media reporting tends to increase resistance to sociological diagnosis. It means that one of the first tasks sociologists have to undertake in approaching a problem of this kind is to cut through the accretion of media definitions, public perceptions and popular understandings, which all too frequently are emotionally and politically loaded, based on superficial knowledge and often simply wrong.

The dominant message of most media reports, especially those of the tabloid press, helps to reinforce the public perception of football hooliganism as always and invariably an extremely dangerous affair. In this way, they contribute to the generation of a moral panic; that is, a reaction to a phenomenon that is perceived as constituting a social problem which distorts and exaggerates its dangers, leading to calls for draconian measures to deal with it – measures of a kind which, as we have suggested, appear to have had the unintended consequence of displacing and reinforcing the problem. As such, reporting of this kind often contains elements of self-fulfilling prophecy.

To the degree that they distort events, exaggerate the threat they pose and play a part in the generation of a moral panic, media reports contribute to the difficulties in penetrating to the roots of football hooliganism in order 'to tell it like it is'. That is, they impede the aim of describing, with as little over- – or under- – exaggeration as possible, what goes on in football hooligan encounters and of assessing as accurately as possible the levels and kinds of violence that are actually involved. They help to create an atmosphere in which cool and rational appraisal is difficult, an atmosphere which makes it seem to many people as if factual analysis is used as an apology for violence and vandalism or as a vehicle for underplaying them. We have no wish to deny that football hooligan encounters are often violent, sometimes lethally so.

Our aim is simply to describe and explain them as well as we can without consciously minimizing their seriousness or embroidering upon it. Nor is it our intention to make moral or political judgments, to apportion praise and blame, to condone or to condemn. Rather by taking what Norbert Elias calls 'the detour via detachment', our aim is to contribute to the advance of factual understanding.[7]

Having said this, it is important to acknowledge that we have been heavily dependent for our knowledge of football hooliganism not only on our own direct observations, interviews and surveys, but also on newspaper reports. That is, our critical appraisal of media involvement in the total phenomenon of football hooliganism should not be read as simply dismissive. If one reads them carefully in order to penetrate beneath the surface rhetoric, newspaper reports can often be seen to contain a tolerably accurate account of particular hooligan incidents. Newspapers therefore are sometimes a useful source of *descriptive* information. It is, however, worth pointing out in this connection that a change of reporting styles appears to have occurred, principally in and after the 1950s; a change, particularly in the popular press, in the direction of less factually detailed and more sensationalistic reporting. As will be seen, this change of reporting styles appears to have played a part in the generation of football hooliganism as we know it today.

Despite the events which occurred in Brussels in May 1985 – the outcome of which was exceptional – the level of violence of football hooligan encounters in Britain, although it is excessive in relation to the currently dominant standards, usually falls short of the savagery and mayhem so often conveyed by press reports. This suggests that it is not the level of violence of football hooligan encounters *per se* which is the principal source of public concern about them so much as the interplay between sensationalizing media reports and the fact that the behaviour of football hooligans offends against dominant standards, leads to a lowering of Britain's prestige abroad and thus incurs the wrath of powerful and 'respectable' people.

In conclusion, what is it about the behaviour of football

hooligans that principally causes offence and 'confirms' for members of the general public what are, in many cases, the media exaggerations? Clearly, prime candidates in this regard are the graffiti that they spray on walls, their vandalism, their heavy drinking and swearing, their obscene songs and chants, and, to an extent, their forms of dress. Probably more menacing, however, is the fact that they tend to operate in sizeable groups, pay little regard to certain conventions about behaviour in public places, and, above all, that they seek out fights – which sometimes result in serious injury – and brushes with the law on match days. The sociological problem is to explain why they should behave like this. What is it in the experiences of these fans that makes them want to fight? Why do they fight in groups and choose to fight in public? Why has the game of football come to be one of the favoured contexts for engaging in what is widely seen as their 'anti-social' behaviour but which, as we shall show, is behaviour that is quintessentially 'social' in the sense that it expresses standards that are, though in slowly changing forms, recurrently produced in particular groups, even though these standards bring them into conflict with the standards that are dominant in society at large? Who, precisely, are these groups and why do they tend to behave in ways that regularly bring them into conflict with the authorities and 'respectable' people? These are among the principal questions to which this study is addressed. Before we begin to tackle them, however, it is necessary to explore the popular and academic explanations of football hooliganism that are currently on offer. It is to these explanations that we shall turn in Chapter 1.

CHAPTER 1

Understanding football hooliganism: a critical review of some theories

Introduction

In surveying the explanations of football hooliganism that are currently on offer we shall deal with four popular views first; those that attribute the phenomenon to excessive drinking, violence on the field of play, unemployment, and the so-called 'permissive society'. After that, we shall look at the theories proposed by Marsh, Rosser and Harré,[1] Ian Taylor,[2] and John Clarke.[3]

Popular explanations of football hooliganism: (i) drinking & violence on the field of play

Probably the two explanations of football hooliganism most widely subscribed to at the moment are those that link it, on the one hand, to the excessive consumption of alcohol by fans and, on the other, to the occurrence of violent incidents on the field of play. Both explanations have severe limitations. However, to the extent that they do contain partly valid elements, they need to be set within a wider explanatory framework. Let us elaborate on this.

Drinking cannot be said to be a 'deep' cause of football hooliganism, for the simple reason that not every fan who drinks, even heavily, takes part in hooligan acts. Nor does every hooligan drink. The leaders of present-day hooligan groups such as West Ham's 'Inter City Firm' (ICF) are a case in point. They claim they do not drink before matches because they need to keep a clear head in order to be able to coordinate the activities of their followers.[4] In fact, such fans often fight even without drink, though a stress not only on fighting but also on heavy drinking is integrally involved in the norms of masculinity that are expressed in their behaviour; that is, ability to fight and 'hold one's ale' occupy an important place in their beliefs about what it means to be 'a man'. Similarly, violence within a match is not invariably followed by hooligan incidents. Nor are all hooligan incidents preceded by violence on the field. This is obviously the case, for example, with pre-match confrontations. It follows that it is erroneous to single out factors such as these as the sole or major determinants of hooligan behaviour.

To say this, however, is not to deny the fact that consumption of alcohol by fans and the occurrence of violence on the field of play can sometimes play a part in the production of football hooliganism. Matches involving English sides abroad, for example, seem to be regarded by many fans as occasions for especially heavy bouts of drinking, a fact which probably helps to shape the form of English-inspired football disorders on the continent. However, as we said in the Introduction, the behaviour usually lumped together under the label 'football hooliganism' is complex and many-sided. In order to understand it, one has to distinguish between different levels of causation, more particularly between what one might call the 'triggers' that 'spark' specific incidents, the immediate conditions that facilitate their occurrence, and the underlying, more deeply-rooted, structures that exert an influence on why it is some fans rather than others who engage most regularly in violent and destructive behaviour. Again, this requires elaboration.

Almost everyone who drinks before or during a football match enjoys a release from inhibitions. One of the effects of this may be that the commission of acts – swearing, shouting, aggressive demonstrations, or even simple drunken mishaps – which run counter to currently acceptable standards and which are defined by other members of the football audience and even the police as 'hooligan' is facilitated. It is probably also the case that some males who drink heavily do so, at least in part, to show themselves and others that, in terms of current standards, they are 'men'. Some football fans who drink heavily probably fall into this category; for them, heavy drinking serves on its own as a sufficient demonstration of masculine prowess. This suggests that it is not the consumption of alcohol *per se* that distinguishes fans who fight regularly in a football context from those who do not. Nor is it the consumption of alcohol as an expression of masculinity. Rather, the central distinguishing feature of football hooligan behaviour appears to be the specific *norms of masculinity* that football hooligans adhere to. These lay stress on heavy drinking as a mark of masculinity. It follows that, whilst drinking can facilitate the occurrence of football-hooligan fighting — for example, by helping to generate a sense of camaraderie in the hooligan group and by aiding fans to combat their fear, on the one hand, of being hurt and, on the other, of being apprehended by the police — it cannot be held to constitute a basic underlying cause. In order to penetrate to a deeper level, one has to look at the *norms or standards* that persistent football hooligans express and at the *social structures* within which these norms or standards are produced. Similar considerations apply to what we have called the 'triggers' of football hooligan incidents.

The occurrence of violence on the field of play can act as a trigger for crowd disorderliness at a football match, in the sense of providing a stimulus, signal or pretext for hooligan behaviour. If, for example, one player badly fouls another or is perceived as having done so, missiles may be thrown at him by supporters of the injured player's team. Some of these supporters may even get on to the pitch in order to attack the offender more directly. However, not *all* fans respond in this way. Nor do violent incidents on the field of play *invariably* act as triggers of hooligan behaviour. They are not, moreover, the *only* triggers of disorder; hooligan incidents can also be 'sparked' by refereeing that is perceived to be biased and unfair, by police interventions that are perceived to be injudicious and unnecessarily harsh, or because fans wish to halt a match which their team is losing. More importantly, they can also be triggered by the dynamics of the interaction between the opposing fan-groups. As is shown by the frequency with which incidents occur outside grounds both before and after matches, these dynamics often have only the most tenuous of links with incidents on the field of play. In fact, hooligan incidents can often be traced to a long history of enmity between particular groups of fans. Examples are the traditional rivalries between the supporters of Celtic and Rangers, Arsenal and Tottenham, Newcastle and Sunderland, West Ham and Millwall, Leicester and Nottingham Forest, and Oxford United and Swindon. This suggests that hooliganism is liable to occur at local Derbies (perhaps especially when the fans involved are drawn from separate *locales*), though in recent years a national, indeed international, dimension has been added to what tended in the past to be a much more local phenomenon.

In short, incidents of football hooliganism can be triggered by a whole variety of situational determinants and not just by violence on the field of play. As we have said, moreover, violent incidents in a match are not invariably followed by crowd disorders, and only a comparatively small proportion of the crowd occasionally reacts to them by engaging in hooligan behaviour. It follows that such triggers cannot be held to constitute an underlying cause of football hooliganism, any more than can the heavy consumption of alcohol. Their occurrence may help to determine whether or not hooligan incidents actually take place and, to a more limited extent, who is involved in them. They may also play a part in determining the relative seriousness of incidents. However, they cannot be said to *cause* such incidents in a literal sense. The common denominator, once more, particularly in more serious incidents, seems to be the interest in *fighting* shown by particular groups of fans and the disrespect and hostility which they display towards 'respectable' groups. Accordingly, it is this which has to be explained if one wishes to penetrate beneath the surface conditions and situational determinants of football hooligan behaviour to the social roots which, in a fundamental sense, produce it.

Although they, too, can be shown to be more or less deficient in certain aspects, explanations in terms of permissiveness and unemployment are at least an attempt to come to grips with this issue, that is, with the *social roots* of football hooliganism. It is to these popular explanations that our attention will now be turned. Again, both can be dealt with fairly briefly.

Popular explanations of football hooliganism: (ii) unemployment and permissiveness

As we shall argue later, there appear to be a number of complex and mainly indirect links between unemployment and the social conditions in which the standards expressed by football hooligans are generated. However, it is easy to show that reference to unemployment *on its own* is insufficient as an explanation. Concern about football hooliganism as a *social problem* – as opposed, that is, to something that was purely and simply a football problem – first began to surface in this country in the mid-1950s. It rose significantly around 1966 when the World Cup Finals were staged in England and reached an early peak in 1968 when the skinhead style became popular on the terraces. Thus football hooliganism first began to emerge as a recognized social problem in a period when the level of male youth unemployment was fluctuating around what is, by present standards, a very low level.

It thus seems to be clear that, although there may be complex linkages between them, unemployment cannot be said to be *the* cause of football hooliganism. The fact that many of the 'super-hooligan' groups who have been active in a football context since the early 1980s – for example, the Inter-City Firm of West Ham and the Headhunters of Chelsea – come from London where unemployment is relatively low also points in the same direction. So, too, as we shall show later, does the fact that the majority of football hooligans on whom data are currently available are in employment.

The idea that unemployment *alone* lies in some simple sense at the root of football hooliganism is one that tends to appeal to commentators of the Left. The idea that permissiveness is *the* root cause, however, tends to appeal to devotees of the Right. They, at least, appear to have history on their side for, whilst the current hooligan problem began to emerge in a period of full employment, that same period – the period starting in the 1950s and early 1960s – is the one to which the label 'permissive society' subsequently became attached. In 1985, for example, Norman Tebbit attributed football hooliganism and 'today's outburst of crime and violence' generally to what he called 'the era and attitudes of post-war funk which gave birth to the "permissive" society which, in turn, generated today's violent society.'[5] And writing in 1979 specifically of football hooliganism, Edward Grayson denied that it had any equivalents before the First World War. In the inter-war years, moreover, he argued, despite high unemployment and the growing size of crowds, there is no evidence of crowd violence. By 1977, however, 'a decade of the permissive society had apparently taken effect as the tartan hordes behaved like animals making cages essential at our national stadium'.[6]

This analysis is quite simply wrong. There is ample evidence that crowd violence was a regular occurrence at football matches in this country before the First World War. Moreover, even though its reported incidence declined in England between the wars, it did not die out completely and remained high in Scotland. This suggests that there is more than a strain of romanticism in the thinking of people like Tebbit and Grayson. They have a mythical view of a violence-free past and they compare this mythical construct with what they see as the violence, permissiveness and moral decline of the present. However, since their view of the past lacks an adequate empirical basis, they are led to misjudge the present. They exaggerate what they take its pathologies to be and come up with inadequate or erroneous ideas of their causes. But this is anticipating our central findings. For the moment, it is enough simply to say that it should be clear from what we have written so far that none of the popular explanations of football hooliganism provides an adequate understanding of what produces it. So let us turn to the main academic explanations that are currently on offer.

Academic explanations of football hooliganism

We have singled out the theories of Marsh et al. and Taylor and Clarke because they are the major attempts made so far to develop a rigorous explanation of football hooliganism. All three represent an advance on popular conceptions and, although we are more or less critical of aspects of each of them, we shall incorporate elements of what they say into our own explanation. We shall start this critical discussion with a brief exposition of the theory of Marsh *et al.*

Peter Marsh and the theory of ritualized aggression

As they are depicted by the mass media and widely perceived in popular consciousness, football hooligan encounters are extremely violent and disorderly affairs. According to Marsh and his colleagues, however, such confrontations are in fact 'orderly' and not seriously violent at all, at least if the participants are left alone. Central to the way in which the Oxford researchers reach this conclusion is the distinction they draw between what they call 'real' or 'proper' violence, and 'aggro' or 'ritual aggressive action'. The former consists of 'physical violence directed in an aggressive way towards another human being'. The latter is 'symbolic' or 'metonymic'; that is, it involves the display of weapons but not their use, and sequences of action that are 'aborted' but which would, if carried through, result in injury or death.[7] The ritual character of 'aggro' is held to derive from consensus on a set of rules, the structure of which is inferable from participants' accounts. In the case of football hooligan encounters, the principal elements of this structure are a set of interpretive rules which establish when an attack is appropriate, rules that govern the course and objectives of the fight, and rules that govern its termination.[8] Analysis of the rules obtained from their interviews with hooligans suggests to Marsh *et al.* that the intention of fans who fight is solely to humiliate and secure the submission of their opponents but not to inflict injury on them.

Marsh and his colleagues further contend that football hooliganism is a present-day variant of a phenomenon that is found in all human societies. Indeed, they conclude from the fact that similar phenomena can be observed in a variety of non-human species that 'the orderliness of aggro' may derive 'from a natural process which ethologists refer to as the *ritualization* of aggression'.[9] They leave open the degree to which human aggressiveness can be said to be innate but suggest that there is probably something in the genetic make-up of human beings 'which provides for an aggressive process'.[10]

At the same time, they recognize that the arousal and control of aggression in humans 'would seem to be very much a cultural affair'[11]; that is, although human aggression may have a biological basis, the situations in which it is aroused, the objects towards which it is directed and the manner in which it is controlled are social. According to Marsh *et al.*, the rules they claim to have detected for limiting the violence of football hooligan encounters are, in fact, a learned equivalent of the inborn mechanisms that have been shown by ethologists to limit the destructiveness of aggressive encounters *within* non-human species.[12]

The Oxford researchers concede that the rules governing football hooligan confrontations are often waived in local Derbies, though, in their view, 'rarely . . . to such an extent that serious injuries result'.[13] They also acknowledge that injuries can occur accidentally or because of a failure of a minority of the participants to abide by the rules. However, Marsh and his colleagues claim that such transgressions are usually censured within the group. Far more important as a source of serious injury, according to Marsh *et al.* are the 'distortions' of the 'normal' course of 'aggro' that result from outside intervention, for example, by the police. This is because such interventions break down the delicate consensus on which the ritual, and hence 'orderly', character of 'aggro' is dependent. As Marsh expresses it: 'By trying to eradicate aggro we end up with something far more sinister. Instead of social violence we get non-social violence which manifests itself in random, gratuitous injury.'[14] And again: 'We should learn that aggro poses only an illusory threat when compared with the very different violence which can be inculcated in the wake of reality-changing outraged censure.'[15] Inherent in Marsh's ideas, as one can see, is a definite view of the history of recent attempts to eliminate violence. As a result of such attempts we are witnessing, he suggests, 'a drift from "good" violence into "bad" violence'.[16] 'Men are about as aggressive as they always were, but aggression, as its expression becomes less orderly, has more blood as its consequence.'[17]

Some criticisms of the theory of ritualized aggression

Before we turn to the theories of Taylor and Clarke, let us offer some preliminary criticisms of the theory of Marsh *et al*. In our view, Marsh and his colleagues are rightly critical of the tendency of the mass media to exaggerate the scale and seriousness of football hooligan violence. However, as we shall show, there is a parallel tendency for the media to under-report it. The Oxford group are also right to point to the ritual component of football hooligan encounters. Nevertheless, their reliance on ethology seems to blind them to the fact that, as far as human beings are concerned, it is wrong to conceptualize 'ritual' violence and 'real' violence as mutually exclusive alternatives. Whilst they correctly see that the arousal and control of human aggression are principally mediated socioculturally and hence are primarily based on learning, they apparently fail to grasp the range and complexity of the forms of violent behaviour that are made possible by that fact. Just because football hooligan encounters have a ritual component and are not as seriously violent as wars does not automatically mean that, in all cases, they are as harmless as non-violent rituals. Moreover, what starts out as a harmless aggressive ritual or game can escalate into violence that is serious and destructive, as the history of sports so amply shows.

More seriously, the model of society adhered to by the Oxford group leads them to conceptualize 'order' and 'anarchy' in simple dichotomic terms.[18] On this basis, they take their identification of the sociologically unsurprising fact that football hooligans obey codes of rules as providing confirmation of the 'harmless' character of hooligan behaviour. But, just as 'real' violence and 'ritual' violence cannot be regarded as simple opposites, so the simple demonstration that an activity is governed by rules does not, *ipso facto*, prove it to be non-violent. It is a question of the *kinds* of rules by which it is governed, the *kinds* of activities that are sanctioned and prohibited by these rules, and the *manner* in and *degree* to which the rules are enforced. The model of society adhered to by the Oxford group apparently blinds them to these sociologically self-evident facts.

Again consistently with their model of society, Marsh and his colleagues fail to probe the manner and circumstances in which the rules that are operative in football hooligan encounters are socially constructed. They also fail to come to grips with some of the structural properties of stratified societies that have to be taken into account in an analysis of rules. Thus, although there are in such societies what one might call 'centripetal' processes that work, for example via the mass media and education, on balance in a unifying direction, the life-situations of different strata lead to the emergence of rules, standards and ways of behaving that vary more or less. More particularly, Marsh *et al.* fail to see in this connection that, in such a society, whether or not an act or event is adjudged to be socially problematic and the degree of seriousness attributed to it are partly a function of the context in which it occurs, partly of the groups involved as participants and observers, and partly of the standards employed. This means, of course, that the standards applied by upper- and middle-class observers to working-class events that have not been officially sanctioned, such as the encounters of groups of football hooligans in public places, are likely to be different from those of the participants themselves.

Marsh and his colleagues' picture of football hooligan fighting as a 'harmless ritual' is also bolstered by some strange omissions. More particularly, the approach they adopted led them to neglect the systematic study of situations and forms of hooligan behaviour that are most likely to be at variance with the ritual aggression hypothesis. For example, they failed to confront the phenomenon of missile throwing. It is difficult to conceive of missile attacks as being part of a symbolic display that is intended merely to frighten and produce submission, and that is not informed by the knowledge that the targets might be injured. Nor can such violence be held to be 'metonymic', since the sequence of actions involved is certainly not 'aborted'. Missiles really are thrown. Other aspects of the Oxford group's research also led them to minimize the extent to which serious violence and injury can accompany football 'aggro'. For example, in the direct observation part of their research they used video cameras to record the behaviour of fans during the course of matches; that is, they focused on a segment of the day's events when, as a result of segregation, penning and police control, the conflict between fan-groups tends, in the words of Marsh et al. themselves, 'in the normal course of events . . . [to] be limited to exchanges of insults'.[19] However, they failed to engage in comparably systematic observations of pre-match and post-match encounters; that is, of those vital segments of what is, for hooligan fans, the 'total football occasion' that are least susceptible to police control and when, as a result, such fans enjoy greater freedom to pursue their objectives. The behaviour of fans in such situations conforms more closely to the idea of self-regulation that is implicit in the ritual aggression hypothesis, and it is our observation that it not infrequently involves forms and levels of violence that are more serious than is admitted by Marsh and his colleagues.

Let us now turn to the theories of Taylor and Clarke.

Taylor and Clarke: football, capitalism and the working class

As we have seen, Marsh, Rosser and Harré conceive of serious violence by football fans as a recent phenomenon that results from inept attempts by the authorities to eliminate a specific form of ritualized aggression. Ironically, although Taylor is critical of the historical perspective employed by Marsh et al., his own approach also suffers from the lack of a satisfactory historical framework. In fact, a feature common to the work of Taylor and Clarke is the assumption that the perception by the media, politicians and the general public of the behaviour of sections of British football crowds as posing a serious social problem is almost or entirely new. Similarly, disorderly behaviour by spectators per se is held by them to have occurred in this country on a substantial scale for the first time in the 1960s. Neither of them attempts to hide the occurrence of violence at football matches in Britain in the past. It is simply their contention that present-day football

hooliganism is unprecedented as far as its central characteristics are concerned. This contention, however, is *a priori*,
based neither on systematic historical studies nor on research-
based comparisons of present-day crowd behaviour with its
counterparts in the past. Such a contention is also accompanied by related forms of explanation. More particularly,
Taylor and Clarke provide explanations of football hooliganism that relate it mainly to recent changes either in British
football and/or British society and the British working class.

According to the view expressed by Taylor in 1971, 'there
are empirical differences between the violence in football in
the 1960s and the violence which characterized earlier stages
in the game's development'. 'Most obviously of all,' he wrote,
'the invasion of the playing pitch by the spectators is quite
clearly . . . new.' Following a report by John Arlott, Taylor
dated this practice from 1961 when a mob of boys rushed
across the pitch at Sunderland following the equalizing goal
scored by the local side in their televised sixth-round FA Cup-
tie against Tottenham Hotspur.[20] Taylor attributed this and
other aspects of present-day football hooliganism that he took
to be new to the effects of what he calls the 'bourgeoisification'
and 'internationalization' of the game on a 'subcultural rump'
of unemployed, unemployable and downwardly mobile young
working-class fans.[21] By the term 'bourgeoisification' he was
referring partly to the changes introduced by the football
authorities from the late 1950s onwards in an attempt to
attract a middle-class and 'affluent worker' audience to the
game, and partly to the transformation in the life-chances and
lifestyles of top players that followed the abolition of the
maximum wage in 1961. By the term 'internationalization' he
was referring to the parallel attempt to develop new, more
international, foci of competition for the game. Taylor saw
these proceses as having begun in the 1950s in conjunction
with the emergence of Britain as an affluent society, a process
which made available a wider range of leisure opportunities to
the working class and which, even at that early stage, led
attendances at Football League matches to decline.

As far, specifically, as fans are concerned, Taylor argued
that traditional working-class football supporters are deeply
imbued with what he calls 'soccer consciousness'.[22] An

essential part of this consists in the belief that the game used to be a 'participatory democracy'[23]; that is, according to Taylor, working-class fans believe they had a closer relationship with their clubs in the past and think they were able to exert a greater degree of control over policies and players. However, they were not consulted over the changes associated with 'bourgeoisification' and 'internationalization', and they experience the increasing orientation of the game to a middle-class and 'affluent worker' audience as a form of usurpation. They also resent the fact that many players have adopted a jet-setting, sports-car driving lifestyle and seem to have severed their links with the working class. Football hooliganism arose in this situation, he suggests, as an attempt by young working-class fans – the 'subcultural rump' – to reassert the 'participatory democracy', that is, the forms of control they believe members of their class were able formerly to exert. In short, according to Taylor, football hooliganism is best understood as a working-class 'resistance movement'.[24] 'Bourgeoisification' and 'internationalization', the processes against which this resistance is directed, are also said to explain the concern of the football authorities; football hooliganism is necessarily problematic from their standpoint since it offers a basic challenge to their perception of the game and the way they want it to develop.

Clarke's analysis is not dissimilar to Taylor's. 'Football's history,' he argues, 'has always been marked by violence both on the pitch and off it.' The present-day pattern of fighting between fan-groups, however, is a 'new extension of the traditional forms of spectatorship'.[25] Clarke attributes this new development to the conjuncture in the 1960s between, on the one hand, what he calls the 'professionalization' and 'spectacularization' of the game,[26] and, on the other, changes in the social situation of working-class youth. These changes, as he puts it, 'have had the combined effect of fracturing some of the ties of family and neighbourhood which bound the young and the old together in a particular relationship in pre-war working class life'.[27] Thus, according to Clarke, working-class boys before the Second World War typically went to football with their fathers, uncles, older brothers or neighbours; in that context, their behaviour was subject to relatively effective control. However, when, from the 1960s onwards, they began increasingly to go to matches in the company solely of lads of their own age, control by older relatives and neighbours could no longer operate. At the same time, as a result of 'profession-alization' and 'spectacularization' and of the emphasis on the game as a commodity to be passively consumed, they found themselves, as far as their football involvement was con-cerned, in a context that was growing more and more alien to the culture of their class. The net result was football hooliganism. Centrally involved – and new – in this connec-tion was fighting between rival fan-groups. However, as part of 'the process of making the game safe for its supposed new, quiescent, middle class, family audience', pushing, jostling, crowd surges and swearing – the first three previously accepted as an inevitable consequence of crowd density, the fourth as 'part of the "man's world" of the football subculture' – came to be seen as 'things that only the hooligan fringe does'.[28] In that way, the problem of football hooliganism was perceptually amplified out of proportion to the increase in violence that was actually occurring.

Let us now turn to the more recent writings of Ian Taylor. In 1982 Taylor set out 'to identify errors and misleading elements' in his own work and that of others.[29] He also expanded his analysis in order, as he put it, 'to theorize the significance of soccer violence in Britain . . . as a displacement of the primary relations of the [working] class and the state'.[30] We shall discuss his understanding of recent history first.

Despite referring in a footnote to 'evidence of pitch invasions by fans in both Scotland and England . . immedi-ately after the First World War',[31] Taylor persists in identify-ing the incident in Sunderland in 1961 as representing the start of football hooliganism as a recognized social problem. However, he now stresses the significance of the fact that this incident was *televized*. Nevertheless, it was, he argues, only in the early to middle 1960s that the phenomenon as we know it today really began to emerge. More particularly, in that period 'pitch invasions escalated, on occasion, into attempts to occupy the pitch in order to force the postponement of games, when the supporters' teams were threatened with defeat'.[32]

More aggressive forms of crowd response began to appear around the same time and there was 'increasing evidence of property vandalism prior to and after the game'.[33] However, it was the emergence of the skinheads at the start of the 1968–9 season that signalled the emergence of football hooliganism proper. It was they who introduced 'fighting gangs' and transformed the goal-end terraces into 'territories' over which rival fans did battle.[34]

According to Taylor, the emergence of football hooliganism into its 'mature' or 'skinhead' form – a form that remains with us today despite the virtual disappearance of the skinhead style - is symptomatic of what he calls 'the decomposition of working class spectator sport'. The key to this, he argues, 'lies in the decomposition of the working class itself',[35] This process of 'decomposition', Taylor maintains, encompasses several features of working-class life, 'from the physical character of its neighbourhoods to the dislocations in its long-standing sporting traditions of boxing and street-fighting'.[36] Underlying this at a more fundamental level, however, are 'recent developments in Western capitalist societies (which) seem to be consigning increasing proportions of the working class to the marginal reserve army of labour'.[37] In simpler language, the unity of the working class is breaking down because more of its members are becoming unemployed and because the unemployed are coming to form an 'under-class' looked on with a combination of hostility, contempt and fear by those who remain in employment. According to Taylor, 'There are grounds for believing that the lived experience of this "under-class" is one of material and psychic frustration and resentment at the continued reproduction of inequality of material and existential possibility.'[38] 'Football gangs', he argues, come from this deprived and 'disorganized' under-class, and the growing violence of their behaviour is a response to their 'material and psychic frustration'. In other words, football hooliganism as we know it today is a consequence of rising unemployment, and more particularly of the destruction of the labour market for working-class youth that constitutes an important component in the contemporary 'crisis of capitalism'.

As one can see, Taylor recognizes that the working class is

internally differentiated. He also argues that those sections of it that have managed to retain a precarious foothold in employment are, in a real sense, increasingly threatened by football hooliganism and other manifestations of contemporary youth violence. In Taylor's own words: 'By the end of the 1970s, a mid week evening or Saturday afternoon soccer match was an event which occasioned fear and anxiety *in significant sections of local working class communities themselves.*'[39] Furthermore, 'the violence around soccer was and is an integral and even primary element in the generalized sense of unease and anxiety over crime and violence that has become part of the reality of working class life over the last decade'.[40] In this situation, according to Taylor, the 'respectable', still-employed sections of the working class began to ally themselves with what he calls the 'authoritarian populism' of the 'New Right', and they did so because of the stress on law and order in the New Right's propaganda. 'The appeal of "Thatcherism" to the British working class, in 1979,' Taylor argues, 'rested in part on the promise it implied of some restoration of order to increasingly disorderly and frequently dangerous working class neighbourhoods.'[41] In short, football hooliganism is, in part, a consequence of the rise in youth unemployment that has accompanied the 'current crisis', and in part a consequence of the 'decomposition' of working-class neighbourhoods and working-class sport that has followed from this. However, it is also a symptom of the growing social disorder, especially in working-class communities, that results from these trends. As such, it has played a part in leading more and more working-class people to sympathize with the policies of the New Right and has helped to bring about a situation in which increasingly repressive measures are introduced by the state as a means of 'policing the crisis'.[42]

Some critical comments

Let us now develop some preliminary critical observations on the theories of Taylor and Clarke. Although we have already offered some criticism of their work, we shall also return in this context to the theory of Marsh *et al.*

In our view, Taylor and Clarke, but particularly Taylor in

his recent work, approach the task of understanding the character of football hooliganism more adequately than Marsh and his colleagues. Although we are critical of much of what Taylor and Clarke have written, they do at least approach the problem *sociologically*; that is, they seek to explain the genesis of football hooliganism and the reactions to it in terms of a particular set of social relations. They see the problem as arising out of specific experiences of working-class youths that derive from their occupancy of specific locations in a capitalist society at a specific and, from the standpoint of the variant of Marxist theory that Clarke and Taylor broadly share, highly critical stage in its evolution. Moreover, neither Taylor nor Clarke can be construed as seeking to deny that serious violence is often centrally involved in football hooligan encounters. They would probably agree with Marsh *et al.* regarding the role of the state, officialdom and the police in sometimes escalating the violence of such confrontations, but they would not want to argue that outside interventions are the *sole* source of serious violence and vandalism in this connection. Taylor, indeed, even contends that 'the mass media have underestimated the extent and character of youthful violence in Britain in the late 1970s'. More particularly, he argues, 'there is a general silence in the national press and especially the popular press, towards the nihilism and violence of white, male, working class soccer supporters'.[43] According to Taylor, what he calls 'the blindness' of Marsh *et al.* on this issue arises because 'they lack any sense of the historical specificity of soccer hooliganism . . . the perspective advanced by Marsh is so general (the history of the species) that it is incapable of addressing particular historical moments in their social and political specificity'.[44]

We agree. Marsh *et al.* do have a highly general view of history. It is, moreover, static. Human beings, they seem to believe, especially human males, independently of the kinds of society they live in, the social roles they perform and the experiences they have, have always and everywhere had the same quantity and kinds of aggressiveness. Furthermore, as the Oxford researchers see it, 'aggro' as a means of discharging aggression into relatively harmless channels is historically and geographically universal, too. It is not, for them, a question of social forms that arise, exist for a while, then change and sometimes die – forms which on account of their changeful character tend to vary from society to society and, within the same society, beween different strata and different historical periods. According to their view, moreover, it is only in the recent past that Britain has witnessed a concerted attack which endangers the existence of 'aggro', threatening to transform it into violence of a more dangerous and destructive kind. They are seemingly unaware of the fact that the struggle to abolish the wild and riotous folk antecedents of modern football can be traced back to the fourteenth century.[45] They also seem unaware of the growing number of studies by historians which document the struggles in the seventeenth, eighteenth and nineteenth centuries to 'civilize' popular culture.

As we suggested earlier, however, Taylor and Clarke are not immune from criticism regarding their historical perspective. They seek solely present-centred forms of explanation and, not unlike the advocates of the 'permissive society' thesis, they have in many ways a romanticized view of the past, particularly of the past of the working class. It is, of course, clear that changes in the working class after the Second World War contributed to the decline in the importance of football for some of its members, but this is a long way from Taylor's idea that working-class football fans believe that, before the 1950s, professional clubs were 'participatory democracies', a thesis that is produced with no empirical evidence to support it. Similarly, Taylor and Clarke both tend to exaggerate the past solidarity of the working class and to contrast it with what they view as the more or less totally 'decomposed' and disunited present of that class; in our view, they underplay the resilience of the working class both as far as the maintenance of old forms of solidarity and the development of new ones are concerned. They also seem to see the working class in the 1950s and 1960s as having experienced an almost complete break with the history of their class and in its relations with the rest of society. More importantly for present purposes, neither of these sociologists seems aware of the work recently undertaken by the historians Hutchinson and Vamplew which documents the occurrence of football hooliganism before the First World War and which, accordingly, raises serious doubts about any theory which assumes that the behaviour of British spectators in the past was mainly 'orderly' and 'peaceful'.[46] Our own findings are broadly in accordance with those of the two historians. We shall begin to present them in Chapter 2. For reasons that should by now be clear, we shall start in that context with a discussion of what is currently known about the social composition of crowds before the First World War.

CHAPTER 2

The football fever (1)

Introduction

Soccer dates from 1863, the year when the Football Association was founded. The game started as an exclusive preserve of the upper and middle classes, but after the 1870s, especially following the establishment of the FA Cup Competition in 1871, it spread down the social scale. However, more than a broadening of the social base from which those with an active interest in football were recruited was involved in this process of diffusion. Members of the working class took to the game primarily as spectators and, with the expansion of football as a spectator sport, it began rapidly to evolve as a professional game.

The process of professionalization started in the Midlands and the North. In 1885, in order to forestall the establishment of a breakaway British Football Association by the newly-emerging professional clubs, the FA agreed to accept professionalism as legitimate, though under 'stringent controls'.[1] The Football League, which was destined to become the principal controlling body of the professional game in England, was formed in 1888. Similar leagues were set up in Scotland in 1889 and in Ireland in 1890, whilst 1892 saw the foundation in the North and Midlands of the Football Alliance, the Northern League, the Lancashire League and the Midland League. The Southern League was formed in 1894. Around the same time, too, numerous crowd-pulling amateur and semi-professional clubs and leagues were formed in various parts of the country. In short, as measured by the rapid expansion of soccer as a spectator sport, Britain around the turn of the century was in the grips of a veritable 'football fever'.

Soccer as we know it in Britain today thus evolved into something closely approximating its present form in the comparatively short space of thirty or forty years. Who were the people who attended matches in that period and what sorts of backgrounds did they come from? Were they exclusively working class, or did members of the higher social strata continue to attend? Did women, children and adolescents go to matches and not just adult males? How was the growth of football as a spectator sport perceived by interested parties? Was it largely a peaceful process or was it contested and hence to a degree marked by tension and conflict? Above all, how, according to contemporary reports, did spectators in the late Victorian and Edwardian periods behave, and how reliable are these reports as indicators of what actually went on? And what were the 'causes' of such disorders as were reported? Were they solely or mainly connected with the 'teething troubles' of a newly-evolving professional sport? These are the sorts of issues that we shall address in this and the two subsequent chapters. We shall start by summarizing what is currently known about the size and social composition of football crowds before the First World War.

The size and social composition of football crowds before the First World War

Data on attendances at 'non-league' and amateur football in this period are not available at present, so, in order to gain an idea of how rapidly football expanded as a spectator sport, it is necessary to rely on figures for attendances at FA Cup and Football League matches. During the first eight years of the Cup, public school 'old boy' teams were in the ascendant and the crowd at the final never exceeded 5,000.[2] Match attendances grew but it was not until the 1890s and early 1900s that they really soared. Crowds in excess of 50,000 annually were recorded as attending the finals at the Crystal Palace between 1897 and 1915. Nor was it only the final which attracted spectators in such large numbers. It was estimated that 200,000 people watched the thirty-one ties in the FA Cup competition proper in 1888–9 but, by 1905–6, sixty-three matches attracted an estimated total of 1,200,000.[3] Attendances at Football League matches showed a similar tendency to increase. In the first season of the competition – 1888–9 – a total attendance of 602,000 was recorded. By 1895–6 the figure had increased to 1,900,000 and by 1905–6 no fewer than 5,000,000 people are said to have attended the matches played in the First Division of twenty teams.[4]

Let us now turn to the social composition of these expanding crowds. According to Taylor, 'the establishment of professional football and the moves which led to it were carried out within the working classes'.[5] However, the research of Mason suggests that such an idea is oversimplified. More particularly, on the basis of a survey of the occupations of 740 men who were directors of professional clubs between 1888 and 1915, Mason has shown that the overwhelming majority were clearly middle class. Wholesalers and retailers formed the largest single group, followed by members of the professions, employers in the drinks trade and manufacturers.[6] This suggests that professional soccer may have been developed far more *for* the working class than it was developed *by* them.

Consistent with this, and suggestive of the fact that Taylor's speculation may be more nearly correct regarding the earliest spectators of professional football than it is regarding the earliest directors, is the conclusion reached by Walvin. He traces the expansion of football crowds in the nineteenth century to the Factory Act of 1847 and the gradual institutionalization of the Saturday half-day. But, he argues, this shortening of time spent at work was not evenly distributed, for 'on the whole, it was granted only to industrial workers and did not apply to the armies of clerks, shopkeepers and agricultural workers whose working hours continued to be almost as oppressive as ever'. The result, he concludes, was that 'those sports, notably football, which came to dominate the Saturday lives of working men, tended to be watched by workers in the heavier industries – textiles, metals, engineering, mining, shipping and port industries'.[7]

By taking greater account of the complexities of nineteenth-century social stratification, Hutchinson and Mason are able to reach a more differentiated and in some ways different conclusion. Hutchinson, for example, basing what he writes on an examination of photographs, accident records and the occupational and class imagery used in contemporary descriptions, argues that, in this period, 'the majority of the crowd was from the upper levels of manual working groups: skilled tradesmen and foremen; and the lower levels of white collar workers: clerks and the minor administrators'.[8] Hutchinson's data also suggest that groups even more socially removed from each other than skilled manual workers and white-collar workers mixed together in the late nineteenth-century crowd. (It has to be remembered that many clerical posts at that time carried higher social status than tends to be the case today.[9]) For example, it was argued in the *Scottish Football Annual* for 1880–1 that:

> At a cup-tie or an international match, it is quite a common thing to see the Convenor of an adjacent county, the city magistrate, the Free Kirk minister, the handsome matronly lady standing side by side with the horny-handed mechanic, the office boy, the overgrown schoolboy and the Buchanan Street 'swell'.[10]

That this kind of social mixing was not confined to Scotland is suggested by a description of the crowd that turned up at the Oval in 1890 to watch the Cup Final between Sheffield Wednesday and Blackburn Rovers:

> The greater part of our country visitors were working men – grinders, riveters, polishers, having something to do, anyhow, with the great hardware industries of their native town; but as enthusiastic about football play as any public school-boy. As for the London contingent, they are nearly all young men, and a great majority seem to be football players themselves, and wear the badges of their respective clubs, in one form or another. But our Sheffield friends are also here in full force. They are mostly working men, rugged and hard as their native steel, and in this respect a great contrast to the London crowd, who are nearly all of what is considered superior social standing.[11]

Mason's findings are broadly consistent with those of Hutchinson. He concludes that football spectators in the late

nineteenth and early twentieth centuries were 'skilled workers
in the main, with relatively high wages and relative security of
employment'.[12] He also provides evidence that admission
charges were sometimes raised in order deliberately to prevent
the 'rougher element' from attending. Thus when Renton, a
team from the Glasgow area, were drawn at home to Preston in
the FA Cup of 1887, they decided to hire Hampden Park, the
ground of Queen's Park FC, to play the match. The officials of
the amateur club agreed, but only on condition that the
minimum charge for admission was one shilling, that is, twice
what the Football League three years later decreed should be
the minimum price. The reasoning behind this stipulation,
according to a writer in *Athletic News* was that 'this, it was
thought, would keep out the rougher sections of the masses'.[13]
Hutchinson suggests that similar reasoning may have lain
behind the move of Glasgow Rangers in 1887 'away from the
slum areas of the city centre' to Ibrox.[14]

Mason does not rely simply on contemporary comment for
his picture of crowd composition but presents more direct
evidence as well. In April 1902, part of the terracing at Ibrox
Park collapsed under the weight of the 68,114 spectators
present for a Scotland–England match. There were some 550
casualties and, in the following week, the *Glasgow Herald*
published occupational details on 249 of the injured. From an
analysis of these data, Mason concludes that:

> the vast majority can be labelled skilled as against unskilled, that
> is to say, having received some formal training, often an
> apprenticeship . . . as against no training at all . . . A corollary of
> this is that they were likely to be better paid and more often in
> work than the unskilled or casually employed workman.[15]

Mason also provides corroboration of Hutchinson's finding
that crowds in this period were often socially mixed. For
example, he cites an article in *Athletic News* in 1877 which
said of the 'immense audiences' which turned up to watch
cricket and football at Bramall Lane, Sheffield, that they 'are
not drawn from one class of people. Each grade of society
sends its quota.'[16] Similarly, commenting on a cup-tie crowd
at Preston in 1883, the *Preston Herald* described it as
composed of 'all sorts and conditions of men, rich and poor,

employers and employed'.[17] A similar degree of social
mixture was reported for the crowds at Sunderland in 1890.
More particularly we hear that, at their League match against
Blackburn Rovers in that year, 'all classes of Sunderland
society were represented, from a prominent MP and a coterie
of town councillors down to the humblest gutter-snipe'.[18]
Social mixture of this kind appears to have been characteristic
of Birmingham crowds as well. For example, in January 1883
the local paper, *Saturday Night*, offered the following
categorization of the occupations of those to be found at a
match in the stand: 'the tradesman who has afforded himself a
holiday to witness the doings of his favourite club; the lawyer,
always interested in a stiff fight . . .; the doctor . . .; the
clergyman . . .; and the schoolboy'.[19] Similarly, at an FA Cup
semi-final at Nottingham in 1884, we hear that 'the gentry of
the district turned out in their carriages in large numbers'.[20]
And, when Sheffield FC played Aston Villa on Shrove
Tuesday, again in 1884 – it was a working day – we are told
that it was mainly 'the well-to-do element of the town' who
turned up.[21]

Mason's data suggest that crowds in this period tended to
be mixed not only in social class and age terms but sexually as
well. For example, reporting on the Darwen–Blackburn Rovers
match of 1882, a writer in the *Blackburn Standard* noted that,
'so lovely was the weather that the fair sex of all classes lent
their charming presence to the extent of upwards of a
thousand'.[22] According to the *Preston Herald*, moreover, there
were at the Preston–Upton Park FA cup-tie of 1884: 'Slim-
waisted girls as fresh as daisies, and sprightly and full of
young life and vivacity . . . adorned here and there with bright
flowers, but, whether or not, exercising a wonderful effect
wherever they turn in reviving seedy spirits.'[23]

In fact, it was standard practice until the mid-1880s to
admit women to matches free of charge. From that period on,
growing professionalization and the need to meet mounting
wage bills meant that such a practice could not survive.
However, even after women began to be charged for admission, many League clubs apparently continued to offer them
season tickets at half price.[24] That the introduction of
admission charges for women did not deter them from

attending matches is suggested from what we hear about Leicester Fosse – the precursor of Leicester City FC – in 1889. Thus it is reported that, at one of their Second Division matches at Filbert Street in that year, 'the fair sex' were present 'in every part of the ground'.[25] Similarly, it is reported that, at Villa Park in 1907, while 'you will find no ladies on the unreserved side, there are almost as many ladies [in the reserved stands] as men'.[26] It is also significant that, according to Gibson and Pickford, Newcastle United had a 'Ladies' Outing Club' run by the women themselves as early as 1906.[27]

Although newspaper reports may have underplayed such class tension and conflict as were evident at matches, the fact that football crowds in this period seem to have been characterized by at least a degree of mixture between the classes, the different age groups and the sexes suggests that teams may have served as symbols of the local community and that identification with the team, and hence pride in the community that it symbolized, may have been sufficiently powerful to overcome to an extent the differences of class, sex and age that acted as divisive forces on other occasions. As we shall show, strong local identifications of this kind appear to have played a part of some significance in engendering the forms of crowd disorderliness that were most frequently reported before the First World War. Before we return to the subject of crowd disorderliness, however, it is necessary to enquire whether the extant data, fragmentary and in many ways unsatisfactory though they are, can tell us anything about possible *changes* in the social composition of crowds in that period.

According to Mason, 'it seems likely that as crowds increased in size and watching became less comfortable through the 1890s, the proportion of women in the crowd would fall'.[28] Similarly, he argues, 'as the crowds grew larger from the mid-1880s on, the evidence suggests that they became increasingly working class in composition with the "stand" a bourgeois island in a sea of working class faces'.[29] The evidence for this is slight and mainly anecdotal. Moreover, we are unsure about 'discomfort' as a deterrent to the attendance of women. Where, for example is the evidence that they had been 'comfortable' at matches before or that 'comfort' was one of the *desiderata*, not only of middle-class women but of those from the working class as well? Nevertheless, in our opinion, Mason's conclusion is probably not without substance. More particularly, although one cannot be sure that there was an absolute rather than a simply proportional decline in upper-class, middle-class and female attendance, it would seem likely that the conflict over amateurism and professionalism in this period – which was, in part, an expression of *class conflict* and not simply a conflict over different views of the morality of sport – would have deterred members of the upper and middle classes from attending matches as frequently as they had done in the past. Moreover, the 1890s were a period of mounting class tension. As a result, the mixing of the classes in non-work situations became increasingly problematic, a fact which seems to have contributed to the switch of more and more males from the higher social strata to the more pristine amateur, socially exclusive and, on the whole, more orderly game of Rugby Union. At the same time, the frequent reports of crowd disorderliness (see Chapter 3) are likely to have had a deterrent effect on the attendance, not only of the higher social classes but probably of women as well. In short, in the 1890s and early 1900s, whilst the stands at British soccer grounds probably continued principally to contain members of the upper and middle classes, together with a fair sprinkling of women, the terraces probably became, for the first time, a preserve almost exclusively of males from the working class.

Let us now turn to the way in which the growth of professional football was perceived by interested parties, paying particular attention to the ways in which the conflict over the professionalization of the game may have affected contemporary perceptions of crowd behaviour. We shall look at some examples of positive opinion first.

Professionalization and the perception of crowd behaviour in the late nineteenth and early twentieth centuries

Writing in 1907, William McGregor of Aston Villa, a leading figure in the foundation of the Football League, suggested that football attracted as spectators men from the middle class and the 'respectable' sections of the working class. In fact, he argued that, since the 1880s, an increase in the 'respectability' of the working class. was detectable as far as matters of dress were concerned and that this was attributable directly to the game. More specifically, McGregor claimed, contrary to popular prejudice, 'the lower class have never taken to football':

> My business premises are situated in a thoroughfare, which . . . cuts through some of the worst slums in Birmingham. The inhabitants of these courts do not patronise football. The game is principally supported by the middle classes and the working man, and the latter are more particular in regard to the wearing of clean collars, than they were 25 years ago. When I first came to Birmingham, the lower classes . . . were much more slovenly in their habits than they are today, and football has undoubtedly brightened them appreciably.[30]

On account of his involvement with Aston Villa and the Football League, McGregor had an interest in establishing the 'respectable' credentials of association football and its crowds. However, he was by no means alone in this period in regarding the influence of the game as mainly beneficial. For one thing, it was widely regarded as a means of luring working men away from the temptations of 'the demon drink'. A writer in *Athletic News* in October 1899, for example, argued that 'it tides a man over that most dangerous part of the week-end afternoon when he does not know what to do with himself, and so he goes and gets drunk, or would do but for football'.[31] Similarly, the President of Aston Villa is reported as having said in 1905 that the game had a 'marked tendency' to produce sobriety among the working class.[32] Even such diehard opponents of professionalism as N. L. Jackson, founder of the Corinthians, and H. H. Almond, headmaster of Loretto Academy, the Scottish public school, were of this view. According to Jackson, for example, there were men who, 'if there were no football, would spend their Saturday afternoons in a public house. Well, these are . . . kept outside for an hour or two if they play or go to look on.'[33] And in an article entitled 'Football as a moral agent' which appeared in 1893 and which was, in the main, concerned to point out the *detrimental* effects of spectatorship, Almond argued:

The roads in the neighbourhood of Manchester and Blackburn
would not be crowded with eager pedestrians if the football
matches ceased; but the public houses, and reading rooms, and
young men's institutes and indoor 'shows' of various kinds would
be more crowded and stuffier.[34]

It was not, though, solely people with a direct interest in the
game as headmasters or football administrators who urged the
merits of soccer as a means of countering drunkenness. Giving
evidence to the Royal Commission on the Liquor Licensing
Laws in 1895, the Chief Constable of Liverpool argued that:

> The working man who would formerly have left his work after
> being paid on Saturday and gone home in a leisurely manner, with
> a number of his friends would have stayed at the first public house
> he came to, stood a drink round, gone on to the next house, and
> then one of his friends would have stood a drink round, and so on,
> until they had had a great deal more than was good for them. I
> think now when there is a match on the Everton or Liverpool
> grounds, a great number of working men, the instant they get paid,
> rush off home as quickly as they can, get a wash and a change,
> leave their wages with their wives, and are off to see the football,
> and I think that has led to a great decrease in drunkenness.[35]

Nor was the social control influence of football believed to be
restricted in its effects to reducing the incidence of drunkenness. According to F. E. Smith, later Lord Birkenhead, it acted
as a counter to social unrest and disorder as well.[36]

Implicit in the body of opinion favourable to football is the
fact that the professional game was contested in the years
before the First World War. No one would have thought it
necessary to defend it had it simply been accepted as a matter
of course. Opinion that was unfavourable to the game in that
period took a variety of forms. For example, a person writing
in the *Labour Leader* under the pseudonym 'Gavroche' put forward a view in March 1904 which was similar to that of F. E.
Smith. However, he was arguing from the opposite end of
the political spectrum. More particularly, while Smith extolled
the virtues of professional football as an antidote to indisci-
pline and disorder, 'Gavroche' argued that it was helping to
induce servility in the working class and was thus inimical to
democracy and progress.[37] In an article published in 1906

entitled 'Sport and Drink', Guy Thorne argued against those
who supported football on account of what they took to be its
sobriety-enhancing effects. Contrary to their views, he suggested that:

> Decent people no longer care to attend football. A new class of
> spectators has been created, men who care little or nothing for the
> sport itself, but who use a match as an excuse for drinking . . . If
> you go into the cheaper part of the field at any big match . . . you'll
> see that every other man has a bottle of spirits in his jacket pocket,
> which he drinks at half time . . . Saturday afternoon matches are a
> curse to the home. It is not the few pence that the husbands spend
> for admission . . . but it is the drinking that follows, often
> protracted till late at night.[38]

However, the majority of the opinion hostile to professional
football in this period came from upper- and middle-class
votaries of the old amateur ethos. Typical expression of such
opinion was given by Charles Edwardes in 1892, Ernest Ensor
in 1898 and H. F. Abell in 1903. Each of them was writing for
'gentlemen's' magazines and they were highly critical of what
they variously described as the 'football fever', the 'new
football mania' and the 'football madness'. What they wrote is
revealing, in particular, for what it tells us about how certain
sections of the higher social classes before the First World War
perceived working-class crowds.

What principally concerned Edwards, Ensor and Abell was
the threat they saw posed to football as a *sport* by the rapidly-
developing professional game. The emergence of football as a
spectacle, they held, was destroying it as a form of play. More
particularly, players were no longer playing for their own
enjoyment but in order to please the crowd. Professionalism,
too, was leading to a 'win at all costs' attitude and was
morally bad for players because it deprived them of the need
to do regular work. It was also morally and physically bad for
the crowd. People ought to play themselves and should not
subject themselves to the dangers of over-excitement and the
temptation to smoke, drink, gamble and quarrel that watching
a football match invariably entailed. According to Abell,
indeed, the 'football fever' was a factor contributing centrally
to the physical deterioration which he perceived as occurring

in the working class and was thus a threat to the nation's capability of defending itself.[39]

This was a period of mounting international tension when the supremacy derived by Britain from being the world's first industrial nation was slowly being eroded by the spread of industrialization elsewhere. This sort of fear, then, was probably genuine enough. At a deeper level, however, it is likely that what led Edwardes, Ensor, Abell and others to project their anxieties on to football was the process of democratization that the development of the professional game entailed, more particularly the fact that what had started out as an exclusive preserve of the upper and middle classes now seemed to them to be engulfed by the masses of 'horny handed artisans'. A crucial aspect of this process, as they saw it, was the threat to public order and 'decent' 'respectable' standards of behaviour posed by large assemblies of the working class. According to Edwardes, for example:

> It all depends upon the measure of civilization in your locality whether there is . . . fighting after the match. Of drinking it may be taken for granted that there is abundance . . . The multitude flock to the field in their workaday dirt, and with their workaday adjectives very loose on their tongues. In Lancashire and the Black Country it is really surprising what a number of emphatic and even 'mysterious expletives' may be heard on Saturday afternoons. Some . . are not fit for a lady's ears.[40]

The sentiments of Ensor were not dissimilar. He wrote:

> The effect of League matches and cup ties is thoroughly evil. Men go in thousands, not to study and admire skill and endurance, but to see their team gain two points or pass into the next round. The end, not the means, is everything. Rough play, so long as it escapes punishment from the referee, is one means to the end, and delights the crowd. Nothing but the firmest action by the Association prevents assaults on referees and players. The passions are excited to the highest pitch of human feeling. Referees in former days . . . were often hunted by enraged partisans and were brutally treated, unless protected by the police or the opposite faction . . . The excitement during the match is epidemic, and 20,000 people, torn by emotions of rage and pleasure, roaring condemnation and applause, make an alarming spectacle. Every Saturday in winter more than a million people

are cheering and hooting round the football grounds. That the tendency of it all is towards brutality cannot be doubted by anyone who has seen the behaviour to a stranger who may have played roughly, and to one of the local champions who has 'floored his man'. In the former case groans and hoots make pandemonium; the foulest curses of an artisan's vocabulary are shouted – and the British workman does not swear like a comfit-maker's wife; murder and sudden death seem to be abroad.[41]

Abell even went so far as to invite his readers to consider the faces of those attending a football match and asked rhetorically:

> Are they the faces of men and youths come to enjoy a good fair tussle of the true English sort, and to hope that the best men may win? Not a bit of it! . . . Once at a famous North Country ground I saw and heard half a crowd of 20,000 people turn upon a poor referee who had done something distasteful, while the other half applauded his action. The spiteful yells . . . the torrents of foul abuse . . . the fierce brandishings of sticks and fists, the almost carnivorous expression on the passion-deformed faces, made up a terrible picture of an English crowd taking its pleasure on a Saturday afternoon which I shall never forget . . . Add to this the extra drinking, the quarrelling, and the opportunities offered for gambling encouraged by the universal concern in the game, and we can only shudder at the immorality immediately associated with it.[42]

According to Edwardes, Ensor and Abell, then, the expansion of soccer as a spectator sport and the correlative process of professionalization were accompanied by forms of behaviour that regularly involved loss of self-control and the generation of fever-pitch excitement. 'Vile' language, gambling, fights between spectators and attacks on referees and players were all common accompaniments of matches. However, these authors were all devotees of a pristine amateur ethos and their prejudice against the working class was scarcely concealed. Hence there are doubts concerning the objectivity of their accounts, accounts which, in any case, are contradicted by members of the 'pro-football lobby'. Let us, accordingly, examine the results of our own historical researches. We shall begin by discussing some aspects of the methods that we used.

Some methodological comments

Our historical data were obtained from two principal sources: a study of the Football Association's records; and an analysis of newspaper reports. As far as the FA's records are concerned, we have systematically examined their Minute Books from 1895 to 1959 (with the exception of the years 1902 and 1903, for which the records are missing). The principal newspapers we have looked at are the *Leicester (Daily) Mercury*,[43] the *Birmingham Daily Mail*, the *Birmingham Post* and *The Times*. The *Leicester (Daily) Mercury* was examined from 1894 – the year in which Leicester Fosse gained entry to the Second Division of the Football League – until 1960. Accounts of spectator disorders reported in the two Birmingham papers were recorded for every fifth year from 1880 to 1975. Data from *The Times* were obtained by searching for relevant articles in its index.

As far as the period before the First World War is concerned, incidents of spectator disorderliness known to the FA and reported in the press were recorded *for every level of the game*. Our decision to adopt such a broad focus was based on the fact that the Football League was only formed in 1888 and hence constituted a new organization in the early years with which we are concerned. Thus it did not then enjoy the degree of unequivocal elite status that it does now and, for much of the period between 1880 and 1914, amateur matches and games involving professional, semi-professional and 'shamateur' clubs from outside the Football League often attracted crowds as large as and sometimes larger than matches held under the auspices of what was destined to become the premier organizational focus of the English professional game. As a result, concentration solely on Football League clubs might have led to a distortion of the frequency with which disorder was reported to the FA and in the press, especially as far as the years around the turn of the century were concerned. We also looked for reports of disorderly incidents that occurred in Scotland and for those involving fans travelling to and away from matches, and not simply incidents that took place in the context of football grounds themselves. Finally, we gathered such material as we could on the changing social composition of football crowds and on the occupational and other social characteristics of fans reported as having engaged in disorder.

We shall first present our data in quantitative form, beginning with an analysis of FA data.

The reported incidence of spectator disorderliness before the First World War

The results of our analysis of the FA records for the period 1895–1915 are set forth in Table 2.1 It was constructed in terms of three principal criteria:

1 that the relevant minutes explicitly mention 'spectator misconduct' or use some synonym such as 'misbehaviour';
2 that the alleged offences were found to have occurred[44]; and
3 that the FA took punitive action, e.g. by imposing a fine, ordering a ground to be closed for a stipulated period, or ordering a club to post notices warning its spectators that closure would follow should the misconduct be repeated.

Incidents are recorded in the year of judgment rather than in the year in which they occurred. Finally, if the FA ordered *both* the closing of a ground *and* that warning notices should be posted, the incident is reported under the former category only.

We have presented the data in Table 2.1 on a year-by-year basis since it seems to us that a time-series of this kind is the simplest way of conveying an idea of trends. Although they are subject to different forms of bias, let us now explore what an analysis of newspaper reports can tell us about the incidence of soccer crowd disorderliness before the First World War.

Table 2.2 shows the number of cases of spectator misconduct and disorderliness reported in the *Leicester Daily Mercury* in the years 1894–1914. Like Table 2.1, it is subject to the proviso that the figures for some years are very low, with the result that the apparent trend would have been different if, for example, in the course of our research we missed even a small number of cases. It is also necessary to stress that we are

Table 2.1   Action taken by the FA in an attempt to curb
spectator misconduct and disorderliness (1895–1915)

Year	Closures	Warnings	Other*
1895	9	9	1
1896	14	11	2
1897	9	5	1
1898	1	1	0
1899	4	2	0
1900	2	3	0
1901	0	7	1
1902	—	Records	—
1903	—	missing	—
1904	0	1	1
1905	0	0	1
1906	2	6	0
1907	1	5	0
1908	0	2	0
1909	1	2	0
1910	0	4	0
1911	2	2	0
1912	1	1	0
1913	0	0	0
1914	0	2	0
1915	0	1	0
Totals	40	64	7

Source: FA Minute Books, 1895–1915. (Includes League and Non-League
disturbances.)
* The category 'other' refers to forms of FA action other than closure or
warning, e.g. the banning of a single spectator.

discussing *reported* cases and are not in a position to hazard a
guess about the rate at which disorderliness may have actually
occurred.

In Table 2.3, our figures from the *Leicester Daily Mercury*
are set forth side by side with those from the FA minutes. The
figures in brackets give the numbers of incidents reported in
the *Mercury* which do *not* appear in the FA minutes.

It is clear from the figures in Table 2.3 that spectator
misconduct and disorderliness at football in England in this

Table 2.2   Incidents of spectator misconduct and disorderliness reported in the *Leicester Daily Mercury*, 1894–1914

Year	Leicestershire	Elsewhere in UK	Annual totals
1894	4	2	6
1895	2	5	7
1896	2	2	4
1897	3	3	6
1898	1	6	7
1899	7	8	15
1900	3	5	8
1901	—	6	6
1902	3	5	8
1903	5	3	8
1904	—	8	8
1905	2	3	5
1906	—	7	7
1907	—	5	5
1908	4	8	12
1909	1	2	3
1910	5	9	14
1911	4	5	9
1912	5	3	8
1913	7	3	10
1914	1	2	3
Totals	59	100	159

period was both *under-recorded* in the FA minutes and *under-reported* by the *Mercury*. More particularly, the FA took punitive action in relation to 116 disorderly incidents between 1895 and 1915. In the same period, a total of 137 incidents were reported in the *Mercury*, fifty-five in Leicestershire and eighty-two in the rest of England. However, only three of the Leicestershire incidents reported in the *Mercury* and twelve of the incidents reported by that paper as occurring elsewhere in the country appeared in the FA minutes. Conversely, only fifteen of the incidents recorded in the FA minutes reached the pages of the *Mercury*. The FA was

Table 2.3   Annual incidence of spectator misconduct and disorderliness, 1895–1914, suggested by analysis of the FA Minutes and reports in the *Leicester Daily Mercury*

Year	FA Minutes	Leicester Daily Mercury	Combined annual totals*
1895	19	5(3)	22
1896	27	4(2)	29
1897	15	6(6)	21
1898	2	5(4)	6
1899	6	13(11)	17
1900	5	8(6)	11
1001	8	6(6)	14
1902	Records	7(7)	7
1903	missing	8(8)	8
1904	2	5(5)	7
1905	1	5(5)	6
1906	8	6(4)	12
1907	6	5(3)	9
1908	2	10(10)	12
1909	3	2(2)	5
1910	4	14(13)	17
1911	4	9(9)	13
1912	2	7(6)	8
1913	—	10(10)	10
1914	2	2(2)	4
Totals	116	137(122)	230

* Combined annual totals were arrived at by adding together the figures from the FA Minutes and the additional (bracketed) incidents that were reported in the *Mercury*.

dependent for its knowledge of incidents on referees' reports. Some of these officials evidently reported incidents which were not regarded as noteworthy by the *Mercury*'s reporting staff or of which the latter were unaware or did not regard as their responsibility to report. Similarly, the *Mercury* evidently reported incidents which some referees either did not see or did not regard as worthy of bringing to the FA's attention or which the FA did not regard as warranting official action. This casts doubts on the adequacy of both sources as measures of the 'real' incidence of spectator disorderliness in this period; that is, of the number of disorderly incidents which *actually* occurred. Nevertheless, taking both sources together means that the total number of reported incidents we uncovered for the years 1895–1915 is 238. The figure rises to 254 if the sixteen cases reported by the *Mercury* as occurring in parts of the UK other than England are included (see Table 2.3). It would probably rise even higher if the FA figures for 1902–3 were available.

The figure of 254 is considerably in excess of the numbers of cases – sixty-three and thirteen – reported by Vamplew and Hutchinson. The significance of these differences becomes even greater when account is taken of the fact that our figures are for a twenty-year period whilst theirs are for periods ranging between thirty-five and forty-five years.

So far the data we have presented relate to the numbers of incidents of spectator misconduct and disorderliness acted on by the FA and/or reported in the *Mercury*. They say nothing about the types of misconduct and disorderliness or the relative seriousness of incidents, whether measured by then contemporary standards or those of today. Nor do they tell us about the incidence of disorderliness at different levels of the game and in different parts of the country. Table 2.4 breaks down the fifty-nine cases reported in the *Mercury* as having occurred in Leicestershire between 1894 and 1914 into four categories:

1 verbal misconduct and disorder;
2 pitch invasions, encroachments and demonstrations;
3 physical violence and assault; and
4 ambiguous and unelaborated references, for example, to 'misconduct', 'disorderly proceedings', 'mobbing', etc.

These categories were either explicit or implicit in the *Mercury* reports and have not been arbitrarily imposed by us. There is a small amount of double counting in the table because, for example, pitch invasions were sometimes unambiguously described as having involved assault or attempted assault. However, in order to keep the amount of double

Table 2.4 Types of spectator misconduct and disorderliness reported in the *Leicester Daily Mercury* as occurring at football matches in Leicestershire, 1894–1914

Types of misconduct and disorderliness	Years		
	1894–1900	1901–7	1908–14
1 Verbal misconduct and disorder e.g. use of threatening, or foul and abusive language; barracking; drunk and disorderly behaviour	10	1	8
2 Pitch invasions, encroachments, interference with play, demonstrations	3	1	15
3 Physical violence and assault e.g. missile throwing, assault or attempted assault in the general match-day context on players, match-officials and other fans	8	4	4
4 Ambiguous and unelaborated cases e.g. references to 'misconduct', 'disorderly proceedings', 'mobbing', etc., without clarification of the behaviour involved	4	5	2
Totals	25	11	29
Numbers of incidents included twice	3	0	2

Table 2.5   Football League clubs against which the FA took action, 1895–1914

Year	Club	Action
1895	Derby	Caution
	Arsenal	Closure
	Sheffield Wednesday	Closure
1896	Crewe	Closure
	Loughborough	Caution
1897	Burnley	Caution
	Lincoln	Closure
1899	Gainsborough	Caution
	Sheffield Wednesday	Caution
1900	West Bromwich Albion	Caution
	Stoke	Caution
1905	Port Vale	One spectator banned
1906	Sheffield Wednesday	Closure
	Bradford City	Closure
	Bristol City	Caution
	Middlesbrough	Caution
1907	Notts. County	Closure
	Sunderland	Caution
1908	Oldham	Caution
1909	Bristol City	Caution
1911	Fulham (Reserves)	Caution
	Stockport	Closure
	Lincoln	Closure
1912	Glossop	Caution
1914	Fulham	Caution
	Lincoln	Caution

counting to a minimum, we have not included cases of assault or attempted assault in the 'verbal misconduct and disorder' category, even though, in most cases, the assault or attempted assault involved verbal as well as physical violence.

Table 2.5 reports the Football League clubs against which the FA took action in the years 1895–1914. It gives an idea of how widespread crowd disorderliness was before the First World War, both geographically and in terms of the different levels at which football was played.

Such as they are, our quantitative data thus suggest that misconduct and disorderliness by spectators were regular accompaniments of United Kingdom soccer in the two decades before the First World War. They took a variety of forms and occurred both throughout the country and at various levels of the game. Support is thus provided for contemporary critics of 'the football fever', and doubt is cast on the historical assumptions of sociologists like Taylor and Clarke. Our data also suggest that there are shortcomings in the work of the historians. Thus, although Hutchinson and Vamplew have correctly argued that football in the late Victorian and Edwardian times was far less tranquil than is nowadays widely supposed, their methods did not allow them to gauge what the dimensions of the problem may have been. However, although they are more detailed, the data we have presented so far still do not say very much about the *kinds* of disorderly behaviour that were involved, how many people took part in them or who they were. Nor do they give any indication of the levels of violence and destructiveness of their actions. Accordingly, in Chapter 3, we shall present an analysis of the *qualitative* data we have managed to unearth.

CHAPTER 3

The football fever (2)

Content analysis of reported crowd disorderliness

The discussion in Chapter 2 gives an idea of the forms of disorderly behaviour which occurred at top-level soccer in the two decades immediately before the First World War. Of course, crowd troubles of various kinds can be traced back to the earliest stages in the emergence of the game as a mass spectator sport, that is to the late 1870s and 1880s. The fact that our quantitative data do not go back beyond the 1890s is simply a consequence of our decision to rely on the FA records and to start systematically collecting data from the *Leicester Daily Mercury* from the point – which happened to coincide almost exactly with the date from which the FA's records have been kept – at which Leicester Fosse gained admittance to the Football League.

The discussion in Chapter 2 also gives an idea of the geographical distribution of crowd disorderliness in this period and of its spread among the different levels of the game. Additionally, it provides an indication of the relevant frequencies with which different forms of disorderliness were reported and, more tentatively, of the rates at which they occurred. However, content analysis of the reports of specific cases will give a clearer and richer picture of the kinds of behaviour that were reported to have been actually involved. It will also provide a means for provisionally assessing the relative seriousness of particular incidents and for 'testing' the adequacy of our preliminary quantitative conclusions. Accordingly, in the present chapter we shall take the discussion of football hooliganism in the years before the First World War one step further by citing some representative examples of such reports. These reports go back to the 1880s. This is because, in our study of newspapers other than the Mercury, we searched for incidents of reported crowd disorderliness from the earliest days of the professional game. The reports we shall discuss were chosen from among the much larger number that came to light in the course of our research. They were selected primarily on account of their relevance for the theoretical issues discussed in Chapter 1. We shall start this content analysis with a selection of reports that document 'verbal misconduct and disorder', that is swearing and the use of 'foul and abusive language' by football fans. The use of foul language may not represent such a serious breach of dominant standards as fighting and the destruction of property but it constitutes, even today, an aspect of fan behaviour that is widely believed to form part of the total hooligan phenomenon.

The language of football crowds

Swearing and the use of foul and abusive language have never, of course, been the sole prerogative either of males or the working class. It would however, seem not unreasonable to assume that, in Britain around the turn of the century, working-class males were probably more likely than the members of other groups to swear in public. It is certainly the case that complaints about the language used at football matches regularly surfaced in the British press in the 1890s and early 1900s. Given the fact that working-class males had by that time come to form the majority of those who watched the game, it seems not unlikely that they were the principal targets of such complaints. This suggests that the pronouncements of men like Edwardes, Ensor and Abell on this score were more than simply expressions of prejudice against the working class. Here are one or two examples.

In January 1899 the Leicestershire FA ordered the ground of Loughborough Town FC to be temporarily closed. Up until that year, the club had been a member of the Football League, having been admitted to membership in 1895. The County FA also forbade the Loughborough team to play within a six-mile radius of its ground. Regarding the FA's decision, the *Mercury* reported that 'The Association are determined . . . to stop the use of foul language on the part of spectators at football matches and that referees will receive the full support of the executors.'[1] In response to this report, a supporter wrote to the *Mercury* urging the Loughborough Committee to do 'all they can to keep the game so that no self-respecting man may hesitate to bring either male or female members of his family.'[2] That this sort of sentiment was not confined to the East Midlands is shown by an article published in the *Birmingham Daily Mail* in November 1899. It similarly complained that 'bad language prevents a decent-minded man enjoying the game and prevents a lady attending'.[3] Evidently the present-day attempt to transform football into 'a respectable family game' has been going on for longer than is generally supposed.

Further light on the issue of 'verbal misconduct' is shed by a report which appeared in the *Mercury* in January 1903. It documents what took place when a commission of the national FA met in Leicester to investigate a complaint issued against the spectators of Leicester Fosse and one of the club's directors. The complaint arose out of incidents in the Midland League match played at Filbert Street between Fosse Reserves and Whitwick on 29 November 1902. In that match it seems that one of the Whitwick players shoulder-charged a Fosse player, who fell and broke his collar bone. This apparently incensed sections of the Leicester crowd and one of the Fosse directors. 'Coarse, violent and threatening language was used,' we are told, and 'dangerous missiles' thrown. After deliberating for two hours, the FA Commission ordered Leicester Fosse to post warning notices, suspended the director for one month and fined the club £5. One of the more interesting aspects of their verdict was that 'visiting teams should in future make their entry and exit from the field of play by the subway now used only by the home team'.[4] This suggests that specific features of the professional game, such as the players' tunnel for entering and leaving the pitch, were originally introduced as much in order to protect the players from the crowd as for spectacular reasons.

That railings around the Filbert Street pitch were also originally introduced at least partly for purposes of crowd control is suggested by a *Mercury* report of 1903. Such railings were erected in the summer of that year and a *Mercury* reporter commented at the start of the 1903–4 season that, as a result, 'there will be no impediment of the linesmen by small boys and youths who allow excitement to carry them from their proper place'.[5] This is just one of many indications which suggest, *pace* Clarke, that substantial numbers of young adolescent males may have attended matches on their own in this period. At least it suggests that they were not subjected to the degree of adult control which, in his opinion, was characteristic of British soccer crowds before the 1960s. This example provides a convenient point at which to move on to the subject of crowd 'break-throughs'.

Crowd 'break-throughs'

Crowd break-throughs before the First World War seem to have occurred partly as a consequence of rudimentary facilities for crowd control. However, break-throughs also seem to have occurred partly because of the inability of clubs to gauge the likely size of crowds. Events at the Aston Villa–Preston FA Cup-tie of January 1888 principally illustrate the latter point. They were reported under the rather dramatic heading 'Military Called Out', and John Hutchinson uses this example to warn against 'exaggerated statements made by the press'. We agree with him. Yet, whilst it is clear that no major violence occurred on the occasion of the Villa–Preston match, the evidence is in some respects ambiguous. The match was scheduled to start at 3 p.m. and an unexpectedly large crowd turned up. Queues apparently started to form outside the ground as early as 10 a.m. It was almost full more than an hour before kickoff and at 2.30 p.m. the order was given to close the gates. However, large numbers of people were still trying to gain admission and, according to a writer in *Athletic News* (10 January 1888), 'such threatening demonstrations were made that it would have been sheer madness to have carried the order into execution. The money-takers then continued the issue of tickets, intimating to everyone to whom they handed a ticket that he would not be able to see the game.' Despite this reference to 'threatening demonstrations', little actual violence seems to have occurred inside the ground. A reporter in the *Birmingham Gazette*, for example, claimed that he could not remember having seen 'a more orderly or good-tempered crowd'.[6] Nevertheless, the police were unable to clear the playing area. Mounted reinforcements had to be called for and the club committee telegraphed for assistance to a troop of hussars then stationed nearby. The mounted police apparently failed to turn up until ten minutes before the end of the game but two mounted hussars arrived more promptly and, together with the police already present, were able to clear the pitch. A writer in the *Athletic Journal*, however, described the police on this occasion as a 'pack of idiots', claiming that they 'pushed and kicked about seemingly enjoying the struggle'.[7]

On the occasion of the Aston Villa–Preston Cup-tie in 1888, the police, the military and the club authorities thus managed, between them, to avoid a major riot and to secure completion of the match. However at the Scotland–England match in April 1890 things were different. An unexpectedly large crowd turned up on that occasion, too, and, although the match was again completed, the crowd was described as 'utterly unmanageable' and, at the close, the ground was apparently a wreck. 'The hoardings were torn down,' we are told, 'and the terraces and railings broken up, while the racing track was trampled out of all recognition.'[8] Evidently some kind of panic took place.

Besides invasions of the pitch that appear to have been principally associated with the size and density of the crowd and the relationship of these variables to such things as ground provisions and the facilities and techniques available for social control, there were also in this period numerous examples of pitch invasions that are more directly attributable to what one might describe as 'match-related causes'. An example is provided by the Blackburn–Sheffield Wednesday match of 1898. On that occasion we are told that, when Lofthouse scored for Blackburn, he was 'enveloped by an over-enthusiastic crowd who invaded the pitch to celebrate'. The field was cleared after five minutes owing, it was claimed, to the 'solid endeavours of the police and the military'.[9] That is an example of what can be called a 'celebratory' pitch invasion. Others occurred for rather different reasons. Thus we hear that the Spurs–Aston Villa Cup-tie of 1906 had to be abandoned after spectators 'swarmed onto the turf at the interval . . . and a mob which was said to be violent [formed] in front of the stand'.[10] Similarly, in 1882 'Everton claimed a Liverpool Cup-tie on account of the unruliness of the Bootle supporters who invaded the pitch during play'.[11]

In the case of the Spurs–Aston Villa and Everton–Bootle matches the reports give no clues as to the reasons for the pitch invasion but, in other cases, the motives of the fans are clear. Thus, when the Blackburn Rovers–Sheffield United Cup match was abandoned in January 1900, sections of the crowd rushed on to the pitch to demand their money back. In the process they 'smashed a portion of the barricades to the ground' and peace was only restored with the arrival of extra police.[12] Another pitch invasion, this time at the match between St Mirren Reserves and Glasgow Rangers Reserves in December 1898, was described as 'a disgraceful outburst of rowdyism'. In the subsequent court case, an eighteen-year-old youth described as the ringleader was sentenced to a £3 fine or imprisonment for thirty days.[13]

Attacks on match officials

The type of crowd disorderliness reported most frequently in this period, however, was neither crowd break-throughs nor pitch invasions but attacks on players and match officials. These could take the form either of missile attacks or direct physical assaults, though particular incidents not infrequently involved both forms of aggressive action. Here are some examples of missile attacks. It is reported that, during the Aston Villa–Wolves match in November 1889 one of the Wolves' best players was felled by a piece of clinker thrown from the crowd. According to the report in the *Birmingham Daily Mail* (25 November 1889), some Wolves fans who were close to the incident claimed they had seen 'a red-headed youth shying stones into the field and [that they had] heard a gang of men urge him on'. Wolves were also the away team in

a throwing incident reported to have taken place in 1897.
More particularly, during their match at Burnley in March of
that year, a collier is said to have thrown a stone at a Wolves
player, striking him on the head and inflicting a serious
injury.[14]

Only single individuals seem to have been directly
responsible for the missile-throwing incidents at the two
matches involving Wolves. However, it is reported that during
the FA Cup semi-final between Blackburn Olympic and Notts.
County played at the Aston Lower Grounds in 1884 'the
crowd hooted and chaffed Notts County and . . . even threw
some sods of turf and packets of yellow ochre at some of the
players'. According to the reporter, the hostility of the crowd
was a 'remnant from all the feeling engendered by Cup-ties in
previous seasons between Notts County and Aston Villa'.[15] In
other words, it seems that, even though the West Midlands
side were not playing in this match, the culprits were Villa
fans with a long-standing grievance towards the Nottingham
side. Moreover, the fact that the missiles thrown on this
occasion included packets of yellow ochre would seem to
indicate a degree of premeditation.

Let us turn now to the subject of attacks on referees.
According to an article in the *Birmingham Daily Mail* on 16
September 1889, the attitude towards the referee is 'always
one of bloodthirsty ferocity'. This view is consistent with the
arguments of Edwardes, Ensor and Abell. Certainly, in the
period before the First World War there were numerous
reports of incidents involving the 'baiting' and 'mobbing' of
referees. For example, at the end of the match between
Worksop and Stavely Olympic in December 1889 the referee,
we are told, was hooted and mobbed by a large crowd. Then
he 'received a nasty blow under the jaw and had to be
escorted to the pavilion by the police, who at the finish had to
get him across the fields, two miles out of his way, as the
natives were waiting for him in different parts of the town'.[16]

Incidents of this kind also appear to have been fairly
standard at the time in the newly-born Football League. For
example, in what was described as a 'disgraceful scene' that
took place at the match between Burnley and Blackburn in
February 1890, it seems that:

the referee was mobbed at the close . . . So demonstrative were the spectators that the police could not clear the field. [The referee] had to take refuge under the grandstand and, subsequently, in a neighbouring house. The police force was increased and eventually the referee was hurried into a cab and driven away followed by a howling, stone-throwing mob.[17]

Similar scenes were witnessed at the end of the Wolves–Everton match of September 1895. On this occasion it seems that, as soon as the referee blew his whistle, the crowd rushed at him and he had to be escorted to the press box by a policeman, two Wolves players and some members of the Wolves committee. He was kept there for half an hour but the police were unable to clear the ground. Eventually it was thought safe for him to leave, surrounded by policemen, but:

No sooner had he stepped out of the box than the crowd commenced to hustle the police and generally to behave like uncivilized beings. When the street was reached, it was found that a car was passing along and the police at once rushed to the doors only to find that the vehicle was occupied by a lady who appeared to be considerably alarmed by the attack. Blows were dealt by the police and the way cleared to a cab, in which Mr. Armitt was placed, a policeman either side of him and two in front, completely sheltering him from view. Finding it impossible to get to the referee as affairs stood, a rush was made for the cabman and an attempt was made to pull him out of his box. His coat was torn from his back, and had it not been for the police and a few others, he would have been soon fetched from his seat. However, he drove away amid loud groans and the shower of a few missiles.[18]

A similar incident is reported to have occurred at the Woolwich Arsenal–Burton Wanderers match of January 1895. On this occasion, according to a report in the *Birmingham Daily Mail* (28 January 1895) the referee 'was savagely assaulted by some ruffians . . . indeed, he was so badly assaulted that he did not recover consciousness for some time.'

Attacks on players

Let us turn now to reports of direct attacks on players. One of the earliest examples we have come across of a crowd attacking players is reported to have taken place at the Aston Villa–Preston match of May 1885. At the end of the match, according to a writer in The Birmingham Gazette (11 May 1885):

> roughs . . . congregated round the Preston team . . . [each of whom] came in for their share of ill-treatment. The Preston men, with commendable courage, turned round upon the crowd surrounding them and retaliated. A free fight quickly ensued, during the course of which several aereated water bottles were hurled into the crowd and smashed, regardless of the consequences. The fight lasted but a few minutes, and the Preston team, with the assistance of the Villa men, made their way to the dressing tent. The roughs continued hissing and hooting and it was a considerable time before they left the field despite the efforts of the few constables of the Perry Bar division who were present.

Not dissimilar scenes occurred at the Walsall–Aston Villa match played in October the same year. On that occasion, it seems:

> the display of feeling on the part of the partisans of the respective clubs was more and more marked. About four minutes from time, the crowd invaded the ground and play was put an end to . . . The Villa team had to be protected by the police and the lovers of good order on both sides as they left the ground . . . [Nevertheless, while they were making their get-away] they were followed and pelted with stones, brickends and turf.[19]

At the Sunderland–West Bromwich Albion match of November 1890, the Albion goalkeeper is reported to have been fortunate to have 'narrowly escaped being half lynched by a savage mob'.[20] Again, following the Wolves–Everton match of December 1890, 'a section of the crowd made an ugly rush at the Everton centre and several cowardly blows were dealt him. A police officer had to use his baton freely on the heads of the nearest and most bellicose of the blackguards.'[21] In another incident, when a player temporarily left the field 'to replace his knickers' during the Oldham–Aston Villa Cup-tie of January 1910, it is reported that, as he approached the dressing room, 'he was violently struck in the face by one of the spectators'.[22]

Occasionally one comes across a report that is even more revealing. A case in point is a report of the drawn match between Spurs and Luton Town played in February 1898. The match was apparently marked by excessive roughness and, according to the *Mercury* (4 February 1898):

> When the players came off the field some ill-disposed ruffians, encouraged to a more practical emulation of the well-dressed yelling yahoos in the grand stand, rushed across and struck some of the Luton men. A few blows were freely exchanged, one of the visitors being particularly smart with his 'bunch of fives'. Although this attracted a deal of attention, the referee did not escape, Mr Rudkin receiving a very hostile reception as he left the ground.

The attack on the referee in this case was caused, it seemed, because he disallowed a Tottenham goal. Of greater interest sociologically, however, is the reference in the report to the 'more practical emulation' by 'ill-disposed ruffians' of the 'well-dressed yelling yahoos' in the stand. Although one cannot be certain of the precise class connotations of the labels used, this reference may possibly be an indication of a degree of identification with the local team that was sufficiently strong to lead to a degree of suspension of the sentiments associated with class differences on other, potentially more divisive, occasions.

That attacks by fans on players did not always take place at or in the immediate vicinity of grounds is suggested by a number of reports. For example, although in this case there is no mention of an actual physical assault, we hear that in 1888, when the Aston Villa team arrived in Liverpool for a match, they received a hostile reception from 'an army of young ragamuffins who met them at the station at Everton, hooting and threatening them'.[23] An incident in Leicester in January 1897 is rather more revealing. It seems that, following incidents at the local Derby between Leicester Fosse and Burton Wanderers, one of the Wanderers' players 'was set upon by seven ruffians who beat him with straps and kicked him'.[24] A few hours later he was found lying in the gutter in a Leicester street and conveyed to the station by two Leicester men. Once there it was discovered that:

> His clothing was covered with blood and dirt . . . [He had] nasty
> wounds on the temples, head, ear and jaw; while his top lip was
> also badly cut as if by a kick. Judging by his appearance, he had
> lost a large quantity of blood and he had no sooner been got into
> the saloon than he became unconscious.

Later, the *Mercury* made contact with a witness to these
events who described the attackers as a 'gang'. More information on 'football gangs' comes from a letter published in the
Birmingham Daily Mail on 26 November 1900. It appeared
under the headline 'Bad Language at the Hawthorns' and
referred to crowd behaviour at West Bromwich Albion:

> I think it would be wise for the Albion Directors to see that in
> future a couple of policemen are stationed in the sixpenny
> stand . . . On Saturday last there were half a dozen of the 'Peaky'
> fraternity from Birmingham . . . in the stand and their disgusting
> language and shouting thoroughly spoiled the spectators' enjoy-
> ment. The Directors should have these fellows kept under proper
> control, or not admitted at all, for ladies (of whom there were a
> fair number) cannot be expected to come and be compelled to
> listen to such filthy talk.

As Pearson has shown, the word 'hooligan' made an abrupt
entrance into English common usage in the summer of 1898
'as a term to describe gangs of rowdy youths'.[25] However,
'hooligans' was not the only term used to describe such
'gangs'. In Manchester they were 'Scuttlers' and in Birmingham 'Peaky Blinders' or 'Sloggers'.[26] The foregoing story about
the 'Peaky fraternity' does not refer to physical violence but it
does suggest the possibility that 'gangs' of this kind may have
been involved in at least some of the football-related disorder
reported in the late Victorian and Edwardian periods.

Vandalism

The aggression of football fans at this time was, of course, not
directed solely at human targets but also against the physical
property and equipment of clubs. In such cases, the vandalism
usually resulted from frustration caused because a game was
either not played at all or took place under conditions
different from those which the crowd had been led to expect.

Such behaviour was clearly not mindless but an indirect attack on the agents adjudged responsible for producing the frustration. For example, when the Everton–Small Heath game in 1895 was terminated prematurely, the crowd 'demanded the return of their money, chaffed the Everton directors without mercy, and finally smashed the face of the clock and the windows of the Committee room. A vanload of police arrived, and the ground was cleared with some difficulty.'[27] According to a report in the *Mercury* (25 December 1890), an even more vigorous reaction was triggered by the abandonment of the Blackburn Rovers–Darwen match on Christmas Day 1890. More particularly, it was reported that:

> Owing to the slippery condition of the ground and the fact that a match was to be played with the Wolverhampton Wanderers, the Rovers sent out their second team to meet Darwen. This exasperated the Darwen team and their supporters, and when it was announced that the match was abandoned the mob became unmanageable, assaulted the officials and others and did a great deal of damage to the grandstand and the dressing room.

Ten years later the Blackburn Rovers ground was again the scene of such protest-oriented vandalism; when their Cup-tie against Sheffield United in January 1900 was abandoned, it is reported that the crowd rushed on to the pitch to demand their money back, in the process smashing 'a portion of the barricades to the ground'. Such was the crowd's fury that order was only restored with the arrival of extra police.[28] However, this, and all the other disorders reported before the First World War that we have come across, pales before events at the Scottish Cup Final between Rangers and Celtic in April 1909. According to Hutchinson, a description of the riot which occurred on that occasion 'ought to be compulsory reading for all those who decry standards of behaviour today'.[29] We agree.

The *Mercury's* account appeared under the headline 'Football Riot at Glasgow'. The rioting, it seems, was occasioned by the fact that, for the second Saturday in succession, the match had ended in a draw. No provision had been made for extra time and, when the teams left the field at the end of the match, thousands of people:

broke into the playing pitch, and proceeded to tear up the goal-posts. Mounted constables arrived, and in the melee that followed, more than 50 persons were injured. When the barricading was broken down, the rioters piled the debris, poured whisky over it, and set the wood ablaze. The flames spread to the pay-boxes, which were only some 20 yards from a large tenement of dwellings. Great alarm prevailed, particularly when the firemen were attacked by the mob, and prevented from extinguishing the fire, for no sooner had they run out the hose than the crowd jumped on it, and, cutting it with knives and stones, rendered the efforts of the firemen useless. The woodwork of the boxes was completely destroyed, leaving only the corrugated iron roofs and lining, which were bent and twisted into fantastic shapes. The club's heavy roller was torn from its fittings, and maliciously dragged across the turf.

Fresh detachments of police and firemen arrived, and a series of melees followed, during which injuries, more or less serious, were inflicted on some 50 or 60 persons.

Stones and bottles were freely thrown, while at least two persons were treated for stab wounds. Over a score of constables were included among the injured, as well as several firemen . . .

The mob repeatedly rescued the prisoners from the police, and ultimately it was deemed advisable to clear the field without taking the rioters into custody. For almost two hours the park was a scene of violence, unparalleled in the history of sport in Scotland . . . The damage to the enclosure amounts to hundreds of pounds . . . Official reports . . . show that fully 70 constables were required to cope with the mob, while nearly 70 firemen, with six motors and engines were on the scene.[30]

A postscript in the same edition of the *Mercury* put the number of injured at 'fully 100 persons' and described how one of them, a police constable, had been 'stabbed in the face and rendered unconscious'. A report in the *Glasgow Herald* corroborated the *Mercury*'s account but referred in addition to 'the destruction of virtually every street-lamp around Hampden', thus showing that the violence spread outside the ground.[31] As we have said, the rioting seems to have been triggered by a failure on the part of the SFA to make arrangements for extra time. Consequently the violence was directed principally against official targets, for example against property in and around Hampden Park, the police, and members of the fire brigade and their equipment. There is no mention in either the *Mercury* or the *Glasgow Herald* of fights between Celtic and Rangers fans. However, the references to stab-wounds and the fact that fire-hoses were slashed with knives show that some fans went to the match armed.

Fighting between fan groups

Let us turn our attention now to the subject of fighting between groups of rival fans. Although there was no mention of fighting between rival fan-groups in the account of the rioting that took place at Hampden Park in 1909, there is plenty of evidence which suggests that such fights were by no means uncommon before the First World War. An example is provided by the report of the semi-final for the Renfrewshire Cup, played between Greenock Morton and Port Glasgow, which took place at Greenock in April 1899. According to the *Mercury* (10 April 1899):

> The latter [Port Glasgow] were the favourites, and when they began to lose goals their partisans became turbulent, and several free fights took place. At the close of the match, Morton having won, the Port Glasgow followers broke into the enclosure, and assaulted the Morton players, and also the police on duty on the ground. In a few minutes the row assumed the proportions of a riot, and extra police were telephoned for. On the arrival of the mounted police the constables were forced to use their batons freely, but the riot continued for over two hours. Nineteen constables were injured, some of them seriously. A number of spectators were also injured. The east end of Greenock was in a state of panic for some time, and when the riot was at its height, shopkeepers closed their places of business. The police arrested four ringleaders on Saturday, and five others yesterday. All the prisoners belong to Port Glasgow.

Spectator disorders in England in this period do not seem to have reached such heights of violence. Nevertheless, they occurred regularly enough. We hear, for example, that at the Norwich–Chelsea match of 1913, 'the East Anglian supporters went on a rampage outside the ground, throwing missiles and damaging property'.[32] Fist fights between rival groups of supporters also quite frequently took place. For example, it is reported that at the Aston Villa–Notts. County match of October 1900:

> a section of the spectators varied the proceedings by engaging in a free fight . . . Matters were assuming serious proportions among the crowd and policemen blew their whistles noisily. Then was seen the spectacle of a football match in progress and three stalwart constables racing across the ground. The unruly folks who had leaped the barriers scuttled. But one less active than the rest was captured and he went back over the palings in a very sudden if undignified manner, the constable acting as assistant, while the crowd cheered.[33]

This report is interesting because it suggests that the policy of the police at football matches in the late nineteenth and early twentieth centuries was not to eject or arrest fans who invaded the pitch and fought but simply to return them to their places and prevent them from interfering with play.

Further testimony regarding fighting between rival fans comes from the *Mercury's* report of the match between Leicester Fosse and Lincoln City on 7 April 1900. According to the report, when fighting between rival supporters broke out, the game 'now seemed to be quite a secondary consideration with an unselect few of the spectators on the popular side and a Lincoln v Leicester proceeded on two occasions in the shape of free fights'. Fighting between rival fans also seems to have broken out at the Derby match between West Ham and Millwall at Upton Park in September 1906. According to the report in the *East Ham Echo* (21 September 1906):

> From the very first kick of the ball it was seen that there was likely to be some trouble, but the storm burst when Dean and Jarvis came into collision . . . This aroused considerable excitement among the spectators . . . The crowds on the bank having caught the fever, free fights were plentiful.

Disorderliness outside and away from grounds

Reports of the kind we have been discussing so far in this chapter appear to confirm the impression given by the analysis in Chapter 1, namely that misconduct and disorderliness by football spectators in the late nineteenth and early twentieth centuries took place principally at football grounds themselves, only occasionally spreading outside into the immediate vicinity. Such reports also suggest that attacks on referees and players were the most frequent forms of physically violent football-related disorder in that period. However, there are reasons for believing that the impressions thus given of the relative frequency of the different types and locations of violent disorder connected with football in the years before the First World War may be to some extent an artefact of the manner in which the reports on which we are reliant were reproduced. Hence, they may not be a reliable guide to the totality of what went on. Let us elaborate briefly on this.

The FA were dependent for their knowledge of disorderly incidents, then as now, on referees' reports. Of course, they probably became acquainted with other incidents through the press but it was only on the basis of referees' reports that they were empowered to act, and the indications are that these officials only reported — and were only required by the FA to report — incidents which threatened their persons, the players or the playing of a match. Similarly, reporters went to football to report on the game and, inside the ground, may only have been interested in incidents which disrupted play.

There are, however, three sources of evidence which suggest that fighting between fan-groups and what we would nowadays call vandalism by football supporters away from the ground may have been more common before the First World War than the predominantly available data seem to imply; namely, letters to the press, reports of court proceedings, and encounters witnessed by reporters who just happened to be present. Here are some examples.

In February 1902 the accidental death at Birmingham's New Street Station of a 'football excursionist' from Derby — he had been to watch the Cup-tie between Derby County and Aston Villa — provoked a man to write to the *Birmingham Post* concerning what he saw as some of the undesirable effects of 'the football fever'. As a witness to the night's events, he said, he had been shocked by 'the immense crowds of drunken people (men and women) who were promenading the streets, singing and shouting'. He could not help, he claimed, 'expressing to a friend that England was becoming more drunk every day'. Elaborating on the scene, he said that he had seen:

> crowds of young girls, about 17 years of age, and also of youths who were in such a state as to be a disgrace to a respectable citizen. Some were rolling about the pavement utterly helpless and seemed to have hardly the strength to do anything but curse, swear and endeavour to sing . . .
>
> New Street . . . and particularly the station, was one huge pandemonium of shouting, blowing whistles and other noisy instruments. Certainly, at a low estimate, 30 per cent of the men were drunk . . . Gentle manners and chivalry were conspicuous by their absence. Police were helpless or powerless. Is all this necessary in the true interest of sport?[34]

That scenes of this type were not atypical of the behaviour of football fans before the First World War is suggested by a report published in March 1894. It described a visit to Birmingham of Blackburn Rovers fans:

> For unrestricted rowdy conduct the Lancashire football follower will require a lot of beating, if the specimens from Blackburn who favoured Birmingham with a visit last Saturday are typical of the bulk. A tremendous number of excursionists from Blackburn and district arrived in Birmingham early on Saturday morning, and long before the business establishments were open indulged in horseplay and shouting in the principal thoroughfare. Several of them, for disorderly conduct in the Bull Ring, were compelled to pay a visit to the Moor Street cells. I am told that some of the saloon parties brought with them large quantities of beer, which they consumed *en route*, and one band, immediately on arrival, entered a public house, where the leader gave an order for '60 glasses of beer'. At the match at Perry Barr the disorderly nature of the 'Lancashire lads' was apparent. The day passed by and the Rovers were defeated but this in no way damped the exuberant spirits of the visitors who made the centre of the city 'hum'.[35]

A letter to the *Mercury* on 18 December 1900, following the visit to Leicester of Woolwich Arsenal, shows that behaviour of this kind was not solely confined to fans from the Midlands and the North. Complaining of the visitors from London, the writer claimed that:

> We noticed early in the day a lot of these sportsmen already dead to the football world. But, at night, the conduct of these people was

most reprehensible, and our local hooligans must have learned a
further lesson in the art. But there is enough drunkenness, filthy
language and disorderly conduct without strangers filling the
number.

The references in these accounts to drunkenness and the use
of 'filthy language' are clear enough but those to 'horseplay',
'rowdy' and 'disorderly' conduct are less so. Fortunately, not
all accounts of the behaviour of fans on their way to and from
matches in this period are similarly ambiguous. There is
ample evidence that the behaviour of football supporters was
often perceived as menacing by people who lived in the
vicinity of grounds or who simply happened to have had a
chance encounter with travelling fans. In 1890, for example, a
correspondent wrote to the *Handsworth Herald* (8 November
1890) complaining that 'residents are in constant terror on big
days. Some day damage to life and property will be done
unless means are taken to keep down the boisterous multitude
who visit us on a Saturday. We want more police on these
days.'

That the perception of football fans as threatening was not
confined to Birmingham is shown by an account of spectator
behaviour at a match played in Shrewsbury on Easter Monday
1899:

> There were many thousands present at Shrewsbury on Easter
> Monday, and the concomitants of betting, drinking, and bad
> language were fearful to contemplate, while the shouting and
> horseplay on the highway were a terror to peaceful residents
> passing homewards.[36]

The following item about a match between Walsall and
Kidderminster appears in the minutes of the FA Emergency
Committee for 30 October–18 November 1908:

> The police force engaged was not sufficient for such a match,
> particularly seeing that feeling ran high when the Walsall team
> visited Kidderminster about a week previously. More strength
> must be engaged for such matches, and the police must be
> instructed to prevent tumult or hostile action in the public roads
> as well as inside the ground.

The fact that the FA was sufficiently alarmed to demand that extra police should be engaged specifically in order to control fans *outside grounds* suggests that disorderly behaviour by fans in that context may have been a fairly widespread and regular occurrence.

That the police in this period sometimes found themselves at the painful end of an attack by 'disorderly fans' is shown by a number of examples. We hear from Birmingham in March 1890 that, when a police constable spoke to a young man who was 'creating a disturbance' along with several companions, the man:

> used a disgusting expression and kicked the officer. Prisoner's defence was that he had been to the football match at Perry Barr and taking three glasses of beer to celebrate the victory, the drink overcame him and he did not know what he was doing. A fine of 10s. and costs was imposed.[37]

On another occasion, a disturbance following a football match led to the arrest of three young men for the wilful murder of a police sergeant and the attempted murder of a constable. Their trial took place at the Gloucester Assizes in February 1896, and they received sentences ranging between one and twelve months' imprisonment.[38]

Although the *Mercury*'s account of the case at the Gloucester Assizes refers unambiguously to a form of football-related violence in the sense that the three accused had attacked two policemen when returning from a football match, it does not seem to be describing an event that was comparable either in form or scale to the sorts of confrontations that we have become accustomed to as football hooliganism today. However, that fairly large-scale fracas between opposing fan-groups similar to those of today did take place at least occasionally before the First World War, and not only inside or in the immediate vicinity of stadia, is suggested by the following account. It appeared in the *Liverpool Echo* on 1 April 1889, and describes the encounter of two rival groups of fans at a railway station in Cheshire. The incident was reported, it seems reasonable to surmise, just because a reporter happened to be present at the time:

An exciting scene took place at Middlewich Station on Saturday evening, after a match between Nantwich and Crewe. Both parties assembled on opposite platforms waiting for trains. They commenced operations by alternately hooting and cheering, and then one man challenged an antagonist to a fight. Both leapt on the metals and fought desperately until separated by the officials. Then a great number of the Nantwich men ran across the line, storming the platform occupied by the Crewe men. Uninterested passengers bolted right and left. The special then came in and the police guarded them off, many of them carrying away marks that will distinguish them for some time.

Indirect evidence that fighting may, in fact, have been a regular but under reported feature of fan behaviour before the First World War is provided by some comments on Lancashire supporters which The Times included in its report on the 1914 Cup Final between Burnley and Liverpool. There were, it seems, well in excess of 35,000 Lancastrians at the match, 15,000 from Burnley, at least 20,000 from Liverpool, and 'whole trainloads from all the other chief towns in Lancashire'. According to the report:

The Northerners were more peaceable than on previous occasions. If they indulged in fraternal fights, they waited until they reached their native platforms. Then perhaps one would say to another, 'Has t' fowten?' and when the answer was in the negative would reply, 'Then let's get fowten an' go whoam!' There is more than a touch of the Celtic fighting-spirit in those solid, enduring, low-statured folk.[39]

It would be wrong to think that fighting was confined to Lancashire fans. Moreover, a distinct regional prejudice is expressed in these remarks. However, the Middlewich incident does provide at least some support for the argument put forward by the reporter.

CHAPTER 4

Football hooliganism and the working class before the First World War

Introduction

So far we have gone some way towards establishing that spectator disorderliness was a recurrent and relatively frequent feature of soccer in Britain in the three or four decades which preceded the outbreak of the First World War. It was, moreover, deeply rooted at all levels of the game, not just at that of the emergent Football League. This suggests that we are dealing with a social phenomenon that was not purely and simply associated with the strains and stresses engendered by the emergence of football as a professional sport.

Perhaps more significantly from a sociological standpoint, the data we reported in Chapters 2 and 3 cast doubt on aspects of the analyses of football hooliganism offered by Taylor and Clarke. Although he has since modified his views, Taylor was quite simply wrong when he asserted in 1971 that pitch invasions by spectators are a new development. Clarke, too, is wrong in suggesting that swearing was accepted in the past as an inevitable part of 'the "man's world" of the football subculture'. It may have been accepted by the majority of working-class males in the late nineteenth and early twentieth centuries but it was clearly not accepted by all members of the crowd. It was also regarded by the football authorities as a problem. Indeed, our data suggest that attempts to transform football into a 'respectable family game' have been going on for a very long time; that is, it is not simply an adjunct of recent processes of 'bourgeoisification' and 'internationalization' – or of 'professionalization' and 'spectacularization' – but forms part of an ongoing process associated with the development of professional football since its early days. Crucial in this regard has been the continuing attempt by those who run the game to gain 'respectability' for themselves and their 'product'. Clarke and Taylor rely on an almost entirely speculative view of the past and this leads them to see too sharp a disjuncture between the processes occurring in the game in the 1960s and 1970s and those which occurred in football in earlier decades.

To say this is not to claim that spectator disorderliness at football in the late nineteenth and early twentieth centuries was identical to the football hooliganism of today. For example, despite our suspicions regarding the existence of a 'dark figure' of disorderly occurrences deep inside large densely-packed crowds and outside grounds, it is probably the case that the majority of incidents in that period *did* take the form of attacks on referees and players of the opposing team; that is, the appearance that this was the case is probably not simply an artefact of the data. Attacks against such targets are perhaps unsurprising in a mainly working-class leisure activity at a stage in the development of British society when local identifications tended to be stronger than is, for the most part, the case today. Such attacks would also have been more likely in a society where opportunities for travel were limited by economic constraints and the comparatively rudimentary state of the transport system. Strong local identifications, reinforced by the fact that a Saturday afternoon at the match was, for the working people who attended, a major leisure outlet, contributed to attacks on referees and opposing players. This was especially the case where the actions of the latter – the match officials as well as the players – were construed as unfairly impeding the achievement of victory by the side in which they had invested so much hope. The focus on these targets would have been intensified by the fact that travel to away matches at higher levels of the game was, for most fans, not a regular, fortnightly affair but limited to important Cup-ties, local Derbies and the occasional annual outing. As a result, away fans simply did not attend matches with sufficient regularity for fighting between groups support-

ing the different teams to attain the degree of – albeit informal
– institutionalization that it has attained today.

Nevertheless, as our data show, fighting between groups of
rival fans did occur before the First World War. Given the fact
that attacks on players and match officials still occur today,
this suggests that one of the things that has happened over the
past 100 or so years in the history of football is a change in the
balance between the different forms of spectator misconduct.
Having said this, however, if it did prove possible to establish
the 'dark figure' for fighting between fan-groups in the years
before the First World War with greater precision, we would
not expect its incidence to be as high as that of today. Our
reasons for arguing this are not restricted simply to the
economic and transport constraints which limited opportunities for football travel around the turn of the century. A whole
constellation of factors in that period seem to have interacted
with these constraints in limiting the extent and regularity of
fighting between fan-groups. For one thing, there were many
other venues apart from football at which inter-group fighting
regularly took place.[1] Central in limiting such fights at football,
too, appear to have been the manner in which spectator
disorders were reported in the press and the way in which
they were approached by the authorities. Let us elaborate on
this.

The reporting of spectator disorders before the First World War

As one can see from the accounts reported in Chapter 3,
disorderly behaviour by football spectators was rarely, if ever,
sensationalized by the late nineteenth- and early twentieth-
century press. There was the occasional dramatic headline but
the incidents referred to were invariably described in a matter-
of-fact and low-key way and, to the extent that moral criticism
was involved, the references tended to be to 'bad sportsmanship' or to a 'disgraceful scene'. The miscreants may have
been labelled as 'blackguards' – a term which carried greater
opprobrium then than it would today – and occasionally as
'hooligans' but they were never described as 'animals',
'lunatics' or 'thugs'. Indeed, there seems to have been a

generalized expectation that working-class crowds would behave in a rough and disorderly manner. A higher level of violence also seems to have been socially tolerated than tends to be the case today. As such, whilst crowd misbehaviour was sometimes regarded as newsworthy, it was not singled out as a cause for exceptional alarm.

At the same time, the majority of accounts of football-related disturbances in that period were confined to the sports pages and hidden away inside match reports. Hence, they probably went unnoticed by substantial numbers of people and, in that context, although there was a body of opinion critical and fearful of the behaviour of football crowds – as expressed, for example, in letters to editors or in the pages of limited-circulation gentlemen's magazines – it did not lead to the generation of a widespread moral panic or a generalized belief that a serious social problem existed, a problem in relation to which action by the state was urgently required. As a result, it remained, by and large, a problem that the football authorities were left to deal with on their own and which the police were allowed to handle using ad hoc justice; that is, they approached the problem without a massive display of force and with only minimal recourse to arrest. For example, fans who invaded the pitch seem simply to have been dumped unceremoniously back into the crowd. As a result, few 'arrest counts' were reported and this appears to have had the consequence of reinforcing the public perception of football stadia as places where 'manly' sporting contests take place and not, as tends to be the case today, as battlegrounds where groups of fans regularly fight and come into conflict with the law. In short, a whole constellation of interacting social processes tended to reinforce the public perception of football as socially unproblematic. Though not always approved of, one expected the use of bad language and a considerable degree of roughness at events that were predominantly attended by working-class males. However, this did not act as a deterrent to the attendance of any except some members of the middle classes and, perhaps independently of their social class, of some women. In any case, if they were interested in football and not attracted to the socially more exclusive Rugby Union game, such people were able to obtain a degree of insulation from the coarseness and roughness of the mass of spectators by paying the higher prices required for watching from the stand. And finally in that period, there were no sensationalizing tabloids and no television to turn such anxiety as existed into a generalized moral panic.

Late nineteenth- to early twentieth-century football hooliganism and the working class

Let us turn now to what the available data tell us about the social origins of the people who took part in football-related disorders before the First World War. In Chapter 2 we showed how the currently available evidence suggests that football crowds in the late nineteenth and early twentieth centuries consisted primarily of skilled manual workers and perhaps of routine white-collar workers. However, a sizeable sprinkling, on the one hand, of men from higher reaches of the stratification hierarchy and, on the other, of women from all social classes also seem to have attended matches. Limited though they are, the currently available data also suggest that, around the turn of the century, processes of what one might call 'proletarianization' and 'masculinization' were occurring as far as the terraced sections of football grounds were concerned; that is, although the development in this direction was probably not simple, unilinear and continuously progressive, by about 1900 the football terraces seem to have become more or less exclusive preserves of working-class men, with the stands the only places where women and upper- and middle-class males continued to attend in numbers of any substance.

What do the available data suggest as far as the social characteristics of the people reported as engaging in disorder are concerned? Table 4.1 collates the few cases we have come across between 1895 and 1914 where the occupations of persons involved in football-related disorders were cited in newspaper reports. These data are sketchy and not particularly revealing. Such as they are, however, they do not seem to suggest that the people who engaged in disorderly behaviour at or in conjunction with football matches in this period were significantly different socially from other, ostensibly more

Table 4.1 Occupations of persons reported as involved in football-related disorders (1895–1914)

Occupations	Offences
Book-keeper	Drunk
Jailor	Theft
Bricklayer	Assault
Colliers (two) (and apparently several colliers)	Assault
Framework-knitter	Drunk and disorderly
Machinist	Assault
Ostler	Drunk/assault
Lock-keeper	Assault
Labourers (four)	Assault (three); Drunk and disorderly (one)

orderly, members of the crowd; that is, with the exception of the four who were described as labourers and who may have come from the very lowest sections of the social hierarchy, they all appear to have come from solidly working-class backgrounds and, in a couple of cases, from the lower-middle class. However, our understanding can be further advanced by an analysis of the social images and categories that are implicit in the language used in that period to describe disorderly fans.

We have already made reference to the involvement of a gang in football-related violence in this period – the gang reported to have attacked a Burton Wanderers player in Leicester in 1897. In addition, there is the mention of 'half a dozen of the Peaky fraternity from Birmingham' attending a West Bromwich Albion match in 1900. Gangs may also have been involved in such incidents as the fight between fans at Middlewich Station in 1889. However, it seems just as likely that the fighting on that occasion simply arose spontaneously out of the encounter of two committed and highly excited groups of rival supporters. Thus, whilst one might suspect that 'youth gangs' may have been involved in some of the fighting between rival football fans which took place in the late nineteenth and early twentieth centuries, that is not something which emerges from contemporary newspaper accounts. Indeed, given the frequency with which fights between gangs of 'hooligans', 'peaky blinders', etc., were reported in the late Victorian and Edwardian press,[2] the lack of frequent references to them in a football context may well be indicative of the fact that they did not attend matches regularly or in large numbers. Had they done so and had they participated visibly in the disorders of those years, it seems likely that it would have been reported and that the anxiety over their activities in society at large would have been transferred to and reinforced the current of concern over the behaviour of football crowds.

The labels that were, in fact, used most frequently in accounts of football-related disorder before the First World War include either the description of specific individuals as 'rowdies', 'roughs', 'ruffians' and, more rarely, as 'hooligans', or references to forms of behaviour such as 'blackguardism' and 'ruffianism'. However, these labels are ambiguous. It is unclear whether they were intended to refer to specific identifiable types of persons, specific identifiable groups, or simply to forms of behaviour that were engaged in in specific situations by people who did not come from a single narrowly-defined social location but who were recruited from a relatively broad range within the stratification hierarchy, though primarily from the working and lower-middle classes.

Such as it is, the available evidence suggests that at the stage in the development of British society reached around the turn of the century, a greater proportion of men, especially of working-class men, would have adhered to more aggressive forms of masculinity than tends nowadays to be the case; that is to say, the norms to which their behaviour was attuned would, in a greater range of situations, have either positively sanctioned fighting or, at least, not discouraged it. As a result, they are liable to have responded with overt physical and verbal aggression more readily and more frequently in situations where they and/or people with whom they identified (such as their representatives on the football field) were threatened with loss in some activity which they valued highly or where they perceived themselves and/or their representatives to have been the recipients of 'unfair' treatment. That, in its turn, is probably to be explained by reference to the fact that the conditions of working-class life generally in that period were, in important ways, similar to those found nowadays mainly in the lowest sections of the working class. In short, around the turn of the century, a degree of roughness in behaviour was probably a more common working-class social characteristic than tends nowadays to be the case. Morever, the distinction between the 'rougher' and more 'respectable' sections of the working class at that time was probably less sharp and pronounced than it later became. Let us elaborate on this.

'Aggressive' masculinity and the 'roughs'

The idea that the working class in the late Victorian and Edwardian periods were generally 'rougher' and, in Elias's sense of the term, less 'civilized' than tends to be the case today, is consistent with the conclusion reached by Bailey that 'respectables' in the mid-Victorian working class were probably 'rarer birds than contemporaries or today's historians have allowed.'[3] Such developments in the mid-nineteenth-century working class as the consolidation of friendly societies on a regional or national basis, Bailey suggests, encouraged contemporary observers in the belief that 'orthodox values of improvement were well on their way to superceding the obsolescent survivals of an older and intemperate way of life, the hangovers from a semi-barbarous folk culture which would soon be extinguished'. According to Bailey, however, such contemporary observers were mistaken, for:

> working-class culture in its adaptation to an urban-industrial setting was more additive than substitutive. What outsiders chose to see as anomalies were its normalities: to members of the friendly societies and other major institutions in common life the concurrent pursuit of 'thinking and drinking', 'virtue and vice' represented not so much a conflict of value systems as a reconciliation.[4]

It is, we feel, reasonable to suppose that the violence reported as engaged in by football spectators around the turn of the century may also have been a hangover from the 'semi-barbarous folk culture' referred to by Bailey. However, it was probably not so much a hangover in the sense that people continued to cling to the traditions of a bygone age simply because they found them enjoyable. It was probably more a consequence of the continued existence of structures, even at the relatively advanced stage of industrialization and urbanization reached by Britain in the late nineteenth and early twentieth centuries, that made violence a more central and public feature of working-class life than it was later to become. This is not a subject that has yet been adequately researched. Nevertheless, there are sufficient data available to suggest at least the outlines of an explanation of why these structures and the violence they engendered continued to persist in only slowly changing forms right into the present century. Let us conclude this chapter by sketching, in largely hypothetical terms, what we take to be the principal structural sources of the relatively high level of violence that tended to characterize the lives of the late Victorian and Edwardian working class.

The structural sources of working-class violence

To our knowledge, most of the data on the British working class at the turn of the century that are relevant for present purposes come from upper- and middle-class sources. They are thus by no means unproblematic. However, those we are familiar with all point consistently in the same direction, namely to the fact that the idea of the working class as 'the dangerous class' was not simply a projection of upper- and middle-class anxieties on to those below them. These anxieties had a number of *factual* sources as well. As propertied 'citizens' with the right to vote, the upper and middle classes identified with and felt proprietorial towards 'the nation' and thus felt profoundly the threat to Britain's international standing posed by the industrial advance of the USA and the industrial-military advance of Germany. Fuel must have been added to their anxieties by the difficulties experienced in prosecuting the two Boer wars. However, these upper- and middle-class anxieties stemmed from domestic sources, too, especially from the processes of democratization that were evidenced in the growing power of organized labour and the struggle for women's rights. In short, there were signs around the turn of the century that the power of the dominant classes in patriarchal and imperial Britain was beginning, at least to a small extent, to wane. The anxieties generated in that connection probably coloured their perception of 'the lower orders', leading to an exaggerated picture of their violence. To recognize this, however, is not to deny the fact that the conditions of life experienced by the majority of working-class people in that period were probably in many ways much as upper- and middle-class writers described them and hence conducive to what was, by the standards of today, a relatively violent tenor of life. Let us examine some of the evidence for this.

Writing in 1908, Baden-Powell offered an estimate which may be taken as a crude first approximation to the relative proportions of the 'rougher' and 'more respectable' sections of the working class in that period. He wrote: 'We have at the present time in Great Britain two million boys, of whom a quarter to a half a million are under good influence outside their school walls ... The remainder are drifting towards 'hooliganism' or bad citizenship for want of hands to guide them.'[5] As founder of the Boy Scouts movement, Baden-Powell may have had a direct interest in over-estimating the number of boys who were 'drifting towards hooliganism'. Nevertheless, allowing for possible distortions and assuming that one of the central characteristics of the 'respectable' working class, then as now, was the degree of control they wished and were able to exert over their children, Baden-Powell's estimate suggests that, around the turn of the century, 'rougher' working-class families probably outnumbered their more 'respectable' counterparts to a considerable degree.

Booth's data on poverty in late nineteenth-century London provide a somewhat different picture. Table 4.2 is taken from Volume Two of his *Life and Labour in London*.

London, of course, was probably not typical of the country as a whole. There is, moreover, no simple, one-to-one correlation between poverty and 'roughness', 'comfort' and 'respectability'. However, taking Booth's data together with

Table 4.2 Proportions of the different classes in London

Classes	Numbers	%	
A (lowest)	37,610	0.9	
B (very poor)	316,834	7.5	In poverty, 30.7%
C and D (poor)	938,293	22.3	
E and F (working class, comfortable)	2,166,503	51.5	
G and H (middle class and above)	749,930	17.8	In comfort, 69.3%
Totals	4,209,170	100.0	

Source: Charles Booth, *Life and Labour in London*, Series 1, Vol. 2, p. 21.

statements like the one by Baden-Powell, it is reasonable to hypothesize that large numbers of working-class people in late nineteenth/early twentieth-century Britain would not have securely achieved 'respectable' status. But, whatever subsequent research on this issue may show, it is certainly the case that the 'rougher' sections of the working class in that period constituted a sizeable proportion of the working class as a whole. It is also probably the case that members of the more 'respectable' working class in turn-of-the-century Britain would have adhered to standards which permitted and even encouraged a greater degree of violence in social relations than tends to be the case today. One of the reasons for this is the fact that, in Victorian and Edwardian Britain, violence tended to be regarded in *all* social classes more fatalistically; that is, as a more or less inescapable fact of life. In that context, an ability to defend oneself against physical attack would, in all probability, have been an even more generally-valued male characteristic than is nowadays the case. Pearson has shown how, during the panic over garotting in London in the 1860s, gentlemen who lacked confidence in the ability of the police to contain the menace, took the law into their own hands and formed vigilante groups. There was even an element of sport in the way in which they perceived their activities.[6] It is difficult to conceive of how matters in this regard could have changed substantially by the end of the nineteenth century.

In short, even though it runs counter to the popular view that late Victorian and Edwardian Britain constituted a peaceful golden age, speculation informed by the currently available data suggests that British society in that period was, on the whole less 'civilized' than it tends to be today. Given that, it is hardly surprising that a relatively high level of violence should then have been a more pervasive characteristic of the working class. The existence of a sizeable 'rough' working class probably exerted a 'de-civilizing' influence on the culture and behaviour of the 'respectable' working class as well. Central among the reasons for this is the fact that, in such a context, more 'respectable' people probably would have had to defend themselves quite frequently against attacks by the 'roughs', for example, at school, when walking through 'rougher' districts, or simply because the degree of residential segregation between 'roughs' and 'respectables' was even less then than tends nowadays to be the case.[7] In any case, regardless of the actual frequency with which attacks occurred, the simple existence of substantial 'rough' working-class neighbourhoods probably contributed to the perception among 'respectable' males that they would have to be able to defend themselves should the necessity arise.

In fact, there is a substantial amount of indirect testimony from upper- and middle-class sources to the effect that the 'rough' working class in late Victorian and Edwardian Britain was sizeable. More particularly, such testimony points to the existence of a well-developed working-class street life in that period, suggesting that a substantial amount of working-class socialization took place independently of the family and the school. That is likely to have been crucial, because there are good reasons for believing that a relatively autonomous street life constitutes one of the most important preconditions for the genesis and maintenance of many of the more aggressive features of the culture of the 'rough' working class. Here are some examples of such testimony.

Writing in 1901, Sir John Gorst suggested that 'The class of lads and young men who spring up in every city have emancipated themselves from all home influence and restraints.'[8] The evidence of Dr T. F. Young to the Inter-Departmental Committee on Physical Deterioration in 1904 was similar. Young members of the working class, he said, tend to 'throw off all parental authority . . . get to congregating around the street corners at night . . . become what we call "corner boys" and get drunken habits . . . [they] have no idea of discipline or subordination.'[9]

An anonymous contributor to Whitehouse's *Problems of Boy Life*, published in 1912, provides further corroboration, maintaining that working-class youths are 'tempted to spend as little time at home as possible . . . The street, rather than the sleeping place, is the home of the average youth'.[10] Writing in 1904, Reginald Bray, a man associated with the settlement movement in Camberwell, suggested that working-class youths tended to stay out on the streets 'until it is dark, and often in summer, until dawn begins to break . . . the street and not the house ought probably to be regarded as the home'.[11] 'Speaking generally,' wrote Bray in 1911, 'The city-bred youth is growing up in a state of unrestrained liberty.'[12]

What is being described here, in our view, is probably more than simply a shared upper- and middle-class prejudice about the working class. Of course, given the residential segregation of the classes, their lack of intimate knowledge about each other's lives, and the threat that the working class were seen to pose to upper- and middle-class interests and values, it was probably partly that. However, although it was almost certainly prejudiced and thus undoubtedly exaggerated the lack of control exerted by working-class parents over their children, such a view was probably also in some ways consistent with the facts. For one thing, it was based on a degree of observation. For another, a pattern of relatively independent street life tends to be characteristic of poor communities generally and arises, in part, as a cultural adaptation to poverty, cramped living conditions and large family size. In other words, it is not so much a question of children 'emancipating' themselves from their families or of a 'breakdown' of parental control as it is of a combination of conditions that constrain people to behave according to such a pattern, leading them to develop highly specific norms and

values. Under conditions of overcrowding, for example, even
parents who value more continuous and home-based forms of
socialization would probably be pressured to push children
and adolescents on to the streets. They would probably also
expect older siblings to look after their younger brothers and
sisters. For their part, the children and adolescents would
probably welcome the escape from cramped conditions and be
attracted to the excitement of the streets. Such a pattern is
liable to be reinforced where parents seek regular solace in
pubs and bars or where there is a high degree of male
dominance and a rigid pattern of sexual segregation. Given the
latter, husbands will tend to spend not only their working
hours but much of their leisure-time as well in male preserves
and, in such a context, the direct burden of housekeeping
and rearing young children will fall so exclusively on
the mothers that they will be liable to want to get their
children from under their feet as soon as the children
are sufficiently independent. Only in that way will they
be able to concentrate on household tasks, the nurturing
of infants and perhaps obtain a degree of 'space' for themselves.

The tendency to push children and adolescents on to the
street in turn-of-the-century Britain would have been further
reinforced to the extent that large family size interacted with a
high rate of infant mortality to produce a lower degree of
parental affection for each individual child than we have
come to expect as 'normal' in advanced industrial societies
today.[13] Of course, such a tendency might have been mitigated
to the extent that older female kin whose own children had
grown up lived in the same neighbourhood and were able to
take some of the burden of child-rearing off their daughters
and younger sisters.[14]

The achievement by working-class youths of a relatively
high degree of independence from their families at a
comparatively early age was also, in all probability, buttressed
by specific aspects of the occupational structure of late
Victorian and Edwardian Britain. Writing of the Edwardian
period, Pearson has suggested that technological developments 'had deskilled numerous working-class jobs', enabling
employers to replace skilled men with unskilled boys at lower

wages. There was also a demand for boys to do simple work in the spheres of transport and communication:

> van boys, errand boys, messenger boys, boys to answer telephones, boys to hold horses' heads and other kinds of trivial but essential work. Finally, respectable England required . . . hotel pages, uniformed door-openers, billiard-cue chalkers, boy golf caddies, and a myriad of other forelock-tugging dogsbodies and serfs.[15]

Pearson makes no mention here of the part played by petty crime in the economy of the lower working class. Nevertheless, he points to one of the principal ways in which the relative independence of working-class youths around the turn of the century was economically buttressed. But how was such a pattern related to the relatively high level of physical aggressiveness in working-class life in that period? It is possible to offer a series of 'grounded speculations' on this score.

It is reasonable to suppose that the roots of the relatively high levels of aggressiveness of males in the late nineteenth-/early twentieth-century working class probably lay partly in the fact that the occupations most of them performed stood at or near the bottom of the hierarchical division of labour and did not require the continuous exercise of foresight and emotional control for their performance. This, coupled with the fact that the then-available technology of production involved a higher reliance on muscular strength than is nowadays the case, would have reinforced a *macho* concept of masculinity. Moreover, such work would have provided a site for its expression. Standards which defined males as the 'protectors' of women would have reinforced this concept, too, as would also the fact that the balance of power between the sexes was skewed more in favour of men. All this was probably reinforced by the relatively high independence of working-class children and adolescents, and the fact that so much of the lives of so many of them took place on the streets. There is insufficient space for us to go into the social and psychological details. It must be enough to say that there is a tendency under such conditions for young males, often under the leadership of the most dominant among them, to bond on the basis of kinship and/or territorial ties and hence for streetcorner gangs to emerge. One of Humphries' informants, for example, recalling his childhood in a Manchester district in the early twentieth century, said if you were born in that area 'you were born in[to] a gang'.[16] Within such gangs there is a tendency for status to be accorded in terms of willingness to challenge authority and ability to fight, and gangs of this kind tend to clash regularly with local rivals. In short, given the fact that a substantial proportion of working-class boys in Britain at the end of the nineteenth and beginning of the twentieth centuries received a considerable amount of their early socialization on the streets, it is hardly surprising that the majority of working-class communities in that period were considerably rougher and more violent than tends to be the case today.

Violent tendencies of this kind were probably also reinforced by the difficulties of the authorities in establishing effective control over working-class communities, particularly over working-class leisure activities and informal 'street economies'. Perhaps the best measure of the limits of official power in this regard in late Victorian and Edwardian Britain is provided by the frequency with which attacks on the police occurred. 'The constable in certain districts,' observed a writer in The Pall Mall Gazette in February 1901, 'is apparently looked upon as the common enemy whom it is right to kick and beat whenever that can be done with safety . . . When he attempts to arrest disorderly persons who have the active sympathy of a crowd of roughs, a policeman's lot is not a happy one.'[17] Such accounts, of course, make little mention of the relationship between police violence and the standards of the working class, but a measure of the fact that opinions of this kind were, again, not simply based on higher class prejudice towards 'the lower orders' is provided by the reports of the Metropolitan Police Commissioner that, in the 1890s, around one in four of London's policemen were assaulted every year. In 1899, for example, when police strength in the capital stood at 13,213 constables and 1,949 sergeants, a total of 3,444 assaults on London policemen were recorded.[18] This is particularly interesting in the present context since, if attacks on policemen were relatively common in that period, it is not at all surprising that attacks on authority figures in a sporting context such as football referees should have been relatively common, too.

Summing up, a relatively high level of violence in social relations seems to have been structurally generated in working-class communities in the late nineteenth and early twentieth centuries. It seems to have been reinforced by the fact that, in that period, violence was more widely accepted in society at large as a simple and unavoidable fact of life than tends to be the case today. Given that, it is hardly surprising that such a state of affairs should have found expression in a football context. However, even though the widely reported fighting between football fans and that between 'hooligan gangs' stemmed from the same or similar social roots, the available evidence suggests that there was little overlap between them. More particularly, as we have seen, although one cannot discount the possibility that 'hooligan gangs' may have gone to matches with the intention of fighting and causing trouble more frequently than the available reports suggest, it seems likely that, in the majority of cases, the football-related fighting and vandalism of that period were generated mainly by more directly match-related causes such as perceived bias on the part of referees, perceived 'foul' and 'unfair' play by visiting players, or simply, at local Derbies and on those relatively rare occasions when a large away contingent travelled to matches, by the dynamics of the interaction between opposing fans.

CHAPTER 5

'An improving people?'

Introduction

By 1922 there were eighty-eight clubs in full or associate membership of the Football League. That, in itself, is a measure of the growing popularity of the professional game. Systematic data on the expansion of spectator support that this growing popularity entailed are not available. However, Green was probably not too wide of the mark when he wrote of football in the 1920s and 1930s that 'The years enclosed by the 1930s saw the graph of football and everthing attendant upon it – crowds, gate receipts, and transfer fees of professional players – move steadily forward on an ever upward curve.'[1]

But how did crowds conduct themselves in this period of expansion? Today, the dominant impression of English football crowds in the inter-war years is an idyllic one of assemblies that were always peaceful and orderly. The example most frequently cited in support of this impression is the 1923 Cup Final, the first held at Wembley, when a crowd estimated at between 200,000 and 250,000 invaded the new 127,000-capacity stadium and spilled on to the pitch. Current memory is liable to stress the orderliness of this crowd and the central part played in clearing the pitch by a policeman on a white horse.[2] What is not so liable to be remembered is the fact that, after the match, fans in search of souvenirs invaded and ransacked the Royal Box.[3] In other words, whilst it would be wrong to describe this as a violent disorder, forms of illegal behaviour did take place at the match that tend not to be recalled in present-day accounts.

The violent incidents which continued to occur at English soccer grounds in the inter-war years appear to have led what is perhaps best called a 'subterranean existence'; that is, they were reported in the press but do not appear to have been regarded as a serious social problem. That this was the case is suggested above all by the fact that editorials and general press comments began to appear quite regularly in the 1920s and 1930s which seem not to have taken account of the sort of incidents which continued to be reported in newspapers and to the FA. Such editorials and reports praised English fans for their good behaviour, on the one hand relative to that of fans in England before the First World War and, on the other, relative to the behaviour of football fans in other parts of the UK and abroad. In short, it seems that it was in this period that there developed the partly mythical view of English fans as phlegmatic and self-controlled compared with those from other countries; that is, as people who are virtually immune from the sorts of wild and uncontrolled behaviour that is to be 'expected' from 'Continentals', 'Latins' and people from 'the Celtic fringe'.

Editorials and general comments of this kind probably form one of the sources of the romantic view of crowd behaviour between the wars. However, as our data show, there can be little doubt that a *factual* improvement of crowd behaviour did occur in that period. In fact, there is reason to believe that the mythical view of English spectators as *always* well-behaved may have interacted with some of the dominant social trends of the 1920s and 1930s to produce this factual improvement. Crucial among these trends was what one might call the slowly growing 'incorporation' of the working class; that is, the gradual acceptance by increasing numbers of them of aspects of the values of dominant groups and, as part of this, the increasing degree to which the more 'respectable' members of the working class sought to comport themselves in public in what they took to be a 'civilized' manner. In its turn, this process of incorporation seems to have depended for its occurrence on the fact that the 1920s and 1930s witnessed the beginnings of the establishment of Britain as a consumption-oriented mass society. A number of complex issues are raised by this analysis. For one thing, it flies in the face of common views of what Britain in the inter-war years was like. For another, it leads us yet again into areas which few sociologists and historians have so far explored. This means that many aspects of our analysis will inevitably have to be hypothetical. Before we attempt to tackle these contentious issues, however, let us explore what the FA records and contemporary newspaper reports can tell us about the behaviour and control of football crowds in the inter-war years.

The reported incidence of crowd disorderliness between the wars

Between 1921 and 1939 the FA records report seventy-one actionable cases of spectator misconduct at Football League grounds, an average of four per year. Sixty-four warranted no more than the posting of warning notices. The period 1930 to 1934 is perhaps worthy of special note since, in those years, only five cases were recorded, none of them in the eyes of the FA necessitating the closure of a ground. Unfortunately, as was the case before the First World War, the FA minutes are usually silent regarding the character of the incidents recorded, their degrees of seriousness and the numbers of people involved. More particularly, in only fourteen out of the total of seventy-one incidents recorded between 1921 and 1939 is there anything more than a vague reference to the occurrence of some unspecified 'misconduct'. Four were references to 'bad language', four to the throwing of missiles in which no target was mentioned, and six to match officials or players who had been assaulted, molested or struck by a missile. Let us, accordingly, turn once more to newspaper coverage in order to see whether that source enables a more complete picture to be built up.

Between 1921 and 1939, the recently retitled *Leicester Mercury* carried a total of 100 reports of football crowd disturbances. Sixty-five occurred at Filbert Street or elsewhere in Leicestershire, and the number of incidents reported annually ranged between nought in 1936 and ten in 1923.

Fifty-nine incidents were reported in the 1920s and forty-one in the 1930s. However, whilst at the beginning of the 1930s the frequency with which incidents were reported was relatively low – a fact which tallies with the finding that only five cases were reported to and acted on by the FA between 1930 and 1934 – the frequency with which they were reported began to creep up once again as the decade wore on. Moreover, in the inter-war years, just as had been the case before the First World War, there was evidently a considerable amount of under-reporting of incidents both by match officials to the FA and in the Mercury. This emerges from the fact that none of the forty-three incidents of spectator behaviour at or in connection with Leicester City's home matches in this period to which Mercury reports took exception makes an appearance in the FA minutes and that, conversely, only six of the seventy-one disorderly incidents involving Football League clubs minuted by the FA were reported in the Mercury. Such a discrepancy points once more to the existence of a 'dark figure' of incidents which escaped the notice of referees and reporters or which were not regarded by them as sufficiently serious to warrant a report.

Let us now compare these findings with our findings for the years before the First World War. Table 5.1 compares the numbers of incidents of spectator disorderliness recorded by the FA as occurring at Football League matches in the inter-war years with the numbers recorded as having occurred in the two decades that preceded the outbreak of the First World War. According to the official record, the incidence of spectator disorderliness at Football League matches in the inter-war years was just under three times as high as the incidence before the First World War. On the face of it, that is rather surprising. However, the figures have not been con-textualized. As we noted earlier, the inter-war years witnessed an enormous expansion in the popularity of the game and, correlatively, in the size of the Football League. Reliable figures are lacking, but it seems highly likely that the apparent increase in the incidence of disorders is, at least in part, an artefact of the growing spectator support that the expansion of the game entailed.

Table 5.1 Incidence of spectator misconduct and disorder-liness at Football League matches recorded by the FA, 1895–1915 and 1921–39

Period	No. of seasons	No. of incidents		
		Closures	Warnings	Totals
1895–1915	18.5	8	17	25
1921–1939	18.0	8	64	72

Perhaps the major point of interest to emerge from Table 5.1, however, is the fact that in the inter-war years the FA made much less use of ground closures as a means of combating spectator disorderliness. Thus, ground closure was ordered in eight out of a total of seventy-two cases reported between 1921 and 1939, whereas such a measure was applied in eight out of only twenty-five cases between 1895 and 1915. In other words, the ratio of demanding that grounds should be closed as compared simply to ordering that warning notices should be posted had dropped considerably, a fact which is possibly indicative of a decline in the perceived seriousness, and perhaps in the factual seriousness, of the events that were being dealt with. Another possibility, of course, is that the FA Disciplinary Committee in the inter-war years may have been taking a softer line. However, the FA minutes are not sufficiently detailed to enable us to determine what was going on in this regard. Let us, accordingly, explore whether or not more light is thrown on to the subject by comparing the two periods using the material we have collected from Leicester's local paper. The results of such a comparison are set out in Table 5.2

The fact that, in the inter-war years, the number of incidents of spectator misconduct and disorderliness reported in the *Mercury* as occurring at Filbert Street (and, in a couple of cases, as involving Leicester City fans travelling to and away from matches) was over twice the number reported before the First World War but that, over the same period, the numbers reported as occurring elsewhere in Leicestershire

Table 5.2 Incidents of spectator misconduct and disorderliness reported in the *Leicester (Daily) Mercury*, 1894–1914 and 1921–39

Period	Filbert Street	Elsewhere in Leicestershire	Elsewhere in England
1894–1914	20	39	84
1921–39	43*	22	35

* Includes two incidents that occurred in connection with travel to and home from away matches.

and elsewhere in England had fallen by about one half is again rather puzzling. However, the picture becomes a little clearer if one moves from a simple quantitative level of analysis to a more concrete, qualitative level and takes the different *forms* of reported disorderliness into account. Thus, of the forty-three incidents of spectator misconduct and disorderliness reported as occurring at or in conjunction with Leicester City matches in the inter-war years, no fewer than twenty-six were reports of 'barracking' or what was perceived as 'unsporting' conduct on the part of sections of the Filbert Street crowd. Eleven were reports of minor misdemeanours, including some incidents of straightforward crime such as pickpocketing, and only six might be described as 'genuine' football hooliganism. Of these, four were reports of individual fans charged with being drunk and disorderly, and only two – one a case of assault on a railway passenger, the other a case of vandalism on a train – involved groups of any size.

The fact that more than half the incidents at Filbert Street reported in the *Mercury* in the 1920s and 1930s fall into the category of 'verbal misconduct and disorder' is probably of some significance. Moreover, none of the reports of crowd behaviour at Leicester City from this period mentions 'foul and abusive' language or uses synonyms for it. References to such language were common in reports before the First World War but, in the 1920s and 1930s, it was forms of verbal misbehaviour such as 'barracking' that were principally described. One of the more revealing instances was reported on 9 March 1937 under the headline 'Barrackers Do No Good'.

'The barracker seems to have come to Filbert Street – at any rate for second team matches,' wrote the reporter. He went on to suggest that, whilst paying spectators had a right to criticize their team, 'barracking' usually did more harm than good. More relevant for present purposes, however, is the fact that his report led a City fan to write a letter equating barracking with 'total loss of control'.[4]

It would be absurd to take the lack of reference to 'foul and abusive' language in the *Mercury's* reports in the 1920s and 1930s to imply that such language disappeared from Filbert Street during the inter-war years. It was certainly reported at other grounds. On 24 December 1921, for example, the *Mercury* reprinted part of a letter sent by the referee of a match between Port Vale and Oldham to the FA Secretary, F. J. Wall. It referred to 'a running fire of jeers, gibes, mixed with the most obscene and filthiest language it has been my misfortune to hear', and was central in leading the headmaster of a school in Newcastle-under-Lyme to prohibit boys from attending League football matches on the grounds that they 'serve[d] the purpose of bringing together the bad characters of the district'.[5] The fact that a fan could equate 'barracking' with total lack of control, that a headmaster could prohibit boys from attending League football on account of 'obscene' and 'filthy' language, and, indeed, the overall pattern of reporting in this period, is consistent with an intriguing possibility; namely, that a decline in the frequency of physically violent crowd disorder may have been occurring, especially relative to the period before the First World War, whilst at the same time there was a heightening of sensitivity towards disorderliness of a verbal kind. The decline in the resort to ground closure as a punishment provides another indication that such a trend may have been occurring. So does press comment, especially in editorials, on the behaviour of football crowds in the years between the wars. As we noted earlier, such comment tended to be based more or less explicitly on a two-way comparison: on the one hand, contemporary fan behaviour in England was compared with the behaviour of fans in this country in the past; on the other, it was compared with the behaviour of fans in other parts of the United Kingdom and abroad. In both respects, the behaviour of English fans in the

1920s and 1930s tended to be held up as exemplary. Let us
examine some of the evidence that led us to form this view.

Newspaper comment and the perception
of English crowds

Commenting on the crowd that attended the 1928 Cup Final
between Huddersfield Town and Blackburn Rovers, *The
Times* football correspondent wrote (23 April 1928):

> The spectators may well have marvelled at the order and restraint
> with which such a vast crowd followed the thrills accompanying
> the defeat of a great side like Huddersfield Town. No less
> remarkable . . . was the quiet behaviour of the crowd before and
> after the match . . . Somehow the old roar of the North in triumph
> or despair was lacking.

There is, undoubtedly, an element of condescension and class
and regional prejudice in the surprise expressed here that
members of the Northern working class could comport
themselves with 'order and restraint'. It is clear nevertheless
that, in the author's judgment, Cup Final crowds had often
behaved less well in the past.

A further indication that crowd behaviour was widely
perceived to be improving is provided by the *Mercury's*
editorial comment on the same match (23 April 1928). It
apeared under the headline 'Orderly Crowds':

> There seems to have been more than usual favourable comment on
> the good behaviour of the great crowds assembled in London to
> take part in the Cup Final and its associated festivities. The
> comment arises, no doubt, from a legendary feeling that big
> sporting crowds are in some peculiar way predisposed to riotous
> and unseemly behaviour . . .
>
> Students of people in the mass will probably tell us that we are
> better behaved, and that we make merry nowadays without the
> discreditable manifestations that were at one time thought to be
> inseparable from these public rejoicings. Rejoicing and sobriety go
> hand in hand, and great crowds distinguish themselves with a
> sense of discipline that is creditable all round. May we infer that
> we are an improving people?

Testimony to the fact that this kind of judgment was not

restricted to Cup Final crowds but had come to be extended to English football spectators generally was provided by a *Mercury* editorial some two weeks earlier (10 April 1928). It was headed, 'Football and Truncheons', and was referring to disturbances at a match in Northern Ireland:

> at Belfast yesterday the half-time interval in a cup-tie between Celtic and Linfield was given up to a diversion which introduced the stoning of the musicians in the band, and the intervention of police who used their truncheons to keep the more heated rivals in the crowd apart. Fortunately the excitement disappeared when the players came out again, and the game was resumed as if nothing particular had happened . . .
>
> In many centres in England during the next few weeks the big issues at stake in the Cup and the League will unite thousands of people in a single thought. Huddersfield's chance of a record 'double', League championships, promotions and relegations – will exact their full measure of hope and anxiety from the thousands amongst whom League football is a dominating sporting interest. And, happily, all these things will be duly settled without a single policeman having to raise his truncheon to preserve the peace.

The growing attendance of women

Further evidence that English football grounds came to be widely perceived as places that were not unduly dangerous is contained in reports which suggest that women were attending matches in increasing numbers. Female involvement in crowd disorderliness was, of course, not totally unknown. This is shown by a report in the *Daily Express* on 22 November 1920. It appeared under the headline 'More Wild Scenes at Football Matches', and the relevant section stated that 'Women have now begun to take a hand in the scenes of misbehaviour by spectators that occur at football matches when the play or the control of the game is not according to their taste.' On the whole, however, one can assume that the increased attendance of women reported at matches during the 1920s and 1930s was largely dependent on the growing orderliness and 'respectability' of crowds. Commenting on the 1927 Cup Final, a reporter in the *Mercury* (23 April 1927) noted that 'A remarkable feature was the number of women who had accompanied their husbands and sweethearts. Many mothers carried babies in their arms and confessed they had brought them to see the cup tie.' On the occasion of the Bolton–Portsmouth final two years later the *Mercury* (27 April 1929) reported in less surprised tones that 'a feature of the crowd was the number of women who were making the trip to Wembley, at least 50 per cent of the train loads being of that sex'. It seems, moreover, that women in this period did not just attend Cup Finals but also went, if not so much to 'bread and butter' League games, then at least to matches in the earlier rounds of the Cup. For example, the *Mercury's* report on the Leicester City–Clapton Cup-tie of January 1922 refers to:

> a never-ending stream of people, including a good sprinkling of ladies [going to the match]. Quite a number of women, in fact, faced the Cup-tie crush without even a male escort. If Leicester is any criterion, then the lure of the English cup is rapidly infecting the female mind.[6]

On 5 November 1923, the *Mercury's* 'Monica's Mirror' column reflected on this growing female interest by printing a feature under the headline 'Women Thrilled by Football – Quite Under Its Sway'. According to the writer:

> It indicates a great enthusiasm when people will stand for half an hour to witness a match, but when women will stand (as they do) for unlimited time with the rain pelting down upon her (sic) pretty clothes, ruining her hat and her comfort, it shows an interest amounting almost to heroism.

In some cases, women in this period were sufficiently committed to supporting a club that they travelled to away matches. For example, it was reported in February 1925 that, out of the 'thousand odd [Hull City fans] that arrived on the 12.20 "special", a good percentage . . . were of the fair sex'.[7] Leicester City's female supporters in that period were no less willing than their Hull City counterparts to travel away – on the grand occasions at least. Thus we hear that, for the Cup-tie in Cardiff in March 1925, 'a large number of women bedecked with Leicester's temporary colours' arrived for the match by train.[8] Brentford FC appears to have enjoyed even greater female support between the wars, for such was the size of the contingent of women who travelled to watch them in a Cup match against Leicester in January 1936 that they were referred to in a *Mercury* report (11 January 1936) as 'the ladies' team'. Such, indeed, was the popularity of football among Manchester women in the 1920s that special transport was provided for them by the City Corporation.[9] The very fact that it was thought necessary to provide segregated transport may, of course, be indicative of the fact that it was regarded as desirable to protect women from the rough and, to them, offensive behaviour of male fans. If that was the case, however, one might have expected segregated provision to be provided in the context of matches as well. However, such issues are less germane for present purposes than the fact that there is a body of evidence which points to the growing attendance of women at football in the 1920s and 1930s, and that this seems to be consistent with the view that football grounds in that period came increasingly to be perceived as orderly and respectable places that were relatively safe. If that was not the case, it is difficult to believe that women, sometimes apparently carrying babies and often unescorted by males, would have been reported as attending matches in increasing numbers.

The way in which crowd encroachments and pitch invasions were reported between the wars is also consistent with the hypothesis that football grounds came in that period to be perceived as comparatively respectable and safe. So, too, are the crowd-control practices of the police and the crowd-control policies of the football authorities. It is to these issues that our attention will now be turned.

Crowd control in the inter-war years

Despite the increasing orderliness of crowds in the 1920s and 1930s, reports of pitch invasions and crowd encroachments at Football League grounds nevertheless continued to appear quite frequently in the press. In none of the cases we have come across, however, do the reports suggest that such incidents were motivated by frustration or violent intent. Rather, they seem to have occurred for one of three principal reasons. First, the admission of a more than capacity crowd sometimes led to the generation of intense pressure and hence, accidentally, to the enforced encroachment of specta- tors on to the field of play. Second, high-spirited fans occasionally invaded the pitch in order to 'entertain' the crowd. And third, fans celebrating the victory of their side sometimes swarmed on to the pitch in order to congratulate and perhaps even touch the conquering heroes. Here is an example of the second type:

> There was an exciting incident when a couple of Swansea supporters jumped over the barrier surrounding the enclosure. They ran to the goal-mouth and one of them attempted to fasten a leek to the crossbar. Immediately three policemen chased across the ground and escorted the men to the touchline.[10]

Examples of a forced crowd encroachment and a pitch invasion in order to celebrate victory occurred at the Cup replay between Leicester and Newcastle in February 1925. The match attracted a crowd of 36,000 and the *Mercury*'s front page depiction of the scene (5 February 1925) is worth quoting at length:

> Three and a half hours before the gates were due to open there were queues at every gate of the Filbert Street ground . . . For an hour after the gates were closed the Leicester City ground was a besieged citadel. It was estimated that there were over 5,000 swarming in the streets around the entrances without a hope of seeing the ball kicked. The walls were lined with spectators and much amusement was caused by the efforts of some youths to climb telegraph poles and look over into the ground. The houses where back windows overlook the playing pitch had their roofs covered with men who had copied the ability of the 'cat' burglar, and every window was crowded with City supporters.
>
> The police had little to complain of in the way of rowdyism, and their only job was to prevent would-be spectators from scaling the walls . . . Several ticket-holders found a difficulty in getting to the entrances, and a way had to be kept clear for them by mounted police . . .
>
> There was still a large number waiting in the streets round the ground after the interval, and nothing that the police could do

prevented them from making repeated efforts to scale the walls . . .
Police strove manfully to keep the struggling crowds off the pitch,
but their failure to give way was due to the pressure of the crowd
behind rather than refusal to accede to the police wishes.

The encroachment which took place during this match thus
occurred as a consequence of the density and pressure of the
crowd. However, there was nothing forced about the pitch
invasion which occurred at the end for, in celebration of
Leicester's victory, there was what the *Mercury* described as 'a
wonderful demonstration . . . spectators carrying the Leicester
players off the field'.

Interestingly, there is no hint here of condemnation of this
invasion by spectators of the 'sacred turf'. It seems, rather, to
have been expected as a natural accompaniment of victory in
an important match. Such incidents may, indeed, have been
encouraged by the sort of language with which this one was
described. The comment that 'the police had little to complain
of in the way of rowdyism' can be read more as a reference to
the disorderliness known to have occurred in the past than to
a current problem that was believed to be of significant
proportions.

In fact, the sorts of incidents described in these reports do
not appear to have caused the club, the police or the
Mercury's reporting staff undue alarm. References to would-be
spectators attempting to scale the walls, climbing up telegraph
poles and clambering like 'cat burglars' over nearby rooftops
in their efforts to gain a view of the match are described in a
matter-of-fact, even humorous way. No arrests were reported.
This is consistent with what we are told about the Leicester–
Swansea match in 1929 when the offending fans who invaded
the pitch were neither arrested nor ejected but simply
returned to the crowd. In fact, there seems to have been an
official emphasis during the inter-war years on crowds as self-
policing; that is, there appears to have been an attempt by the
football authorities to minimize the reliance on formal control
and to enlist the help of the majority of spectators in securing
order. Thus, following disorderly incidents at one of Liverpool's matches in 1930, the FA Emergency Committee decided
that 'their spectators must understand that they have a

responsibility in maintaining order, and that it is their duty to aid officials and police to suppress disorder, and that failure to do so may result in the grounds being closed'.[11] Similar decisions are recorded in relation to spectator disorders at West Ham in 1922 and Stoke City in 1924.[12] Evidence that crowds in the inter-war years did sometimes act as self-policing bodies is provided by a note in the Everton match-day programme for 3 April 1937:

> You will be glad to know that the spectators at the rear of the Gwladys Street goal took violent exception to the bottle throwing incident, and gave the offender a 'hot' time. He was sorry for himself long before the end of the game. Every little helps, and your 'good citizenship' in checking such incidents as this is very much appreciated. Only by your help can the nuisance be completely stopped. But stern measures will be taken against anyone who is proved to be an offender.

Clubs in the inter-war years were also sometimes critical of the police. This was the case even when an invasion of the pitch was or was likely to be involved. A case in point was reported in the *Mercury* on 24 April 1937, after Leicester City's victory over local rivals, Nottingham Forest, had secured for them promotion to Division One. On that occasion, following the match it seems, the police prevented the crowd from entering the pitch to congratulate the players and Frank Wormack, the City manager, was reported as saying 'We certainly asked the police to take precautions to prevent the players being hurt but it was not expected these would have been carried out to such an extent.' George Smith, the club secretary, was reported to have added 'You can tell the public it won't happen next Saturday.'

Despite occasional excesses such as this, the tactics for controlling crowds employed by the police in the inter-war years, the policy on crowd control of the football authorities and the clubs in those years, the reporting practices of that period and, of course, the generally-growing orderliness of the crowds themselves, all seem to have worked together against the generation of an overt moral panic over the behaviour of football crowds, at least a moral panic of significant propor-tions. Newspapers portrayed football grounds as comparatively safe places and matches as sporting contests rather than as 'battles'. Even hazardous or potentially hazardous incidents tended to be reported in a relatively calm and sometimes humorous way. For their part, the clubs and the football authorities encouraged crowds to be self-policing, and the police continued to effect rough justice in an *ad hoc* manner much as they had done before the First World War. As a result there were few arrests at matches. This, in its turn, would have reduced the number of serious incidents that could be reported, with the consequence that the growing public perception of grounds as relatively safe places would have tended to be reinforced.

Public concern about crowd behaviour between the wars

Despite these predominant perceptions, however, there are some indications that there was, in the inter-war years, an undercurrent of concern about crowd behaviour which may even have been rising during the 1930s. Here are some contemporary comments on and descriptions of fan behaviour which point in that direction.

Following an FA Cup Semi-Final at Filbert Street in March 1928, a correspondent wrote to the *Mercury* (26 March 1928) complaining of the behaviour of the visiting fans:

> It is true that when the Magistrates declined to grant an extension of licenses for the semi-final I was rather indignant . . . But after being about the city a good deal on Saturday evening I am thankful that the Justices stood firm . . .
>
> I am not a teetotaller, but I believe in moderation. Whether some of our Cup-tie visitors were flushed with victory or despondent because of defeat I cannot say, but I know from what I saw on Saturday evening that the Magistrates' decision was a wise one.

A reference to alcohol also appeared in the *Mercury*'s account of the behaviour of Everton fans when they visited Leicester in January 1933 (14 January 1933):

> a long special train brought over 600 boisterous [Everton] supporters, who crowded out of the station and made a terrific din

with rattles, whistles and sirens. 'Here we are, Leicester,' they yelled. 'One step nearer Wembley,' and they held up trams and buses and scores of cars as they pushed their way across London Road. One party stopped in the middle of the road and held up a stream of traffic while they were photographed . . . With shouts of, 'Good old Everton,' and 'Everton up for the cup,' 600 visitors surged down Granby Street behind one of their number, who carried a large jar of beer on his shoulder.

A similar account appeared in the *Mercury* on 12 January 1931, after Brighton and Hove Albion had despatched Leicester City from the Cup:

> 2,000 men and women of Brighton gave Leicester one of the noisiest nights it has known during the past few years. After they had seen their team hustle the City out of the cup competition, they became 2,000 souls with one ambition. All they wanted was to move, ribboned and rosetted, through the streets and to be recognized as bits of Brighton. Towards train time, Granby Street was what the film men would call 'an all talking, singing and dancing spectacle'. It echoed with bells, rattles and sing-songs. 'Sussex by the Sea' and 'Who Killed Cock Robin' were being raucously rendered in every bar each side of the street. At nine o'clock the glass roofs of the L.M.S. Station rang with ecstatic song. The community of 2,000 was dancing, cheering and bellowing in the booking hall and on the platform. Passengers mildly making their way to branch line trains were seized by the hand and embraced as if they were long lost friends . . . The last line of coaches disappeared under the London Road bridge. The rattles and bells and frantic enquiries into the death of cock robin grew faint and faded into silence. Railwaymen sighed with relief, perfunctorily moved bottles from prominent positions on the platform and Granby Street was like part of a city in mourning.

In the latter case, the reporter was evidently not offended by the celebrations he had witnessed. He seems to have regarded the exuberance of the Brighton fans as a source of amusement. A similar tone pervades the report of the behaviour of Everton fans in 1933, although in that case the reporter was more ambivalent, presumably because the antics he described were more openly disruptive in intent and potentially more serious in their consequences. However, the critical letter written to the editor of the *Mercury* in 1928 shows that the behaviour of football fans could still be viewed as a cause for concern during the inter-war years, particularly if it was seen as principally alcohol-inspired. In fact, as we shall show, seriously violent and sometimes vandalistic behaviour did continue to lead a 'subterranean' existence on the football terraces of England in this period, sometimes also surfacing on the trains that carried supporters. Had such incidents been highlighted by the press, it is difficult to believe that the contemporary myth of English football fans as invariably orderly and peaceful could have survived. In other words, the reporting practices of that period seem to have interacted unintentionally with police strategies and the policies of clubs and football officials to inhibit the escalation of concern.

CHAPTER 6

'Incorporation' and English football crowds between the wars

Crowd disorderliness in the 1920s and 1930s

A report in the *Daily Express* on 1 November 1922 shows that referees in the inter-war years were not always as immune from the wrath of crowds as present-day mythology would have it. The report described scenes following a drawn match between Brighton and Luton. It appeared under the headline 'Mob Breaks Loose at Brighton: Policeman Stunned by a Spectator':

> There was a disgraceful scene on the Brighton ground on Saturday . . . the referee being chased and a policeman stunned by a blow from a corner flag . . .
>
> Immediately after . . . the match, hundreds of the 11,00 spectators jumped the barriers and rushed across the ground. The police barred the way to the players' and officials' quarters, but it was only after an exciting melee that the hotheads calmed down and dispersed.
>
> A policeman was stunned by a blow from a corner flag hurled by a hooligan, and was carried behind the West Stand in a dazed condition.
>
> The 'sportsmen' who joined in the baiting should be utterly ashamed of themselves.

It is interesting to note how, despite the reference in this report to 'hotheads', 'a hooligan', a 'mob' breaking loose, and an attack on a policeman, criticism of the offending fans was directed against their transgression of the ethics of 'sportsmanship' and their inability to exercise self-control. That is, it was not, as tends to be the case today, couched in terms of a dehumanizing rhetoric that denounces their behaviour as 'animalic', 'lunatic' and 'barbaric'.

Another report of disorderly behaviour by a group of football fans appeared in the Mercury on 17 March 1930. It described how a number of Leicester City supporters en route to a match in Birmingham rushed a train at Leicester's London Road Station and how the chief culprit among those caught by the police was fined forty shillings with twenty shillings damages. It seems that the accused had attempted to enter a first-class compartment for which he did not have a valid ticket and which was already occupied by two passengers. As he tried to board the train, we hear that:

> one of the two passengers put his foot on the handle inside to prevent the door being opened. As this prevented [the accused] opening the door, he smashed the window, and then, when further efforts were made by the two passengers to keep him out, he threw a handful of broken glass at one of them, severely cutting his leg, which had to be stitched by a doctor.

The Mercury's account does not contain sufficient information to enable one properly to contextualize these events. A report from 19 March 1934, however, is rather more revealing. It describes a return of Leicester City fans from Birmingham on a football special:

> Everything had gone smoothly from the time of the departure at New Street and it was feared that something extraordinary had happened to cause the train to pull up in such a manner only 300 or 400 yards from its destination. After a thorough search of all the coaches, it was found that the communication cord had been pulled. It is understood that the railway representatives questioned a number of people regarding the matter.
>
> From other sources, it was ascertained that the hooligan element sometimes found on the trips had caused not a little damage to the rolling stock, some of it almost new. Windows were smashed, seats cut and torn and the leather window straps slashed with knives.

After presenting this inventory of damage, the report immediately moved on to a description of the 'gay scenes in the centre of the city'. Although Leicester had been defeated, fans were described as 'shouting, singing and dancing', and youths and girls, it was said, 'paraded up and down Granby Street between the clock tower and the Midland Station until nearly midnight'. It is interesting that the police are not mentioned in a report which dealt with what is, even by present-day standards, a serious hooligan incident. Perhaps they were not called in to investigate? The style and tenor of the report also contrast markedly with the sort of sensationalizing treatment that tends to be accorded to incidents of this kind today. For example, and unlike the account in the *Daily Express* in 1922, the reference to hooliganism was brief, unheadlined and buried towards the end of a general report on the match and the crowd that attended it. This is particularly interesting in that some of the culprits were apparently armed with knives. The account also suggests that this was not a one-off affair, since a 'hooligan element' was said to be 'sometimes found on the trips'. This, in its turn, poses the question of why, if hooligans travelled to matches with some regularity during the inter-war years, their activities were not reported more frequently in the press? The answer, we suspect, lies partly in the fact that journalists in that period were not looking for them, partly in the relatively weak channels of communication they had at their disposal, and partly in the fact that the railway authorities and the police – if the latter were brought in at all – felt that they were capable of handling matters without recourse to the courts. Hence, there were few arrests. In any event, the dynamics of the overall social configuration within which football hooligan incidents occurred, were reported and dealt with by the authorities in the inter-war years were evidently not conducive to the amplification and correlative escalation of the phenomenon itself.

Missile throwing and fighting

Reports of missile throwing and fighting also occasionally surface in the newspaper reports of the 1920s and 1930s. A graphic account is provided by the testimony of an oxyacetylene welder from Birmingham in a report which appeared in the *Birmingham Post* on 14 October 1920. It refers to the court action that he took against Birmingham (now Birmingham City) FC.

> The affair happened on 'Spion Kop' . . . Immediately after the interval, 'bottles were flying around like hailstones'. Witness tried to get away, but he was struck on the head, and received an injury which necessitated seven stitches. He had seen other disturbances on 'Spion Kop', and on one occasion a week or so before he was injured, he saw men using bottles as clubs instead of using their fists. The bottles were half-pint stout bottles.

This incident happened, in all likelihood, deep in the crowd and was thus the sort of event that a reporter could easily have missed. We are dependent for our knowledge on the fact that the fan who was injured took legal action and that his case was reported. Perhaps the most interesting feature in this instance, however, is the fact that the victim's testimony suggests that the incident which led to his injury was not an isolated occurrence and that fighting took place fairly regularly on the Birmingham terraces in this period. It suggests in other words that, just as before the First World War, there is a 'dark figure' of hooligan incidents which occurred at or in conjunction with football matches and which it is, again, impossible to quantify.

The report on the Birmingham case of 1920 provides no clues as to whether the fighting referred to took place among Birmingham City fans or between them and the supporters of visiting teams. However, the fact that confrontation between rival fan-groups did take place in the inter-war years is suggested in Pardoe's study of Spurs–Arsenal rivalry. He asks rhetorically in this connection, 'Why were supporters in the early 1920s so incensed, so fanatical as to indulge in street fights, the more belligerent armed with iron bars and knives?'[1] We have not come across any references to armed street clashes between rival English football fans in this period. However, we have come across cases which refer unequivocally to fighting between rival fans at matches. A case in point was reported in the *Birmingham Post* on 24 February 1930. The report describes incidents alleged to have taken place at a match between Clapton Orient and Queen's Park Rangers, and suggests, once again, that we are dealing with a phenomenon that was no by means a completely unusual occurrence in the inter-war years:

> Towards the end of the match at Homerton . . . the police had to stop fighting between rival spectators behind the goal which the Rangers were defending. There was no demonstration against the referee or the players. Only last Wednesday, the Rangers ground was closed owing to the unruly conduct of their supporters.

The incident at Loftus Road which led to the closing of QPR's ground, however, *had* involved a 'demonstration' against the referee. More particularly, writing in the *Birmingham Post* on 20 January 1930, a reporter described how, at the end of the match between QPR and Northampton Town, the referee had to be:

> escorted to his dressing room by the police. A large section of the crowd booed, and some missiles were thrown. One spectator seized a plank of wood, and with this cracked the window of the referee's dressing room. A mounted constable then helped to quell the disturbance and the crowd gradually dispersed.

Pearson, too, notes the frequency of attacks on referees and players in this period.[2] Moreover, our researches show that, as had been the case before the First World War, such incidents – and other forms of disorderliness, too – were not confined solely to matches in the Football League but also continued to occur at the lower levels of the game.

Despite the fact that there may have been a tendency for the frequency with which football hooliganism was reported – and perhaps for the frequency of the behaviour itself – to rise in the 1930s, it certainly did not rise to a level that approximated to the levels of today. Nor was great public anxiety generated on this score or football-crowd behaviour defined as a serious social problem. Nevertheless, as we have shown, a substantial, perhaps in the 1930s even slowly increasing, amount of disorderliness continued to occur at English football grounds in the inter-war years. At least two things would seem to follow from this: firstly, that the sort of idealizing comment by our own contemporaries that we discussed at the beginning of Chapter 5 exaggerates the order-liness of English crowds between the wars; and, secondly, that the current tendency to romanticize the inter-war spectator is an idealization based upon an idealization.

The behaviour of Scottish fans between the wars

So far we have attempted to demonstrate how, despite probable fluctuations, the incidence of football hooliganism in England declined between the wars. In Scotland in that period, however, the incidence seems to have remained high and may even have increased. In fact, there is reason for believing that the continuing high incidence of football hooliganism in Scotland may have formed part of the backdrop for the idealizing judgment by contemporaries of English supporters in the inter-war years. Here are four accounts of the behaviour of Scottish football fans in the 1920s and 1930s. As will be seen, forms of behaviour are revealed in these accounts that are strikingly similar to the behaviour of the football hooligans of today.[3] Intense sectarian rivalry between Catholics and Protestants, of course, especially between supporters of the Celtic and Rangers clubs, formed one of the principal sources of such hooligan behaviour. It was above all central to its more organized character compared with the forms of disorderliness exhibited by English football fans at that time.

On 10 October 1927, the Mercury published an account of a court case in Glasgow. It was stated that 'when the rival factions clashed, they were separated by the mounted police, many people rushing up streets and into shops for safety'. One of the accused, a Rangers supporter, 'rushed at a man who was wearing a green scarf and had a green handkerchief in his pocket'. Fines of one and two guineas were imposed on the offenders, fines which would have been substantial in the 1920s and reflected the evident anger of the magistrate in this case.

A report published in the Mercury on 20 November 1932 suggests that the combatants in these confrontations were sometimes armed and that fighting did not only take place at matches in the Scottish Football League but at the lower levels of Scottish football, too:

Eight young men, most of them with their heads bandaged and showing signs of having received a rough handling, appeared at Glasgow Central Police Court today, in connection with the scenes at a football match on York Hill Park, Glasgow, on Saturday afternoon. They were charged with having formed part of a disorderly crowd and conducted themselves in a disorderly manner, shouted, cursed and swore and brandished bayonets, knives and other lethal weapons and committed a breach of the peace. With one exception they were remanded in custody until Wednesday. One of them was seriously injured. The charges arose following the Scottish Juvenile cup-tie match between Partick Glencairn and Townhead Street. The fight began shortly after the start of the game and nine men were hurt and had to be treated at the Western Infirmary.

The confrontation between Morton and Celtic fans which took place at Cappielow Park in April 1922 is described by Bill Murray as 'one of the worst riots Greenock had ever seen'.[4] Excited Celtic fans apparently arrived at the match in large numbers, parading flags and banners. The police attempted to prevent these from being taken into the ground but the fans simply threw them over the walls. 'These flags,' according to another Scottish historian, 'became rallying points for large groups of supporters'. Early in the match fighting took place on the terraces at the 'Wee Dublin' end but this soon quietened down. At the half-time interval, however, 'this west terracing suddenly exploded into violence':

> The Celtic 'Flag Men' were seen to line up and charge across the empty no-man's land. Utter confusion followed, stones and missiles of every description rained on groups of struggling rival fans. To add to the confusion a band of supporters carrying green and white banners invaded the park from the Sinclair Street end and ran to join the fray. They were confronted by local supporters and forced to retire with abandoned banners strewn on the park. It was apparent that the blue and white supporters were gaining the upper hand and it seemed that the police were powerless to deal with a situation which had escalated to a most alarming extent. Hundreds were still on the pitch when the teams reappeared and many unfortunates were being helped away for treatment for head and face injuries.
> As the crowds poured out of Cappielow fighting was renewed in Port Glasgow Road. Stones were thrown and many shop

windows in the area were smashed. Morton supporters had gained possession of Celtic banners and were burning them in the streets. The approach to Cartsdyke Station was a scene of utter disorder as struggling fans made for the Special trains. There was more trouble on the trains travelling back to the city; communication cords were pulled and one frenzied fan who had been brandishing a razor was taken from the train and arrested at Paisley . . .

Some accounts have suggested that Morton supporters had taken enough over the preceding years, and sick of the confusion caused at Cappielow by the city fans, had organised themselves for a confrontation. Local shipyard workers had been seen to come into Cappielow armed with bags of rivets and other missiles.[5]

As one can see from this and the earlier accounts, the level of violence of football-related disorders in Scotland in the inter-war years appears to have been considerably higher than that of their counterparts in England. Perhaps more importantly, however, the confrontations between fan-groups reported as recurrently taking place north of the border in the 1920s and 1930s seem to have been more organized and to have involved a greater degree of planning and premeditation than any we have come across in England before the 1960s and 1970s. One of the social bases of this greater degree of instrumentality seems to have been what were called the football 'brake clubs'. These were groups of fans who travelled collectively to matches by hired transport, first of all in horse-drawn brakes but, later, increasingly in motorized vehicles such as chara-bancs and lorries. On 11 September 1922, under the heading 'A Bayonet Charge', the Mercury described the participation of members of one of the Rangers brake clubs in disorderly incidents that took place following a match involving the Glasgow team:

> Remarkable scenes were witnessed in the evening during the return journey of the Glasgow Rangers' club brakes. Bottles had been thrown from one brake and a third vehicle was assailed with stones as it was passing.
>
> The occupants, all young men, dismounted, and marching back to where the stones were thrown, many carrying heavy iron bars, swords and bayonets, they attacked the people in a row of miners' houses, one old man being badly assaulted.
>
> The men spent nearly an hour skirmishing in the vicinity of

wash-houses and outbuildings in search for those who threw the stones and eventually returned to the club brake and drove off.

The brake clubs seem to have been principally community-based and their rivalry was fuelled by the fact that there was a high degree of residential segregation in Glasgow between Protestants and Catholics. They were also an organizational base, as indeed were the teams themselves, which allowed football to serve as a vehicle for the expression of sectarian rivalries. However, the brake clubs were not the only structural source of football hooliganism in Glasgow between the wars. As Murray has shown, 'street gangs' were operative in a football context in Glasgow as early as 1924, the year in which 'the Bridgeton Billy Boys', a Protestant gang named after their leader 'King Billy' Fullerton, were formed. According to Murray the 'Billy Boys' had a membership of up to 800, were prominent at Orange Walks and Rangers matches, and were noted for 'picking fights before, during or after the exploits of their sporting heroes'.[6]

The pattern of football hooliganism in Scotland between the wars was thus similar in many ways to one of the principal patterns evident in England today. There was, that is, a persistent tendency for working-class gangs to fight at and over football, and for them to use the game as a context in which to express a masculine ethos in which ability to fight, courage, group loyalty and heavy drinking were regarded as essential masculine attributes. The organization of these gangs around the division between Protestants and Catholics and, at a lower level, around the religiously exclusive brake clubs was, of course, a feature peculiar to Scotland. We do not wish to understate the importance of sectarianism in the Scottish context. Bill Murray shows how discriminatory practices by 'the Old Firm' clubs helped to fuel football rivalries. Nevertheless, despite these specific features, the masculine ethos which underpinned the activities of the Scottish football gangs appears to have been rooted in certain structural characteristics that are commonly found in lower working-class communities. We shall conclude this account of the inter-war years with a brief discussion of what we take to be the principal reasons why, in England in that period, the disorderliness of football crowds declined relative to the levels reached in the years before the First World War. Our analysis of this issue will focus on the evidence which suggests that crowds in the 1920s and 1930s were growing more 'respectable'.

'Respectability' and the growing orderliness of English crowds

As we suggested in Chapter 5, the size of Football League crowds grew considerably between the wars. The evidence currently available on the social composition of these expanding crowds is slight and anecdotal but, such as it is, it tends to support what one might call 'the respectability thesis'. Here are a few examples.

When Leicester City won the Second Division Championship in 1925, a public ceremony was held in the city's de Montfort Hall to present the shield and medals. A *Mercury* reporter (9 May 1925) described the audience at this ceremony as follows:

> A pretty typist stands on her feet, throws her Paris model in the air, stamps her feet and yells hysterically . . . All around, tier on tier, there are packed rows of cheering people, men and women, boys and girls. In the crowd the shoe hand sat next to the solicitor, and the miner next to the magnate.

Whilst one cannot assume that the sorts of people who attended this ceremony were necessarily representative of those who regularly went to Leicester City's matches, it is reasonable to suppose that the success then enjoyed by the East Midlands team would have led it to serve, for a fairly wide cross-section of the Leicester public, as a unifying symbol. As such, it would have drawn together people from different walks of life through discussions, in pubs, clubs, at work and elsewhere, about the progress of the team. In fact, the FA Cup Final was sometimes explicitly seen in this period as performing such a unifying function nationally. For example, according to the *Mercury* editorial of 27 April 1935, 'It is a sign of the times that the Cup Final no longer splits us into classes, but unites all classes in a bond of mutual interest.

Like the Derby the Cup Final seems to have become everybody's business.'

That the success of Leicester City was locally perceived to perform a unifying function, perhaps broadening the social base from which the club drew its support and leading it to recruit spectators from what, in the terminology of the time, were referred to as 'the classes' as well as from 'the masses', is hinted at by an article which appeared in the *Mercury* on 7 September 1927. Its subject was the comparative attractions of the soccer and rugby codes:

> The tremendous growth of Soccer in Leicester in recent years raises many interesting points. The crowds at Filbert Street are two or three times the size of pre-war 'gates' . . . [The club] commands a regular following of 30,000 enthusiasts.
>
> An old-time Leicester sportsman, who . . . has always been in touch with the two games in Leicester, attributes the remarkable popularity of the City to a change in public opinion.
>
> 'There have been times,' he said, 'when the Tigers [Leicester's rugby club] had bigger gates than the Fosse. There was a lot of prejudice against Soccer. Rugger was thought to be a game for the classes, the other for the masses.
>
> 'Perhaps this prejudice still exists in some quarters . . . In some respects, no doubt, it was a case of amateurism and professionalism.
>
> 'There was even something snobbish about the affectation of superiority of the one over the other.
>
> 'I do not think there is much of that feeling about now, because all sportsmen are pleased with the progress of the City, who have so splendidly won their way to the front.
>
> 'The improvements to the ground, and the vastly better and more comfortable accommodation compared with the old days have helped to draw the people, and a successful team has done as much as anything.'

In other words, even though the 'snobbishness' about rugby relative to soccer still exists today and was at its peak in the earliest years of the century, this author is suggesting that it declined in Leicestershire between the wars. One implication of this argument is that a proportion of Leicester City's gate in that period may well have been increasingly recruited, not just from the working class, but from higher up the social scale as well.

Finally, that the trend towards the greater respectability of crowds may not have been restricted solely to Leicester is suggested by an article published in the *Birmingham Post* on 3 January 1939. The article consisted centrally of an attempt to analyze why what is called 'the nuisance of partisan crowds' was growing and, apparently paradoxically, it explained this phenomenon principally by reference to the fact that watching football had become a 'respectable and fashionable entertainment'. The greater 'respectability' of crowds had this effect, it was alleged, by drawing in people who were ignorant of the finer points of the game. The article continued:

> Soccer grounds, nowadays, have lost the old cap-filling, collar-lacking 'gate'. Your average spectator has a hat and a collar. He remains a partisan – we suggest he is even more a partisan because, being of the 'hat and collar' crowd, he knows less of the game than the old 'cap and muffler' brigade. As Burns might have said: 'A man's a man for a' that'. And Burns never thought of the woman spectator.

Also possibly pointing in the same direction is the fact that, whereas accounts of crowd disorders in the years before the First World War frequently referred to 'rowdies', 'roughs', 'ruffians', 'hooligans' and 'blackguards', this kind of socially stigmatizing label is almost entirely lacking in contemporary accounts of the disorders that took place between the wars. Instead, a rhetoric of sport was used to castigate as 'unfair' and 'unsporting' the behaviour of a 'minority' or 'section' of the crowd, although, occasionally, groups of boys or youths were explicitly singled out as the main culprits.

The evidence available to us, then – slight and anecdotal though it is – suggests that football crowds between the wars tended to be perceived by contemporaries as mixed in their social composition. Indeed, as the 1939 account from the *Birmingham Post* suggests and as our earlier discussion shows in greater detail, they tended to be perceived as mixed sexually and not just in social class terms; that is, an increase in the attendance of women seems to have taken place and reporters thought of this as sufficiently remarkable to highlight it in their reports. The apparent decline in the extent to which obscene language was used points in the same direction.

Football crowds in that period also seem to have been *perceived* to be growing more 'respectable'. It seems reasonable to hypothesize that one of the consequences of such a perception would have been to increase the 'respectability' of crowds still further by making the game more widely 'fashionable', a process that would, in all probability, have been enhanced by the fact that, throughout this period, the King regularly attended FA Cup Finals. That, in its turn, may have drawn members of 'the establishment' into regularly watching the game, perhaps leading some of them to become involved in its administration. A corollary of this was the fact that leading FA officials in this period themselves became minor establishment figures. In fact, a variety of social conditions existed in the 1920s and 1930s that would lead one to expect the appeal of the game to have spread up the social hierarchy. Working in all probability in the same direction, too, and further increasing the 'respectability' of crowds, was the growing 'incorporation' of the working class. Let us elaborate.

The growing 'incorporation' of the working class

We are using the term 'incorporation' in a non-evaluative sense to refer to a long-term social process in the course of which growing numbers of working-class people came to embrace aspects or variants of the values of the 'hegemonic' upper and middle classes. As part of this same overall process, members of the working class came to be accorded more of the rights of 'citizenship', trades unions and other working-class organizations came to be accorded greater legitimacy in the eyes of socially-dominant groups, and more working-class people became, slowly at first, to become more affluent. It was a social process full of conflicts, but as it occurred, more and more members of the working class came to see class relations less solely in oppositional terms, and the resistance the majority of them continued to offer to their subordinate status came increasingly to be directed into formal channels, to be more concerned with issues of wages and conditions of work, and less characterized by open violence. At the same time, although current wisdom usually locates the start of this process wrongly in the 1950s, more members of the working class began, slowly but increasingly, to become more 'home-centred', 'privatized', and oriented towards material consumption. The process of incorporation did not begin between the wars; it was, however, speeded up and took firmer root in that period, affecting far wider sections of the working class than had been the case before the First World War. This deepening, widening and speeding-up of incorporation seems to have occurred because British society in the 1920s and 1930s began, in preliminary form, to take on the contours of what is now recognizable as an affluent mass society.

Industrial relations between the wars

In order to illustrate our belief that incorporation was increasing between the wars, let us first examine developments in the sphere of industrial relations. They are crucial because they show that one is not dealing with some simple, unilinear and progressive process. They also show that incorporation was accompanied by considerable tension and conflict. Indeed, it seems to have depended to a large extent on the fluctuating balance of power between the social classes and how this affected patterns of economic growth.

Although there were signs of increasing militancy after the mid-1930s, there was, it seems, a broad tendency for industrial relations in Britain to grow more peaceful between the wars. At face value, such a trend – as measured, for example, by strike statistics – is in many ways consistent with trends in spectator disorderliness at football.[7] In both cases, one is dealing with a form of collective behaviour the reported incidence of which was high at the beginning of the 1920s but which subsequently fell, only to rise again from the mid-1930s onwards. The correlation is far from perfect and it could, of course, be spurious. There are, however, reasons for believing that it may be indicative of a deeper underlying trend.[8]

The years 1918 to 1926 in Britain were years of intense class conflict. The period 1922–5 was relatively quiet as far as *manifest* conflict was concerned, at least as expressed in strikes but, that the underlying issues had not been resolved, is shown by the explosion of 1926. The fact that recorded spectator disorderliness at football in those years was also relatively high may, it seems reasonable to suppose, have been in part another manifestation of the intensity of class conflict at the time. *Both* may have been signs of disaffection from the established order of the members of a subordinate class. Both certainly involved violent outbursts. However, whilst strikes usually involved behaviour with a relatively high instrumental content, football match disorders involved behaviour of a more affective kind; that is, they were largely unplanned, relatively spontaneous outbursts by groups that were not formally organized. To say this is to deny neither the element of short-term *ad hoc* rationality involved in spontaneous outbursts nor the affective content involved in strikes that are planned.

In both these spheres of British social life conflict was thus intense for around a decade following the end of the First World War. The diagnosis of this conflict offered by Cronin is illuminating. The Labour Party and the unions, he suggests, were largely on the defensive between the 1890s and 1914. During the war, however, 'momentum swung back to the workers and their institutions'. This power shift, together with the privation suffered in the war years, the revulsion that the war itself engendered, and the effects of the Russian Revolution 'combined to produce a massive insurgency by 1917–18'. This 'posed a fundamental challenge to British society'; it was a measure of how deep the underlying social antagonisms were and 'its resolution shaped the course of social relations for a generation or more'.[9]

What seems broadly speaking to have happened, in other words, is that at least the power *chances* of workers relative to those of their rulers in industry and the state received, in some respects, a boost in the context of the First World War.[10] That is, faced with the need to mobilize the nation for the defeat of a common enemy, the socially-dominant groups grew more dependent on the industrial and military services of the working class. At the same time, members of the working class became politically radicalized in growing numbers as a result of war-time deprivations. Disaffection from a social structure that had enabled such a catastrophe to

occur played a part as well, and this whole process was
accelerated by the success of the Russian Bolsheviks in 1917.
In that context, too, the fact that the state became increasingly
involved in industry during the war provided for the working
class a single common domestic enemy that was highly visible
to growing numbers of them, hence contributing to the
emerging *national* character of the protest movement. Of
course, when the war came to an end, the pattern of
dependency changed once more and this meant that the
power chances of the working class were, on the whole,
correspondingly reduced.[11] However, the fact that the promised 'land fit for heroes' failed to materialize after 1918 and
that workers found themselves at the bottom of a still very
unequal and rigidly hierarchical social order meant that the
radical discontent that large numbers had experienced during
the war was, if anything, reinforced.

The general power shift towards the working class in the
First World War and the process of political radicalization
which many of them underwent during and after it formed the
principal social structural and ideological roots of the intense
class conflict in British society which reached its climax in
1926. In that context, fearing revolution, and in the short run
doubting their capacity to suppress it, members of the
government and other dominant groups relied at first principally on a policy of compromise and containment. From 1920
onwards, however, encouraged by the weakening of the
unions which occurred in conjunction with rising unemployment – by June 1921, for example, the level among union
members had reached 23 per cent[12] – they embarked on a
policy of more direct confrontation and, following the
collapse of the General Strike, succeeded in securing a shift in
the balance of power at the national level once more firmly
in their favour. Simultaneously, they managed to secure a
widespread 'deradicalization' of the working class, together
with a moderation in the demands made by the majority of
workers. As Cronin has expressed it:

> Having restored order in the unions and banished the spectre of
> direct action, the Government achieved stability of a sort in
> industrial relations. The outcome of the contest created a sanitised

system of free collective bargaining between well-organised employers and responsible and cautious trade unions.[13]

In this situation, Cronin concludes, the government was able to reduce its involvement in industry, and one of the spurs that had contributed to a broader class consciousness during the war was removed. Cronin is moving in largely uncharted territory here. Such a cut-and-dried formulation cannot capture all the complexities of these changes. Nevertheless, it seems to provide important clues. What seems to have happened is that, following the collapse of the General Strike, the government began to retreat from direct involvement in industrial affairs, thus removing a crucial precondition for the consciousness of working-class people of themselves as a class on a national level – an easily identifiable common enemy, the state. In that situation, class issues began to become more geographically localized and specific to parti-cular industries once again. That, in its turn, was a precondi-tion for the occurrence of further incorporation because it meant that members of the working class were less likely than they had been between 1917 and 1926 to see class relations solely or mainly in simple oppositional terms. As a result, increasing numbers of them became less inclined to think in terms of outright resistance and more inclined to think in terms of accommodation with and integration into the *status quo*. In that context, too, the stage was set for a resumption of economic growth and that, by making material acquisition seem more feasible and attractive to growing numbers of working people, formed another precondition for the continu-ing occurrence of incorporation. Let us elaborate on how that seems to have been the case.

Unemployment and economic growth between the wars

Contrary to popular memory, which tends to see only the high levels of unemployment, the British economy grew quite rapidly and substantially between the wars. In fact there are several indications that Britain's experience of the world recession of the 1930s was less severe than that of other major industrial countries. For example, according to Aldcroft, 'The United States . . . suffered declines (respectively) of 37, 36 and 31 per cent in real income, industrial production and employment, whereas the corresponding figures for Britain were 0.8, 11 and 4.7 per cent.'[14] In Britain, moreover, not only incomes but consumption levels tended to hold up. Thus as Aldcroft again has shown, consumption was principally maintained by 'a substantial increase in the real incomes of wage earners largely as a result of improvement in the terms of trade, a shift in the distribution of income in favour of wage earning groups, and an overall increase in the average propensity to consume'.[15] In fact, despite the very real privations suffered by many people, the comparative mildness of Britain's overall experience of the depression 'helped to ease the way for an early and vigorous recovery'.[16] Between 1932 and 1937, for example, real income increased by 19 per cent, domestic output by more than 25 per cent, industrial production by nearly 46 per cent, gross investment by 47 per cent, and exports by 28.4 per cent.[17] To say this is not to hide the reality of unemployment. Throughout the inter-war years the rate rarely fell below 10 per cent of the insured labour force and, when unemployment peaked in the third quarter of 1932, the level rose to nearly 23 per cent. Translated into absolute figures this means that, even in the 'best' years of the depression, something like a million people were out of work. At its depth the figure was closer to 3 million, and countless thousands were forced to work short-time.[18] However, there were great disparities in rates of unemployment, particularly between regions, with the North of England and 'the Celtic fringe' suffering rates about twice as high as the Midlands and the South. Such were the discrepancies that existed in this regard that Aldcroft, characterizing the inter-war years as a whole, is able to write of:

> the sharp contrasts that emerge[d] between the growing sectors of the economy and the declining industries, the prosperous regions and the depressed areas, and the high unemployment and poverty alongside expanding real incomes for the majority of the population and improved social and welfare conditions.[19]

In other words, despite the continuance of poverty and

chronic unemployment, the inter-war years were a period in which the real incomes of the majority of British people grew. The result was that 'on the whole the nation was better fed, clothed and housed than before the war'.[20] There was even, it seems, a modest movement towards a more equal distribution of income, though the process of levelling up seems to have been confined largely to the middle- and lower-income bands with people in the top income-bracket, by and large, holding on to their share.[21] Probably experientially more important in contributing to incorporation, however, was the absolute increase in real incomes and living standards that occurred between the wars. Cronin has estimated that between 1914 and 1937–8 the income available to the working-class family increased by some 30 or 40 per cent.[22] Since, over the same period, the size of the average working-class family declined from 4.65 to 3.77 persons as a result of deliberate family limitation,[23] such increased earnings made possible an improvement in average working-class living standards of somewhere in the region of 70 per cent.[24]

Technological development, growing affluence and incorporation

The technological developments and correlative changes in the occupational structure that took place between the wars were probably also conducive to incorporation. For example, the share of manufacturing in the British economy probably peaked around 1914. Since then, although the process has been relatively slow, growth has centred principally in services and white-collar jobs. It has been estimated that manual workers made up 80 per cent of the employed population in 1911 but this figure had fallen to 77 per cent by 1931 and less than 70 per cent by 1951. Between 1920 and 1938, government employment alone increased by 27 per cent.[25] In that period, furthermore, proportional changes were occurring within the broad category of manual workers in favour of those employed in semi-skilled and perhaps also in skilled occupations.[26]

Other developments in the 1920s and 1930s were working in the same direction. For example, hours of work were reduced from an average of 53–4 per week before the First World War to around an average of 48 hours in the 1930s. By the middle of 1939, in addition, some 11 million workers were receiving paid holidays.[27] Moreover, some 4 million new houses were built in the inter-war years, a fact which had a number of implications. Slum clearance and the provision of public housing, for example, meant on the one hand an improvement in the living conditions of many members of the working class and a breakdown of informal 'street economies'. On the other hand, it led to an increase in the power of local authorities to assert control over the lifestyles of the working class, for example by demanding 'respectability' and ability to pay as preconditions for being granted a council house. Both aspects of this development were conducive to growing incorporation.

The demand for new furnishings, electrical goods and other consumer durables which the house-building programme generated was conducive to growing incorporation, too. In 1920, for example, the number of electricity consumers stood at 730,000 but by the late 1930s the figure had risen to around 9 millions. The result was that 'by the end of the period the majority of households owned an electric iron and radio, one in seven a vacuum cleaner and electric cooker and one in fifty a refrigerator and washing machine'.[28]

Comparable changes occurred in the inter-war years in the field of leisure. Between 1920 and 1938, for example, employment in sport and entertainment rose from 101,700 to 247,900.[29] By the late 1930s, moreover, some 10 million people were, between them, staking around £40 million a week on the football pools. And by 1939, there were some 5,000 cinemas in the country attracting total weekly audiences of some 20 millions.[30] Although he clearly did not approve of what he saw, George Orwell grasped the significance for incorporation of the changes that were occurring when he wrote sarcastically that 'It is quite likely that fish-and-chips, artsilk stockings, tinned salmon, cut-price chocolates . . . the movies, the radio, strong tea and the football pools have between them averted revolution.'[31]

In short, the inter-war years witnessed the beginnings of Britain as an affluent mass society with an increasingly privatized, home-centred and consumption-oriented working class. As part of this process, growing numbers of working-class people became more incorporated into the social order and began generally to behave more in terms of what they took the criteria of 'respectability' to be. Another way of expressing it would be to say that, in conjunction with the emergence of Britain as an embryonic affluent mass society, the proportion of more 'respectable' families in the working class began slowly to increase whilst, correlatively and equally slowly, the proportion of 'rougher' families declined. Underlying this process, as we have suggested, was the fluctuating balance of power between classes and the associated patterns of economic development and growth. On the one hand, the defeat of the working-class insurgency of the years immediately following the First World War pushed growing numbers of working-class people into seeing class relations more in accommodative and less in simple oppositional terms. They came, accordingly, to favour more 'moderate' and restrained forms of trades union activity. The continuing threat of unemployment pushed them in that direction, too. On the other hand, the economic growth, rising living standards and expanding leisure and consumption opportunities of the 1930s acted as a spur to more accommodative behaviour by providing material rewards for conforming to the *status quo*. By present-day standards these rewards may seem modest, but to working-class people, many of whom had experienced British society before the First World War, the hardships and deprivations of the war itself, the struggles of the 1920s and, whether directly or indirectly, the mass unemployment associated with the slump, they must have appeared considerable.

Occupational change, the changing balance of power between the sexes and incorporation

The process of incorporation thus seems to have been fundamentally buttressed by such deep-structural developments as the changing balance of power between classes and patterns of economic development and growth. Also probably pushing in the same direction and leading to more 'conformist' and 'civilized' behaviour on the part of growing numbers of working-class people were both the slowly changing occupational structure and the less unequal balance of power between the sexes that was gradually emerging. The changing occupational structure would have had such an effect in two main ways: firstly, by contributing to the decline of informal 'street economies' and by incorporating more working-class males into the ranks of formal wage labour; and secondly, by reducing the dependency of men on physical strength for performing their work. In both these respects, the attachment to the more *macho* culture of earlier times of the men who were affected would, in all probability, have been loosened.

The growing power of women received its most obvious expression through their occupational involvements in the First World War and when they were given the vote in 1928. However, it was probably also manifested in more subtle ways; for example in the fact that, between the wars, growing numbers of working-class women were able to persuade their men to use 'artificial' birth control, thus contributing to a decline in family size. The increased planning of families was indicative of greater mutuality in the relations between the sexes and hence of the growing power of women. This would have been 'civilizing' in its effects to the extent that it drew more men more firmly into the home, hence reducing their exposure to the influences of an all-male culture and 'softening' the behaviour learned in such a setting. The other side of this coin would have been a greater involvement and visibility of women in social settings outside the home, including, of course, at football. At the same time, parental supervision over the early socialization of children would have been increased, on the one hand as a result of the growing involvement of men in the family and, on the other, as a result of declining family size. In that context, less and less of the early socialization of more and more working-class males would have taken place in the street under the principal influence of their age peers, hence lessening the tendency both for male adolescent street gangs to form and for more extreme forms of aggressive masculinity to be a dominant pattern. The lengthening of the time spent in formal education between the wars and the formation and expansion of youth organizations of various kinds would, in all probability, have worked in the same direction. Of course, these changes would have occurred relatively slowly and unevenly, and would have been experienced to different degrees in different regions. Nevertheless, this thumbnail sketch is, as far as we can tell, a reasonably accurate general picture of the main relevant social changes that occurred in Britain between the wars.

Summary

Let us now summarize our main conclusions concerning football crowd behaviour in that period. Although in many ways sketchy and incomplete, our data on football crowds in the inter-war years all point broadly in the same direction. More particularly, they suggest that, in England, football crowds grew more 'respectable' in a factual sense. As we have shown, such a process of increasing 'respectability' seems to have depended partly on the changing social composition of crowds and partly on changes that were taking place, in conjunction with a complex of more fundamental social developments, in the working class and in inter-class relations. For example, it seems that English football crowds in the 1920s and 1930s were recruited to a greater extent than had been the case immediately before the First World War (though not than in the period up to about 1890) from higher in the stratification hierarchy. They remained predominantly working class so far as their overall social composition was concerned, but more members of the middle classes, and perhaps of the upper classes, too, seem to have attended matches. More women seem to have gone to football as well. At the same time, as we have argued, the process of incorporation probably led growing numbers of working-class people to adopt what they considered to be 'respectable' values and to behave in what they thought of as a 'respectable' manner. The fact that the behaviour of English football crowds was, for the most part, portrayed as orderly and peaceful by the press probably reinforced the tendency of people who considered themselves to be 'respectable' to attend matches. So, too, did the manner in which football crowds were policed. In fact, one could say that the social composition of football crowds in the inter-war years, the manner in which they were reported and controlled and, hence, perceived by the general public, seem to have interacted to enhance their 'respectability', both in terms of their factual composition and behaviour.

However, as we have shown, crowd disorderliness continued to lead a kind of subterranean existence at and around football grounds between the wars. There appear also to have been a slight rise in crowd misbehaviour and a rising degree of concern about it in the late 1930s. This suggests that the potential for a move in the opposite direction was already there. As we shall show in Chapter 7, it was precisely that which tended to happen after the Second World War, particularly from the middle 1960s onwards.

CHAPTER 7

'Soccer marches to war'

Introduction

At the end of the Second World War in Britain the appeal of soccer as a spectator sport reached unprecedented heights. The 1949–50 season, when a total of 77 million people are estimated to have attended matches, saw the peak of this rising trend. Of these, some 40 million were attendances at matches in a Football League now expanded to ninety-two clubs. Since then, however, with the exception of the years 1967–70 which saw a partial recovery following England's World Cup victory in 1966, the story as far as Football League attendance is concerned has been one of steady decline. More particularly, total attendances fell to around 33 million a year in the 1950s, to 25–9 million in the 1960s and to 24–5 million in the 1970s. In the 1980s they have dropped below the 20 million mark and at the time of writing (1985–6) they are continuing to fall.[1]

Asked to attribute causes to this decline, many people would probably assign pride of place to football hooliganism. However, whilst there can be little doubt that football hooliganism has contributed to this process, perhaps accelerating the decline, there are a number of reasons for believing that its roots have primarily to be sought elsewhere. Among them is the fact that attendances started to decline long before football hooliganism was widely defined as a serious social problem. Moreover, attendances have declined at Football League matches but not, at least to anything like the same extent, at matches in other competitions. This suggests that it is not football hooliganism alone that has been causing the decline – it occurs just as frequently at Cup as it does at League matches – so much as the form of competition on which the Football League is based and the fact that the attractiveness of the matches that this leads to has declined for an increasingly home-centred, consumption-oriented and discriminating working class faced with an expanded range of leisure choices. The fact that the decline has been greatest for the lowest divisions of the League adds weight to this conjecture.

More compelling evidence, however, comes from the fact that football hooliganism began fundamentally to take its present shape and to give rise to a persistently high level of anxiety in the years 1969–70, more precisely in the only years since 1949–50 when attendances rose. Clearly, popular wisdom regarding the reasons for declining attendances at professional football is pretty wide of the mark.

Popular wisdom is also wide of the mark regarding the behaviour of British football crowds in the years immediately following the Second World War. It is probably the case that it is this period, more particularly the years from 1945 to 1960, that the majority of people have primarily in mind when they think of the halcyon days of the 'sporting' English crowd, the years when football hooliganism was regarded as a peculiarly foreign 'disease'. However there is substantial evidence of spectator disorderliness and misconduct at soccer matches in this country in the early post-war years and, from a point somewhere in the mid-1950s, a combination of social changes began to interact and to start producing the situation in which we find ourselves today. Changing attitudes to violence, particularly a growing sensitivity towards the behaviour of working-class youths, appear to have been important in this connection. So, too, does the fact that the football authorities, in a period of inexorably declining crowds, began to grow increasingly anxious about the image of the game. Such concerns were augmented considerably around 1966 when the World Cup Finals were staged in England, helping to produce a situation in which relatively minor incidents of crowd disorder began to be blown up out of proportion to the seriousness of what was actually going on. The emergence of a more sensationalizing media, the regular televizing of matches and the growing use of military rhetoric in the reporting of matches and crowd behaviour appear to have worked in the same direction, more particularly by 'advertizing' football as a context where fights regularly take place. Between them, changes such as these appear to have been active in producing, first of all in embryonic form, football hooliganism as we know it today; that is, a situation in which large-scale *fracas* between opposing fan-groups, outside as well as inside football stadia, have become a regular feature of the association game.

The reported incidence of crowd disorderliness in the immediate post-war years

Let us become more concrete and start to unpack this complex process. Although there were fluctuations from year to year – for example, peaks seem to have been reached in 1947–51 and 1956–9 – the level of football crowd disorderliness in the 1940s and 1950s, when match attendances were at their highest, seems to have remained relatively low. The dominant perception of football crowds by contemporaries in those years was one of orderly assemblies and this seems to have worked together with the behaviour of fans *per se* to keep the factual incidence of disorderliness down. To say this, however, is not to claim that the period was devoid of incidents. Between 1946 and 1960, 195 cases of 'disorderly behaviour by spectators' were brought to the attention of the Football Association, an average of 13 per season. By contrast, 'in the following six seasons 148 cases were reported, an average of 25 per season'.[2] In our view, this increase in the incidence of spectator disorderliness was, in all probability, partly a consequence of the moral panic over football hooliganism that began to gather strength in the mid-1950s but also partly a 'real' phenomenon; that is, referees and members of the Football Association's disciplinary bodies probably grew more sensitive in the context of the developing moral panic to what they perceived as violent acts by spectators and were hence more ready to take disciplinary action, in that way expanding the number of reported cases. For reasons we shall explore later, the actual incidence of violent and disruptive behaviour by spectators appears to have increased as well. What one might call the 'perceptual' and the 'real' dimensions of the problem seem to have been conducive to a process of mutual escalation, the moral panic contributing to an increase in the rate at which football hooligan incidents were both reported and occurred, and the increase of reported and actual football hooliganism intensifying the moral panic.[3] That is, the feedback process constituted by the interaction of images and public representations of spectator behaviour, and spectator behaviour itself, began to work in a direction opposite to that which appears to have been characteristic of the 1920s and 1930s.

Table 7.1 presents a year-by-year incident-count of the cases of spectator disorderliness recorded in the FA minutes for the period 1946–1959. The overall number of cases in this table is higher than that reported by the Chester Committee because we have included cases reported as occurring outside as well as inside the Football League. The number of cases recorded for the Football League is lower because we have excluded all cases that refer simply to 'an alleged incident' and/or where no disciplinary action was taken.

In the Football League the dominant trend in the early 1950s was a more or less consistent decline from the relatively high levels recorded between 1947 and 1951, stabilization at a lower level for a while in the mid-1950s and then, after 1956, a more or less consistent tendency to rise. Two points are of immediate relevance here. The first is the question why, given the relatively high levels of recorded disorderliness in the years 1947–51, the media chose not to react with expressions of concern. The second is the fact that the rise in recorded misconduct after 1956 has to be understood in the context of the fact that match attendances fell by some 7 million in the course of the 1950s. This only reinforces our impression that the greatest factual increase in the incidence of spectator misconduct at and in conjunction with Football League matches began to occur, although at first only relatively slowly, from the middle of the 1950s onwards.

Table 7.2 breaks down the incidents of spectator miscon-

Table 7.1 Incidents of spectator misconduct and disorderliness reported to the FA, 1946–59*

Year	Football League	Outside Football League	Totals
1946	2	2	4
1947	15	5	20
1948	7	11	18
1949	11	13	24
1950	15	4	19
1951	10	11	21
1952	8	7	15
1953	6	6	12
1954	6	8	14
1955	6	4	10
1956	9	11	20
1957	10	7	17
1958	21	8	29
1959	12	3	15
Totals	138*	100	238

* Includes twenty-eight incidents recorded as occurring at reserves matches.

duct and disorderliness recorded in the FA minutes for this period into four categories: 'missile throwing', 'direct assaults', 'pitch invasions and incursions' and the catch-all category of 'misconduct'. Perhaps the most interesting point to emerge from the figures in Table 7.2 is that the recorded incidence of misbehaviour in all categories except for general 'misconduct' was higher in the 1940s than the 1950s. The incidence of missile throwing, for example, was considerably higher in the 1940s when the average number of cases dealt with by the FA per year was just under nine, as compared with an average of less than 5 per year in the 1950s. Evidently the Football Association was concerned about this problem for, in 1947, an edict was circulated to clubs informing them that the FA was 'disturbed at the growing practice of throwing missiles at officials and players' and warning them 'of the serious consequences which may result from such disorderly conduct'. Among the missiles mentioned were orange peel, apple

Table 7.2 Types of incidents recorded in the FA Minutes, 1946–59*

Year	Missile throwing	Direct assaults	Pitch invasions and incursions	Unspecified misconduct
1946	2	2	0	0
1947	14	6	2	2
1948	7	3	6	8
1949	10	8	4	9
1950	10	2	5	9
1951	5	8	0	10
1952	1	0	1	13
1953	0	0	0	12
1954	3	2	1	10
1955	3	4	2	2
1956	8	3	3	7
1957	7	2	2	8
1958	15	5	5	10
1959	0	0	1	14
Totals	85	45	32	114

* The figures in this table are higher than those in Table 7.1 because incidents that involved, say, both missile throwing and assault have been recorded separately under both categories

cores, a potato, ice-cream cartons, cushions, mud, sand, snowballs, fireworks, teacups, lumps of ice, stones, gravel, shale, clinkers, coal, nails, a piece of iron and, finally, a pellet fired from an air gun. The air-gun pellet struck the chest of a linesman at the match between Preston North End and Burnley on 26 December 1947.

This discussion again raises the question of why the media did not react with expressions of concern. As we shall show, the picture began slowly to change from sometime around 1956. The point, however, is to explain what it was about the mid- to late 1950s which led to such expressions of concern, whilst in the 1940s incidents which would later have been reported as serious were apparently allowed to pass off without attracting the attention of a hostile press. Two sets of changes seem to us to have been crucial in this connection:

firstly, the growing expression of concern about working-class youth, especially, in the first instance, about 'teddy boys' and later about 'mods and rockers'; and secondly, the increasing gloom felt about Britain's position in the world, a gloom that was intensified in the sporting sphere by England's defeat by Hungary at Wembley in 1953 – the first such defeat on English soil – and, in the political-military sphere, by the Suez débâcle of 1956. However, before we attempt to come to grips with these issues, we shall first briefly turn to the *Mercury*'s coverage of spectator misconduct.

Coverage of spectator misconduct in the *Leicester Mercury*

A total of fifty-five incidents were reported in the *Mercury* as occurring in England in these years; that is, around one-fifth of the number recorded in the FA minutes. It is reasonable to suppose that such under-reporting may have been one of the conditions for the widespread belief in that period that crowds in this country were invariably well-behaved. Such a belief tended to receive reinforcement from two further sources: on the one hand, from positive comments made by foreigners about English crowds; and, on the other, from reports of disturbances abroad. Here are some examples. Following a two-match tour of England by the Argentine national side as part of the Festival of Britain celebrations in 1951, the Argentine captain commented effusively on the fairness of English crowds. His views were reported smugly in the *Mercury*.[4] Another accolade came the way specifically of Leicester fans in 1955 when six Italian police officers confessed to being 'amazed how a handful of Leicester police officers manages to control large football crowds. In Italy,' they said, 'the area would be "flooded" with police officers to keep order.'[5]

A number of stories of football-crowd disorders abroad were printed in the *Mercury* in this period. Only occasionally did they refer to matches involving English clubs. The reports came from such diverse countries as Sweden, Kenya, Switzerland, Portugal, Italy and Yugoslavia. Principally, however, they came from South America. One of the most striking features of these stories is the absence of explicit comparison with the behaviour of English fans. 'It couldn't happen here' and 'What will these crazy foreigners do next?' appear to be the assumptions shared by reporters and readers alike, but the assumptions were not spelled out. Clearly, to have been more explicit would have been tantamount to stating the obvious.

In the mid- to late 1950s, however, things slowly began to change and stories of widespread misbehaviour by English fans started to appear. The following articles were published in the Mercury on 4 November 1957 and 12 September 1959 respectively, under the headings 'This Soccer Trend Must Cease' and 'Don't Fence Our Players In':

You can call the average Leicester City fan what you like . . . but he is a toff compared to the characters that line the terraces in many other areas . . .

Take Goodison Park where Everton have been putting on the magic in recent weeks. In front of spectators who, if they aren't the worst sports in the world, seem to be heading for that qualification.

On Saturday hundreds of them jeered West Bromwich Albion and assaulted some of the players as they went for their coach after the game . . .

This season, some six teams have been booed and jeered for long periods at either Goodison or Anfield. Bottles have been thrown at several players . . . and Teddy Boys have run out onto the pitch and played 'practice' matches in the goal mouth before the match at Preston when Everton were playing away.

Everton fans have wrecked an excursion train and had free fights with other gangs following Liverpool.

It makes you wonder . . . especially when you hear that similar things can happen elsewhere. Even in Regency Brighton.

For there, on Saturday, Reading manager Harry Johnson was hit on the jaw by louts and two of his players were also struck as they left the field at the end of the game.

It's a trend that is increasing. They even threw fireworks at a goalkeeper at Highbury on Saturday.

It's a trend we don't want in Leicester. And, thank goodness, you Filbert Street types seem to feel just that way too.

Will the time ever come when our Football League matches have to be played in, say, 'cages' of wire netting to protect the players and officials from the fans? Such an idea seems unthinkable, although some Continental and South American countries already have been forced to go to these lengths to protect the footballers from the volatile crowds when things have gone wrong on the field.

Admittedly there has been a minor outbreak of acts of hooliganism this season on the part of individuals here and there, but for the most part English soccer crowds are good-natured and well behaved, comparing favourably with any in the world.

So far no method of dealing with the rowdies has been offered.

Club officials can scarcely advise violence when they are so anxious to stamp it out, and a tongue-lashing is unlikely to bring an improvement. No, the answer rests with the clubs themselves . . . Queen's Park Rangers have told their crowd that they are considering taking legal action against any person guilty of disorderly conduct at their Shepherd's Bush ground.

So, at least as early as the mid-1950s, reports began to appear of English soccer fans wrecking trains, engaging in free fights and attacking players and officials. Significantly, the reports single out Merseyside fans as the principal perpetrators of these disorders and one of them referred to the participation of teddy boys, the principal 'folk devils' of the period. In fact, commenting on the race riots of that year in Nottingham and Notting Hill, a *Times* editorial on 5 September 1958 drew links between assaults on blacks, the activities of teddy boys, student 'rags', the behaviour of Scottish football fans in London, and the wrecking of football specials. After doubting whether the race riots were 'merely the lawlessness and thuggery of a certain social layer of vicious young people venting themselves against a new target', the editorial continued:

It may seem a far cry from the fact that undergraduates have been known to bombard statesmen with garbage and that Eros has to be boarded up on some of the days when international matches are played in London to the present debased and savage outbreaks. But the cry can nevertheless be heard from one extreme to the other, and now that the evils of hooliganism among one social class stare us in the face we should ask ourselves whether the time has not come to deal with it severely in all social classes. The university students who wreck theatrical performances, the football spectators who seem to feel that their afternoon's enjoyment is not complete unless they rip up the railway carriages that take them home are – just as much as the Teddy Boys who, whether harmlessly or lethally, are obstreperous in public – all manifestations of a strand in our social behaviour that an adult society can do without.

Generally speaking, however, such connections were not made, and the overall tone in which the disorderliness of football spectators was reported was reassuring and the language far from alarmist. At that stage the problem was recognized as a minor one and draconian measures were regarded as unnecessary. Within the space of the next ten years, however, the situation was dramatically reversed and football hooliganism came to be accorded the status of a major 'social problem'.

The emergence of football hooliganism as a social problem

Let us trace the gradual build-up of the moral panic about the behaviour of English football fans and the correlative escalation of the phenomenon of football hooliganism itself. This process took place in a period of mounting concern about the behaviour of working-class youths. (In the twenty-seven-month period starting in August 1957, no fewer than thirty-one editorials appeared in the Mercury dealing with such issues as teddy boys, violence and the supposed leniency of the courts.) It was a period, too, in which the regular televizing of football began and in which the football authorities – faced with continually declining crowds and attempting to replace those sections of the working class who were deserting the game with a new, more 'up-market' clientele – became increasingly concerned about the image of the game. The watershed, however, seems to have come, as we have said, in the period of build-up to the 1966 World Cup Finals for, in that context, all these different sources of anxiety appear to have fused and football hooliganism was propelled into its current phase. From that point on it became a self-perpetuating social problem with the actions of the youths and (mainly) young men who were centrally involved and the media and official reactions to what they did feeding each other in a vicious spiral.

We shall start by examining the train-wrecking exploits of Liverpool and Everton fans in the mid-1950s and early 1960s. Although such behaviour was not unknown between the wars, the infliction of damage to railway carriages by travelling fans was held in *The Times*, as can be seen from the following report, to have 'reached a peak' in March 1956:

> A British Railways official today described damage done to a number of trains by Liverpool football enthusiasts returning from the Everton v Manchester City match at Manchester on Saturday, as the worst in the history of the railways.
>
> He listed this damage, done to the last of six football excursion trains which arrived at Liverpool at 11.20 p.m.: 8 door windows smashed, 5 side windows smashed, 14 pictures broken, 2 mirrors cracked, 1 whole door missing, another door damaged, a door-handle missing, dozens of light bulbs removed, several compartments heavily bloodstained, luggage racks pulled from the walls as though people had been swinging on them, and a number of slashed seats.
>
> The official said: 'It is impossible to estimate the amount of damage because it is so detailed and widespread. Nearly every train coming into Liverpool after 8.15 on Saturday had some damage. It will take several weeks to repair the coaches.'[6]

Although this report does not give a detailed picture of the behaviour involved in these 'vandalistic' acts, it is clear that several of the fans were armed with knives. However no action seems to have been taken and when, in December 1957, fans from Liverpool were again involved in such behaviour, it was announced by British Railways that they did not intend to stop providing football specials because 'it would not be right to penalise the many hundreds of decent people who travel on them, because of a handful of hooligans'.[7]

The train-wrecking exploits of Liverpool and Everton fans continued into the 1960s, earning them the title in the popular press at the time of the 'Merseyside maniacs'. Their antics probably constitute the first emergence of football hooliganism as a *regular* phenomenon in one of its recognizably modern forms. Underlying it appears to have been the fact that the away followings of the two Liverpool clubs were at that time larger than those of the majority of other teams. Possibly underlying it, too, was the emergence of a greater assertiveness in public on the part of working-class youths, an assertiveness which showed itself in demonstrative support for a football team and hence for the local community and culture that it represented. It is certainly the case that, in the early 1960s, the arrival of the fans from Merseyside began to be widely anticipated with apprehension. 'Shopkeepers lock up when Everton are in town', it was reported in November 1964.[8] Around the same time, too, the Stoke police promised local people a 'get tough' approach for the impending visit of Liverpool.[9]

However the incipient emergence of football hooliganism in its present-day form, that is as an activity involving large numbers of travelling fans, was not restricted to Liverpool and Everton supporters for very long. As early as 10 November 1963, *The Sunday Times* was able to comment generally on an 'undeniable increase in irresponsible crowd behaviour' and to describe a situation in which 'scarcely a week goes by without a report of incidents'. Merseyside fans soon came to share the spotlight with those from Glasgow, with its long history of violent rivalry between supporters of Rangers and Celtic. The sectarian and other social divisions which led to the attraction of a violent support to the two Glasgow clubs in the 1920s and 1930s showed few signs of diminishing in the 1950s and 1960s. In 1961, for example, following crowd disturbances at a match in Dundee in which fifty fans were allegedly slashed with bottles and one died later in jail, a Scottish MP called for the liquidation of the Celtic club.[10] In this period, too, 'Scottish style' fan violence began to be exported to England. Thus, when 'Catholic' Everton entertained Protestant Rangers in December 1963, in a match for the unofficial 'Championship of Britain', there was, according to the *Daily Herald*, 'bound to be trouble'.[11] Their prediction was right, for fighting between Everton and Rangers fans is reported to have occurred on that occasion *outside* the Goodison ground.

This was, to our knowledge, the first time in England after the Second World War that a confrontation between fan-groups was widely reported. Although such fights had taken place in England previously, they tend to be less visible and less disruptive of a match than pitch invasions or missile attacks on referees and players, and it was these forms of disorder in that period which still continued to generate the greatest media and official concern. Following a spate of missile throwing at its ground, and under the threat of closure by the FA, Everton FC in November 1963 became the first English club to erect fences behind its goals. At that stage, however, the media remained largely ambivalent. On the one hand they were beginning to point more regularly to the 'growing menace' of football hooliganism, but on the other they were still demanding a traditional 'British approach'. It was the latter side of this ambivalence that predominated in the press reaction to the Everton fences. 'Hooligans?' queried a puzzled *News of the World*. 'They're so friendly!'[12] The *Daily Sketch* agreed. Under the headline 'Brave Fans – You Don't Need Cages', the *Sketch*'s account of fan behaviour on a football weekend in 1963 continued ironically (25 November 1963):

> What? No darts? No invasions? No sendings off? No fights on the field? No protests? No menacing mobs awaiting the exits of referees? What is British football coming to? And what dull reading for the violence-hungry this weekend! . . . Everton can remove the hooligan barriers at Goodison Park, and those who plead for cages and moats and barbed wire can weep in their beer, for the British football fan is showing he can correct the stormy situation of recent weeks in the good old British manner – by common sense.

As late as 11 February 1964 the *Daily Mail* was even benignly expressing its preference for 'hooliganism rather than indifference'. Henceforth, however, reacting to the increasingly violent and destructive activities of a minority of the hooligans themselves, the media began more and more to portray hooligans unequivocally as major 'folk devils'.

Possibly underlying the positive side of the media's ambivalence towards football hooliganism in the early 1960s was the belief that most of the behaviour involved was harmless schoolboy excess. However it is probably significant that groups like the National Federation of Football Supporters' Clubs argued that 'boys don't cause trouble. It is youths of 18–20 who are the culprits.'[13] There was also evidence of even older perpetrators of hooligan acts. For example, a thirty-seven-year-old labourer was convicted for throwing a bottle at a visiting goalkeeper at one of Middlesbrough's matches in December 1963.[14] Three months later Manchester United banned a twenty-four-year-old from Old Trafford for six months. And in November 1965, in one of the first major incidents of the post-war period to be reported, the average age of thirteen Liverpool fans charged with offences at a match in Sheffield was more than twenty-seven years.[15] Clearly, while school-age fans were often involved in hooligan incidents around this time, not all disturbances involved only very young supporters. Nor is it clear that schoolboys were usually responsible for the most serious offences.

Despite evidence of this kind, the earliest attempts to implement preventive measures were certainly aimed primarily at very young fans. Early in 1964, for example, in an attempt to combat what was called 'the schoolboy threat', British Railways stopped issuing half-price tickets for 'football specials' from Liverpool.[16] Later the same year Everton FC deliberated over a proposal to ban unaccompanied children under fourteen years of age from matches at Goodison Park.[17] And in December 1964 the FA published proposals recommending the segregation inside grounds of boys paying half price.[18] To the extent that they were followed, it seems likely that such recommendations would probably have contributed to the initial formation of the 'youth ends' which began to emerge in their recognizably modern form around the end of the 1960s.

Towards the end of 1964 a joint FA/Football League enquiry into the state of the game pinpointed 'soccer rowdyism' off and on the field as the game's major problem.[19] The continuing slump in attendances, it was widely believed, was due almost entirely to the game's 'violent image'. 'The game has reached an extraordinarily low level in the eyes of the public,' argued FA Chairman, Joe Mears. 'We must take immediate steps to remedy it.'[20] Mears' concern was understandably shared by many contemporaries. In 1964 football's spectator problems were still small beer compared with the disorderliness of youth in other contexts. It was precisely in that year, for example, that the confrontations between 'mods' and 'rockers' at coastal resorts were having their fullest impact, generating a 'moral panic' which amplified and distorted the seaside confrontations.[21] Not surprisingly, football's administrators were concerned lest such gang violence should begin to surface in and around football grounds. In particular, they were worried that the regular TV coverage of League and Cup matches might, on the one hand, spread the word about crowd disturbances, hencing inviting imitation elsewhere, and on the other, by widely publicizing the disorderliness of the crowd, contribute even further to the game's worsening image. Moreover, those who ran the professional game were beginning to become convinced that, in an increasingly competitive market in which football's traditional audience was shrinking, new and aggressive techniques would have to be adopted to sustain high revenues. In these new conditions spectator misbehaviour of any kind – especially if it was accorded extensive media-coverage – would severely damage the capacity of football to sell itself to an increasingly discriminating public.

As we have seen, football match attendances in England had been in decline since the boom years of the late 1940s. Other popular leisure pursuits which relied on a largely working-class audience – the cinema and greyhound racing, for example, – suffered even more dramatically. The reasons for the relative decline in the popularity of these cultural forms are complex but they probably lay mainly in changes in the structure and experience of the working class. These came about, at least in part, as a result of the increasing affluence of the 1950s and the widening range of consumer and leisure options. The spread of television and car ownership were probably crucial in this connection. As far as football was specifically concerned, the fact that a growing number of working men could now take their families out on Saturday afternoons and watch football on television in the evening helped to weaken the ties which had grown up earlier between local football clubs and their principal audiences, the more 'respectable' sections of the working class. The post-war consumer boom and the rise in real wages, particularly among routine white-collar workers and the skilled and semi-skilled sections of the working class which made it possible, contributed to this reordering of class practices and meant that, by the early 1960s, the huge football crowds of ten years before were gone, almost certainly for good. Probably also underlying this process and working in the same direction was the growing power of women. More particularly, to the extent that the power of working-class women grew, they would have been enabled to demand that their men should spend more time and money on the family and less on predominantly all-male pursuits such as football, in that way advancing the formation of a more privatized and home-centred working class.

Changes in the game itself in the early 1960s mirrored in a rather exaggerated way some of the more significant changes that were then occurring in the wider society. The abolition in 1962 of the maximum wage, for example, enabled the game's stars to escape into a new and hitherto uncharted world of high earnings. Although nearly all players remained working class in manner, tastes and background, their new conditions of employment thrust at least some of them into a social milieu that had as one of its major defining qualities a veneer of youthful classlessness. This was especially pronounced in the entertainments industry around that time, and football had, by then, come to be defined as a branch of 'entertainment'.[22] This meant that its stars could be used, along with those from show business generally, much more than previously in 'ghosted' features and promotional and advertizing ventures of various kinds. Increasingly, moreover, they were used to appeal to more than just a working-class audience. In a word, footballers became celebrities and they mixed increasingly with celebrities from other walks of life. Non-football celebrities, however, also started to become increasingly involved with football stars and, in that context, more and more of them began to be publicized as watchers of the game. In other words, at a point when football's traditional audience was declining, the game, on account of its new, supposedly classless image, began to become fashionable among members of the newly-emerging cultural elites and some sections of the older ones. As a result, commentators were able to point to the manner in which the changing association game was 'usurping the position of cricket as the sport which is socially OK'.[23] Here was a potentially lucrative market and some clubs reacted with a variety of initiatives aimed at tapping football's new high-spending followers. Fears persisted, however, that the game's new public might be lost should its fashionable image be tarnished by widely publicized spectator misbehaviour. In other words, football's latest attempt to present a more 'respectable' face had the effect of throwing into much sharper relief the disturbances which were already occurring both inside and outside the grounds, hence increasing the concern about them.

The 1966 World Cup

The prospect of England staging the World Cup Finals in 1966 intensified this effect. As Cohen has pointed out, the probability of football hooliganism being accorded the status of an explicitly recognized social problem was considerably heightened in that context because it now began to be perceived as a potential threat to the country's prestige abroad.[24] More particularly, if football crowd disturbances in England were beamed around the world, the nation's tranquil self-image of civilized 'Englishness', a self-image which was believed to obtain one of its chief expressions in our orderly sports crowds, would be called into question. And, as we suggested earlier, in the 1950s and 1960s, the English, perhaps especially members of the ruling elites and media personnel, began to grow increasingly anxious regarding Britain's position in the world. The England football team's defeat by Hungary in 1953 and the Suez debacle of 1956 were among the events that were crucial in this regard, but underlying the doubts and anxieties at a deeper level were the gradual loss of empire and the relatively poor performance of the British economy.

As early as November 1963 newspapers were expressing dire warnings of the consequences that would follow from spectator misbehaviour during the World Cup Finals. The *News of the World*, for example, lent its support to the erection of fences at Everton in that year by reminding its readers that 'Goodison is one of the principal venues for the World Cup in 1966. Complete discipline and control must be established.'[25] In the months which followed, several incidents of spectator misbehaviour in England were accompanied by similar warnings or prescriptions: '18 months from now,' wrote the *Daily Mail* (16 December 1964) 'the widespread and curious world of Association Football will look at the game in the land where it was born. They will shudder to see how tired, worn, even wicked it is.'

At this stage, however, the press were still able to point to crowd troubles abroad as a means of keeping the domestic 'crisis' in perspective. The continental game was widely regarded by English officials, players and supporters with a mixture of suspicion, distrust and, as far as some continental stadia were concerned, outright fear. Such feelings were not the product of simple xenophobia. The violence and accusations of bribery that accompanied Liverpool's European Cup defeat by Inter Milan in April 1965, for example, typified for many commentators in England the English experience in Europe.[26] Off the field, the behaviour of some continental crowds could still easily put that of their English – if not their Scottish – counterparts in the shade. The crowd violence during the visit of Chelsea to Rome in October 1965, for example, found the English press puzzling over the:

> seemingly unaccountable reactions of the massed spectators to almost any sort of play, culminating in the exhibitions of violence and lawlessness that took place during Chelsea's match in Rome this week. It is difficult to imagine passions rising to such heights in this country, or to envisage the need for wire fencing to protect players from spectators.[27]

The writer had evidently forgotten the furore of two years before which had led to the erection of fences at Goodison. *The Times* even went so far as to recommend the withdrawal of British clubs from European competition until the continentals 'had put their house in order'.[28] Two days later, however, on 11 October, following fighting between opposing fans at Old Trafford and between police and youths at Huddersfield, the press had apparently become convinced that English supporters had become 'infected' by what was now a universal 'disease'. *The Times* displayed suitable humility in its comments: 'Let us not be chauvinistic about it. Disorder does not only occur at the football grounds of Italy, Argentina,

Brazil or elsewhere. It now seems to be a universal disease . . . but now more widespread and given greater publicity than before.'[29]

By November, according to the *Sun* (8 November 1965), Manchester United fans were staging their own 'Roman Riots'. Events involving Millwall fans at Brentford in the same month, however, threatened to put even the aggressive displays of United's growing away following into the shade. Despite the long history of crowd disorderliness at the Den, Millwall fans in 1965 found themselves firmly in the shadow of the exploits of some of the emerging groups of travelling supporters from the North, especially those who followed the more successful clubs of the period such as Liverpool, Everton and Manchester United. By the end of that year, however, Millwall fans were ready to reclaim some of their former 'glories'. During a local Derby against Brentford, on 6 November, a dead hand grenade was thrown on to the pitch from the Millwall end. Predictably, perhaps, some sections of the press chose to misread the meaning of this symbolic gesture. 'Soccer Marches to War!' screamed the *Sun* on 8 November. The story continued:

> The Football Association have acted to stamp out this increasing mob violence within 48 hours of the blackest day in British soccer – the grenade day that showed that British supporters can rival anything the South Americans can do.
>
> The World Cup is now less than nine months away. That is all the time we have left to try and restore the once good sporting name of this country. Soccer is sick at the moment. Or better, its crowds seem to have contracted some disease that causes them to break out in fury.

There was fighting at this match both inside and outside the ground, and one Millwall fan sustained a broken jaw.[30] However, the reporter chose to concentrate on the symbolic violence of the hand grenade and implicitly equated this incident with the full-scale riot that had taken place at the match between Peru and Argentina in 1964 when some 318 people were killed and more than 500 injured! Appeals like this and from the *Daily Sketch* (10 December 1965) aimed at ending 'the creeping menace which is blackening the name of soccer', reached a crescendo in the months immediately before the Finals. On 21 April 1966 it was the turn of the *Sun* again. Following violent scenes during the visit of Celtic to Liverpool, its editor commented:

> It may be only a handful of hooligans who are involved at the throwing end, but if this sort of behaviour is repeated in July, the world will conclude that all the British are hooligans . . . Either the drift to violence must be checked or soccer will be destroyed as an entertainment. What an advertisement for the British sporting spirit if we end with football pitches enclosed in protective wire cages.

Young fans from abroad did not attend the 1966 Finals in large numbers. This was probably a major reason why the widely-feared spectator misbehaviour failed to materialize. However, large away contingents *had* now begun to travel regularly to matches in Britain's *domestic* competitions and, in that context, the media and official fears were more firmly based. Nevertheless, there was still a tendency to exaggerate the frequency of the disorders that were occurring. Several aspects of media production conspired to produce these distorting effects. For example, it was around the time of the 1966 World Cup that the popular press started sending reporters to matches to report on crowd behaviour and not simply on the game itself.[31] Previously, football reporters had tended to report only the most visible incidents. Now, less visible incidents, incidents that were less obviously disruptive, began to be reported too, and the increase in the frequency with which they were reported contributed to the impression that football hooliganism was increasing more rapidly than was, in fact, the case.

Sensationalization by the press

Around the same time, too, reflecting the intensifying moral panic about youth violence – part of which consisted of opposition from the predominantly conservative press to the de-criminalizing legislation that was being debated in Parliament in the second half of the 1960s – and perhaps because it helped to sell newspapers in an industry that was growing more competitive, the popular press started to report incidents sensationalistically, often using a military rhetoric. We have already noted the *Sun*'s 'Soccer Marches to War!' Here are a few more examples: 'War on Soccer Hooligans', (*Daily Mirror*, 16 August 1967); 'Courts Go to War on Soccer Louts', (*Daily Mirror*, 22 August 1967); 'Soccer Thugs on the Warpath', (*Sunday Mirror*, 27 August 1967). At the start of the 1967–8 season, after describing how potters' clay had been added to the list of missiles recently thrown by fans at the Stoke City ground, the *Sun* (11 November 1967) even asked its readers rhetorically: 'What Next? Napalm?' By 1969, *The Times* and the *Guardian* had begun to use a similar rhetoric and were informing their readers of the Home Secretary's determination to 'make war' on soccer hooligans.[32] In effect, football grounds became increasingly defined as places where openly violent conflict regularly occurs, hence increasing their attractiveness to youths and young men who found such incidents rewarding and exciting.

There were signs, too, that the media coverage of football hooliganism was contributing *directly* to its escalation. Trouble in and around London grounds, for example, gathered momentum towards the end of 1967 and, as this happened, so the role of the press in helping to trigger incidents became more pronounced. A Chelsea fan convicted of carrying a razor said in court in his defence that he had 'read in a local newspaper that the West Ham lot were going to cause trouble'.[33] This sort of predictive reporting was now becoming commonplace. So, too, were the threats passed between groups of rival fans. With the year drawing to a close, football, it was announced in the *Daily Mirror* (26 September 1967), had entered a 'new era' of terrace rivalry:

> Soccer violence . . . has entered a new era . . . of planned trouble on the terraces. On Friday, 10 November, Oldham Athletic and Stockport County meet in a Third Division match. And already there are threats of trouble being passed between supporters of the two clubs . . . Oldham's young fans have already been told to stand by for major trouble from Stockport supporters when the clubs meet.

As a result of reporting of this kind, supporters who did not hear about planned confrontations on the local grapevine began to be informed about them in the press. By the mid-1970s popular newspapers had even begun to publish 'league tables' of fan violence. Manchester United's Stretford End, for example, was placed at the top of the 'League of Violence' published in the *Daily Mirror* in May 1974. On 12 September the same year the *Daily Mail* joined the bandwagon by publishing a 'Thugs League' of clubs in the metropolitan area:

> Chelsea, London's soccer violence champions for 2 years running, are in line to land the hat-trick. They share the lead with West Ham in Scotland Yard's league of violence – 97 fans having been thrown out of each ground up to 24 August . . . Arrests in and around Spurs' ground at White Hart Lane, Tottenham, put the North London club as Chelsea's main rivals for a title no football club wants.

Tables of this kind may have been intended to shame fans into behaving in a manner more acceptable to 'respectable' groups. In fact they probably had the opposite effect by playing a part in creating a national status hierarchy of football hooligans, giving a more formal character to the emergent status struggle between the different 'football ends'. Henceforth, hooligan fans began to fight increasingly for reputations which, as they saw it, were 'celebrated' by the media. In short, there came into existence two league tables: one official and about matches won or lost; the other unofficial and about who ran, where and from whom and about who were currently branded as the most 'evil' hooligans in the country.

Although the popular press was probably most decisive in this unintended process, television probably played an unwitting part as well. For example, as TV coverage of the game increased, so viewers began to see some of the violent incidents that were occurring inside grounds. They also began to see the new patterns of often obscene chanting that were beginning to develop. On the one hand, this added to the concern of the football authorities and the general public, especially when 'four letter words' began to become clearly audible during transmissions. On the other hand, it acted as a further invitation to youths and young men who were attracted to such behaviour to come and get in on the verbal and physical aspects of the confrontations between fan-groups that were now beginning to occur with increasing regularity.

Football hooliganism and social class

Underlying these developments was the continuing gulf between the 'rougher' and more 'respectable' sections of the working class, a division that was probably intensified as growing affluence led increasing numbers of working-class people to become more privatized, home-centred, consumption-oriented and hence more incorporated into 'respectable' values. The youths and young men who wanted to fight at football were drawn predominantly from the 'rougher' sections of the working class and, as they were recruited to the game, the social composition of its crowds began gradually to change. Quantitatively, this change was not all that great. Football crowds in this country have always been recruited primarily from the more 'respectable' sections of the working class and they remain so to this day. However, the fact that – as a result of official decisions and their own relatively autonomous choices – young males from the 'rougher' sections of the working class began in this period increasingly to congregate on the goal-end terraces of grounds made it appear, both to people in direct attendance and who were watching the game on television, that crowd behaviour was changing significantly 'for the worse'. As a result, from the middle of the 1960s, hooliganism and its coverage by the media were added to the other causes that were leading 'respectable' workers increasingly to desert either the game per se or direct attendance at matches. Simultaneously, however, though not in numbers sufficient to compensate for the loss of more 'respectable' workers, growing numbers of youths and young men from the lower working class began to be attracted to football by the incidents that were now regularly taking place in that context and by the publicity these received.

Summing up, what we have argued in this chapter is that towards the middle and end of the 1950s, in conjunction with the continuing emergence of Britain as an 'affluent society', sections of the working class, especially working-class youths, began to grow more publicly and visibly mobile and assertive. One of the contexts where this found expression was football. At that stage football was less favoured as a context for such behaviour than dance halls, cinemas, pubs and, on bank holidays, seaside resorts. However in the early and middle 1960s the mounting concern of officials and other 'respectable' people over youth misbehaviour, coupled with the fears of the football authorities (at a time when crowds were declining) that hooliganism might lead them to lose both the *nouveaux riches* customers they had started to attract and members of the 'respectable' working class on whom they had traditionally relied, contributed to alarmist reporting which distorted the scale and seriousness of the incidents which were occurring, adding to their apparent frequency. The emergence, in the context of growing competition for readers, of a sensationalizing tabloid press worked in the same direction. So, too, did the connections made by these sections of the press between liberalizing policies and the rising tide of violence and crime. However, the staging of the World Cup Finals played a decisive part in intensifying these anxieties because it was felt to involve the prospect of showing to the world how badly English spectators were behaving. In that way, it was argued – at a time when national self-confidence was declining – it would lower the prestige the nation was felt to enjoy internationally on account of the orderly behaviour of its sporting crowds.

From that point on the media came increasingly to play a part in shaping the behaviour of football hooligans, contributing to a *factual* escalation of spectator misbehaviour. Through the use of a military rhetoric, football grounds began, in effect, to be 'advertized' as places where fighting and not just football regularly takes place. Fans were also told of the likelihood of trouble at particular matches, and the media helped to define a national status hierarchy of football hooligans and a struggle for superiority between the emergent 'football ends'. All this helped to draw in young males from the 'rougher' sections of the working class, probably in greater numbers than ever before, adding to the existing momentum for 'respectable' workers to withdraw their support, especially from the goal-end terraces, and contributing to the position that we find ourselves in today: namely, a situation where hooligan incidents are larger in scale and a much more regular accompaniment of matches than used to be the case; where spectators are increasingly fenced in and heavily policed; and where the English hooliganism problem has been exported to an extent sufficient to lead the terms 'English football fan' and 'hooligan' to be widely regarded on the continent as coterminous.

CHAPTER 8

From the teds and the skins to the ICF

Introduction

In the present chapter we shall extend our analysis of the emergence of football hooliganism in its distinctively modern forms by looking in greater detail at the underlying developments in the working class. We shall also look at some of the ways in which the policies adopted to combat football hooliganism interacted with trends occurring in the youth subcultures of the working class to produce the distinctive 'football ends' and 'fighting crews' of the 1960s and 1970s. Finally, we shall examine the emergence of the more organized 'superhooligan' groups that began to become active in conjunction with football in the late 1970s and early 1980s. We shall also look at the evidence for the belief that the greater organization of such groups can be attributed to the actions of extreme right-wingers.

Before embarking on such an analysis, however, it is necessary to pay rather more attention to the ways in which the development of the working-class youth movements of the 1950s and 1960s – of the teddy boys, for example, and the mods and the rockers – was connected with the wider social developments of that period. It is also necessary to enquire into why such movements generated a high degree of social concern. An analysis of this kind is necessary in order to set the stage for showing how and why the skinheads, the immediate successors of the teds and the mods and the rockers, were the first in this series of working-class youth collectivities to use football as one of their principal stages. We shall begin by recalling a few simple economic facts.

Economic developments in the 1950s and 1960s

The inter-war years in Britain are rememberd by most people as the years of the depression; the years immediately following the Second World war as an era of austerity. The 1950s and 1960s, however, tend, by contrast, to be remembered mainly as the years of affluence. In fact, as we have seen, although this process was interrupted by the war and post-war reconstruction, the foundations of Britain as an affluent society had begun to be established in the 1930s. It was in the 1950s, however, that the most fundamental and far-reaching development of this country as an affluent society oriented towards mass consumption began to take place. Despite the significant reforms in education, health and welfare that were implemented by the Labour Government of 1945–51, it is probably correct to say that virtually no redistribution of wealth occurred in conjunction with this process. Nevertheless, general living standards rose and there was some substance to Harold Macmillan's slogan in the 1959 general election campaign that 'You've never had it so good'. Let us enquire into the evidence for this.

During the 1950s, buttressed by the expansion of the world economy, industrial output in Britain rose at a rate of 3.7 per cent per annum. In the same period, investment consumed some 15 per cent of GNP.[1] Moreover, between 1950 and 1965, earnings increased by more than 40 per cent and real wages by more than a quarter. In that context, 'prosperity slowly lifted virtually the whole of the working class to a higher standard of comfort and well-being and, with some lag, workers' expectations about what constituted a reasonable standard of living also rose'.[2] However, more than factually improving living standards and rising expectations were involved in this overall process for, correlatively, the balance of power between classes had begun to shift in some of its dimensions more in favour of the working class. Although significant in its effects, this power shift was neither permanent nor decisive. It had begun to occur during the war and, just as had happened between 1914 and 1918, it took place in the first instance because members of the dominant classes became more dependent in that context on the working class. Centrally underlying the shift in the post-war period, however, were developments such as the following: the weakening of 'establishment' confidence and unity that occurred in conjunction with the dismantling of the British Empire and the need to adjust to a post-imperial role; the level of working-class unity expressed in electoral support for the Labour Party and through the membership of trades unions; and the power increment relative to employers that workers obtained from low unemployment. It was, in all probability, this overall power shift that lay at the roots of the increased working-class assertiveness that we referred to in Chapter 7. The greater sense of freedom made possible by their growing purchasing power was probably working in the same direction.

Cronin has expressed this greater working-class assertiveness by suggesting that, after the Second World War, the demeanour of the working class began to become 'less tolerant of privilege, hierarchy or deference'.[3] Such a 'decline of deference' received cultural reinforcement from a spate of novels, films and plays in the 1950s and 1960s which gave prominence to a variety of non-deferential working-class heroes.[4] In fact there are a number of indications that this decline of deference occurred more widely across the social spectrum as Britain underwent the drift from the so-called affluent society of the 1950s to the so-called permissive society of the 1960s; that is, the power shift towards the working class which occurred in Britain after the Second World War seems to have embraced all or most sections of the class.[5] Thus the relatively low level of unemployment of that period seems to have enhanced the power chances not only of organized labour but of unorganized labour too.

The growing power of 'youth'

The affluent full-employment society of Britain in the 1950s not only witnessed a slight but significant shift in the power-ratios of the social classes. There also occurred a shift in the balance of power between the generations. The most obvious manifestation of the latter shift was the rise in youth wages; by the early 1950s, 'the average young worker, male or female, had half as much again spending money as his or her counterpart in 1939'.[6] It was this, most fundamentally, which made possible the creation of a specific teenage market. On his visits to Britain in 1954 and 1956 the American Eugene Gilbert, who had become rich through exploiting the teenage market in the United States, concluded that there was no potential for setting up a permanent office in this country. By 1959, however, Mark Abrams had estimated that the total spending power of British youth was no less than £330 million a year.[7] At the same time, the raising of the school-leaving age and the spread of secondary and higher education (which were, of course, constraints on the development of the teenage market), increased the numbers of young people who had not yet entered the adult world of work. In such ways as these, 'youth', more particularly in the first instance working-class youth, began to become a more distinctive and visible group than had been the case before. Centrally underlying this development was the emergence in the 1950s of a commercial-ized youth culture centred around pop music and, connected with it but at the same time having a degree of autonomy, the emergence of a highly uniform national working-class youth style, the style of the 'teddy boys'.

The concept of 'adolescence' as a distinctive life-stage between childhood and adulthood had, of course, long been taking shape in conjunction with industrialization and urbani-zation and the lengthening of the early socialization and education processes that this entailed. The concept of 'youth', however, and more particularly that of the 'teenager', are relatively recent additions to the stock of cultural categories.[8] The degree of national uniformity of the youth styles that emerged in and after the 1950s is also relatively new. Although they were variations on a stock of common themes, the 1880s and 1890s had 'the larrikins' and 'the hooligans' in London, 'the scuttlers' in Manchester and the 'peaky blinders' or 'sloggers' in Birmingham.[9] There were, in all probability, many more locally named 'folk devils' in that period who have not yet come to light. Similarly, in the 1930s people from the more 'respectable' classes were complaining, for example, of youths of seventeen years of age 'imitating adults, wearing long trousers, smoking pipes and swaggering with a girl on their arm'.[10] In the 1950s, however, it was the greater cultural, stylistic and financial *independence* of the working-class young, especially of males – the fact that their clothing and behaviour were *not* imitative of adults – which lay at the heart of much of the concern about 'teddy boy gangs'. At the heart of it, too, lay the fact that, within a comparatively short space of time, adherents to this style emerged across the country and that this was reported by the mass media, including importantly at this stage by television. Indeed, television coverage was probably one of the preconditions both for the diffusion of the teddy-boy style and for the degree of national uniformity that it entailed.

The teddy boys

The evidence about the sorts of youths who were involved in the more serious public order offences attributable to the teds suggests that they were unqualified early school leavers in the main, most of whom were destined for a life of manual labour. Their style emerged initially in the working-class neighbourhoods around the Elephant and Castle in South London. The early teds could hardly be mistaken for the 'pampered' children of an affluent society and certainly not of an increasingly 'classless' one. 'They were market porters, roadworkers, a lot of van boys, all in jobs that didn't offer much – labourers could cover the lot.'[11] In Leicester the teds were drawn mainly from the council estates and the run-down areas of the city centre. Again, 'labourers' were prominent among those reported as having been arrested.[12] In fact the gang fights and vandalism of the teds seem to have owed at least as much to the long-established masculine and territorial traditions of the areas from which they came as they did to what were popularly perceived at the time as the effects of growing affluence and the progressive relaxation of discipline on the lives of young males from the unskilled and semi-skilled sections of the manual working class.

In pointing to such continuities with the past, we are not suggesting that the 'gang' practices of the teds were identical in all respects with earlier forms. It is clear that, in the 1950s, there took place a degree of restructuring both within the working class and in the relations between the working class and the wider society. Relative prosperity, consumerism, greater cultural penetration from the United States, the effects of universal state education on working-class children, and, of course, the power shift that we discussed earlier, were all important in bringing this process about.[13] Although they touched the lives of all working-class people, these changes had their most visible effects on the more 'respectable' sections of the class where they played a part, for example, in leading to their declining interest in traditional class pursuits such as attendance at the Saturday afternoon football match. They were also often experienced as contradictory and expressed in the form of *intra*-class tension and conflict as well as – although this was a partly conflictual process, too – through *inter*-class accommodation and incorporation. The activities of the teds and their followers played an important part in this connection. They formed one of the principal sources and foci of this conflict within the working class and they probably helped to push more 'respectable' people more firmly in the direction of incorporation, in that way again increasing the social distance between themselves and 'rougher' elements. Seabrook and Blackwell shed light on to this conflict when they wrote that the teds revealed 'too many of the faintly grotesque associations with the old working class. They were in part a reincarnation of the dangerous classes and were believed to be carrying coshes, knuckle-dusters and razor blades.'[14]

The 1950s and 1960s also witnessed something approaching a cult of 'working classness'. One of its effects was to push the working class into a position of greater cultural prominence. At the same time, the rise of a music market catering specifically for youth served to give young working people the appearance of having a 'particular hegemony' over many aspects of popular culture.[15] It was, of course, mainly appearance because the prospects for mobility and exercising control available to working-class youths in that context were severely limited. However, the growing power and affluence of the working class, coupled with more general changes in the cultural significance of the class, combined to produce a number of profound effects. One of them was the growing assertiveness which showed itself in the behaviour of the teds as well as among more 'respectable' members of the working class. It is important, though, to note that the avenues which were available or regarded as appropriate for expressing this new-found assertiveness varied. Among the central sources of such variation were the position of groups in the internal stratification hierarchy of the working class and the traditions of particular families and communities. This is a complex issue but generally speaking it can be said that the growing assertiveness of young working-class people from more 'respectable' backgrounds tended to be reflected, for example, in the rise of the working-class grammar-school boy and girl, in the growing numbers of white-collar workers who were originally working class, and in the rise of a whole variety of working-class pop stars. By contrast, the growing assertiveness of young people – especially young males – from the 'rougher' sections of the working class was more liable to find expression in activities that were interpreted as a threat to dominant standards. Such threats were most clearly symbolized by the rise of groups like the teds and, later, by the mods and the rockers, the skinheads and the football hooligans. The scale of the threat such groups were perceived as posing was exaggerated both as a result of the growing uncertainties which beset members of the socially-dominant classes and because of the mounting conflict between 'roughs' and 'respectables' within the working class. Media amplification intensified this effect.

Given both their character and the general context in which they arose, it is understandable that the emergence of the teds should have provoked intense anxieties among the members of more 'respectable' groups. The visible spread of the teddy-boy style and, above all, its emergence as a nationwide phenomenon regularly reported by the media, were clearly central among the processes which led to the intensification in the 1950s of concern about the 'unmanageability' of youth. As a general phenomenon, such concern continued almost unabated in the years which followed. The particular foci of concern, however, shifted as – within the framework of the changing political, economic and racial contours of British society – working-class youth styles themselves evolved and changed.[16] First of all, national concern about youth behaviour shifted briefly to the involvement of black and white youths – the latter allegedly teddy boys – in the so-called race riots in Nottingham and Notting Hill in 1958. After that, it focused for a while on the seaside skirmishes of the mods and rockers. Then, towards the middle of the 1960s, a more permanent focus began to be provided. More particularly, as football hooligan stories began to move more into the headlines, so stories about the continuing seaside antics of the mods and rockers began to fade from public view. At the same time, a new youth style, that of the skinheads, was beginning to emerge. As we have said, these particular 'folk devils' operated with much greater frequency and regularity in a football context than any of the earlier groups. Indeed, so great was their degree of involvement that, even today, the idea of the 'football hooligan' and 'the skinhead' as coterminous remains firmly imprinted in the public consciousness.

It is to these developments that our attention will now be turned. We shall start with an analysis of the emergence of the 'football ends'.

The emergence of the 'football ends'

It is difficult to date the initial emergence of the contemporary 'football ends'. Nevertheless, the main outlines of this process are fairly clear. We have seen how Liverpool and Everton seem to have been the first clubs regularly to attract large away followings. We have also seen how, on account of the train-wrecking exploits they engaged in, Liverpool and Everton fans in the late 1950s and early 1960s earned the label from the media of 'the Merseyside maniacs'. In other words, some Liverpool and Everton fans were the earliest publicized forerunners of the present-day football hooligans. However, that was not their only contribution to the present-day football scene. Liverpool and Everton fans in the 1960s also played a leading part in the development of what has since become a prominent feature of terrace subcultures up and down the country; the replacement of the (to present ears) rather stilted songs and chants of the 1950s and earlier with a larger, often obscene, irreverent and symbolically violent repertoire. These two developments seem to have been different manifestations of the same underlying development; the emergence in Liverpool around that time of what we have called a greater 'assertiveness' among working-class youths and of a burst of irreverent, anti-establishment, anti-'respectable'-society oriented cultural creativity on their part.

The advent of the new forms of singing and chanting probably had the effect of intensifying the tendency towards segregation by age inside grounds. Such a tendency was probably further hardened by the policies of differential pricing for young fans which were common in the early 1960s. The new styles of singing and chanting were, of course, largely the preserve of the young and, by March 1965, newspapers were referring to the 'unhappy incidents' after an FA Cup Semi-Final at Villa Park in which 'a jeering mob of young Liverpool supporters . . . gloatingly chanted over and over again, "Ee, aye, addio, Chelsea's out the cup!"'[17]

As far as we have been able to ascertain, however, it was the start of the 1966–7 League programme which saw the first references in the national press to the activities of 'hooligan gangs' inside and outside stadia. Ad hoc match-day alliances forged between groups of lads and young men from local estates and suburbs began in that period to stake out (mainly) the goal-end terraces as their territory and to act in ways which either deliberately or inadvertently discouraged the presence of older spectators. Previously it had been common practice for young fans to switch ends at half-time. Now, more and more they began to watch from a fixed location. Just as the goalkeeper defended 'their' goal against the attacking man-oeuvres of the opposing side, so, as an almost natural extension, they defended the territory behind it from the opposing fans. When the teams changed ends or if the opponents started the match with the 'home end' behind them, such a position also enabled young fans to attempt, either verbally or by throwing missiles, to put the opposing goalkeeper off his game.

The wider margins provided by the larger terraces at some grounds meant that they were still able to an extent to cater for an age-mixed clientele. But from this point on, the favoured positions – on the 'home' terraces, slightly above and behind the goal – increasingly became the preserve of those young fans who were identified by the media and the game's administrators as the chief perpetrators of football hooliganism. Robins and Cohen point out that the 'youth end' on Arsenal's North Bank at Highbury was born in the 1966–7 season.[18] In October 1966 the Burnley club began to receive complaints from disgruntled fans about 'a number of young supporters creating trouble at matches, particularly behind one goal'.[19] Increasingly, too, major incidents no longer involved the small numbers reported as having typically taken part in disturbances earlier in the decade. Rather, they were now reported to involve 'hundreds' of rival supporters, as in the 'pitched battle' between Everton and Manchester City fans in November 1966, in which '30 to 40 spectators [were] removed from the ground'.[20] At Blackpool in December the same year, 'a gang of about 200' young Blackpool fans were reported to have attacked the coaches carrying Fulham supporters 'long after' the end of the match.[21] By the end of the 1966–7 League campaign, too, the growing numbers of incidents reported inside and in the immediate vicinity of grounds began increasingly to be supplemented by accounts of confrontations between groups of rival fans at railway stations. Knives and other weapons were reported to have been used in some of the worst railway station incidents which took place around that time.

It was also in the 1966–7 season that Northern fans 'arrived' in London, an event which played a part in stirring the embryonic London ends into developing greater levels of cohesion. In the early 1960s, the away travel of young fans had still been restricted by parochialism and cost. In addition, such Northern visitors as had made the journey to the capital had, up until then, retained a healthy respect for home territories, especially in the East End dockland areas where the reputation, especially of Millwall fans, had for a long time induced caution on the part of outsiders. By 1967, however, these fears had evidently begun to diminish for, in the May of that year, Manchester United went to Upton Park, taking with them a large travelling contingent. Young United fans, fast

gaining notoriety at the expense of their Merseyside neighbours, arrived in London seemingly intent on claiming the
North's first terrace success in the capital. Their efforts
marked the beginning of what was to become one of a number
of bitter and long-standing rivalries between football 'fighting
gangs' from London and the provinces. At the West Ham–
Manchester United match, damage was widespread as fighting
spread inside and outside the ground, and twenty people were
hospitalized. It was the day, according to the press, when
British fans finally succeeded in outstripping their continental
and Latin American rivals. Under the headline, 'Soccer's Day
of Shame', the News of the World of Sunday 7 May 1967
proclaimed: 'For years we have despised the Latins for their
hysterical and violent behaviour. In 1967, British fans are
themselves held in disgrace by the rest of the world.'

Penning and segregation

The response of the police and clubs to what, by the end of
1967, was a growing network of inter-end rivalries, still with a
strong local base but with increasing signs of expansion
beyond regional confinements, was to attempt to segregate
opposing fans. At that stage, segregation took two forms: on
the one hand, the use of lines of policemen to keep rival fans
apart; and on the other, the erection of dividing fences on
terraces shared by home and away contingents. At West Ham
in 1967 the emphasis was still on the use of police officers to
provide a barrier between the rival factions. Following their
match with Manchester United in that year, an officer on duty
at the game told a London court that the police had 'great
difficulty in keeping a gangway clear between a large number
of West Ham supporters and about 500 Manchester United
supporters on the North Bank of the stadium. Abuse and
threats were passing between the two opposing factions and
beer cans and pennies were being thrown.'[22] Later in the year,
when United visited Chelsea, a similar strategy was used by
the police in the Shed, where visiting fans were reported to
have outnumbered the home contingent by two to one.[23] At
White Hart Lane, once a 'comparatively quiet backwater for
hooligans' according to The Sunday Times on 15 November

1967, newly-erected steel fences failed to prevent large-scale fights developing between members of the emerging Tottenham and Chelsea ends. The match was held up for ten minutes and there were forty-four arrests, an early record.

At this stage, the pattern of segregation was still largely voluntary, in the sense that it depended on members of the rival fan groups choosing to watch from separate locations in the company of their fellows. As a result, it was rarely totally enforceable. However, although it failed to have a noticeable preventative effect, it did, even in this early form, have a number of unintended consequences. For one thing, it had the effect of demarcating home and opposing territories inside grounds with a greater strictness and clarity than young fans could have achieved on their own. For another, by opposing the separate fan-groups, not only with each other but also with the police, it helped to reinforce their solidarity. It also almost *invited* violation by opposing fans. As early as September 1967, West Bromwich fans were reported to have intentionally positioned themselves in the 'opposing end' of the nominally segregated Hawthorns grounds for the visit of Nottingham Forest. Almost inevitably, fighting broke out between the rival factions.[24]

The introduction of segregation and the increased numbers of policemen that were necessary to enforce it also had the effect of increasing the tendency for hooligan fans to seek confrontations with their rivals *outside* grounds and *away* from the attentions of the police. In short, the phenomenon began to be *displaced* and the incidence of hooliganism at railway stations increased, at that stage it seems especially in London.

It is not difficult to see why hooligan confrontations away from grounds should have occurred increasingly in London. For one thing, there were eleven Football League teams in the metropolis in the 1960s, considerably more than in any other urban area. For another, the tube and rail links to these grounds are difficult for the police and transport officials to cover adequately. Hence, hooligan fans are provided with greater opportunities in that respect. Added to this, the arrival from 1967 onwards of increasing numbers of Northern 'hard cases' in London on match days stung the emerging London crews into taking violent defensive and/or pre-emptive action. Traditional working-class animosities between London and the provinces may also have been indirectly spiced in the mid-1960s by the emergence of the notoriously violent Kray and Richardson 'protection gangs'.[25] More particularly, the 'cool' violence of these London racketeers may have provided role models for working-class teenagers and young adult males who moved around the fringes of the London under-world, in that way helping in the formation of a partly older 'street smart' backbone for some of the major London ends. These sorts of influences would probably have been most strongly felt at clubs which best espoused the dynamism and supposed 'classlessness' of London in the mid-1960s. Chelsea FC was the capital's brightest, most go-ahead club in that period; with its modern showbiz image, it certainly attracted the attentions, not only of the image-conscious 'Martini set', but also of some of the early violent mods with criminal connections or pretensions. Compared with those of their London and provincial rivals, the style of even the early Chelsea ends was distinctively smart *and* violent. It remains so to this day. In the late 1970s and early 1980s it was Chelsea fans who pioneered the movement of violence into the seats, away both from what they regarded as the *gauche* posturing of the 'styleless rabble' on the terraces and from the unwanted attention of the police. It was not deliberately planned, of course, but in the late 1960s the Shed and its various supporting casts were already building for the major rucks of the early 1970s.

The emergence of the skinheads

If Chelsea FC in South London provided one of the focal points for the 'cool', 'smooth' violence of what Cohen has called 'the upwards option' offered by the style of the 'hard mods' and their followers,[26] in the North and East of London in 1968 the distinctive style of the skinheads was beginning to emerge. The stylized hardness of the skins and their celebration of the traditional concerns of the 'rough' working class – their violent masculinity, their community loyalty and collective solidarity, their violent opposition to outsiders and any males who looked 'odd' (including, of course, those like 'queers' whom they saw as posing a threat to their feelings about masculinity) – stood in stark opposition to the images that they held of 'mainstream' mods. To them (and, of course, to the rockers as well) 'mod' meant effeminate, 'stuck up', snobbish, phoney, aspiring to be competitive, emulating the middle class.[27] 'Hard mods', most of whom came from society's lowest strata, did in a sense provide a stylistic link between the mods and skins. Some of them wore jeans and industrial work-boots and were, perhaps, the forerunners of the latter. The majority, however, managed to combine elements of 'the upwards option' provided by the mod style with at least some of the skins' predilection for group loyalty and violence. Herein, at least in part, lay the emergent differences in character between the East London ends and those in the South; between, say, West Ham's North Bank and the Shed; between the early skins and the style-oriented 'hard mods'.

Whilst the skinhead movement cannnot be adequately explained without reference to the sorts of changes discussed by theorists such as Clarke, it seems to us reasonable to suppose that the distinctive aggressiveness of their style was probably more fundamentally connected with the threat to traditional lower-working-class conceptions of gender and masculinity that was posed in the 1960s, on the one hand, by the mods and, on the other, by 'the hippies'.[28] With their fetishistic concern with style, their sexually mixed gangs and use of drugs, the mods were offensive enough to the 'heavy' masculinity of lads at the unskilled end of the labour market. But the emergence in Britain in the mid-1960s of the popular bohemianism of the hippies was probably among the major stimuli for 'the skinhead offensive'. The 'work-shy' 'dirty' hippies, with their pro-drug pacifism and the fact that many of them were 'pampered' university and polytechnic students, must have been anathema to lads from the poorer working-class estates. Moreover, the pronouncedly 'effeminate' aspects of the hippie style were probably important both in provoking many aspects of skinhead symbolism (which was, of course, diametrically opposed to the symbolism of the hippies) and in providing the skins with what they took to be justification for extending their 'queer-bashing' practices to all males who offended their rigid conceptions of what constitutes an 'acceptable masculine style'. Although they were wheeled into violent and increasingly prominent action in the late 1960s under the full glare of an attentive media, such conceptions are deeply rooted in the traditions of lower-working-class communities. The skinhead movement may have constituted, in part, a response to the economic insecurities experienced in particular by East End working-class youths in that period – insecurities connected with the containerization of the docks, for example, and which were played upon and accentuated by 'Powellism' and the 'race crisis' of the 1960s. However the violence of the skins, their hostility towards 'outsiders' and the 'defence' of the community that they engaged in – albeit at football, on a new, national scale – also represented a continuation of *traditional* class practice.[29] As one of the East End's original skins told Daniel and Maguire, 'When people kept saying skinheads, when they're talking about the story of us coming up from the East End, this has happened for generations before . . . I mean, where does skinhead come into it?'[30] According to these authors, 'the Collinwood gang' from which the above interviewee was drawn:

> sees itself as a natural continuation of the working class tradition of the area, with the same attitudes and behaviour as their parents and grandparents before them. They believe that they have the same stereotyped prejudices against immigrants and aliens as they believe their parents have and had.[31]

Whatever the balance in this regard between continuity and change, it is clear that the skinhead movement had a number of profound effects on the emerging football ends. For one thing, the severe image of the skins with its expression of a standardized and very 'hard' masculinity was one that lads from 'hard' neighbourhoods could easily adopt. For 'core stylists' the Ben Sherman, the braces and the Doc Martens were compulsory but the skins had little of the narcissism and stylistic exclusionism of the mods. Hence the constraints on either adopting the style as a whole or on taking up aspects of it were relatively few. Moreover, the skins' stylistic message was simpler than that of the mods. The 'prison crop' hairstyle and, to a lesser extent, the boots and braces, were all that was necessary to express the central tenet of 'the skinhead message' – hardness. When in 1969 the label 'skinhead' became synonymous, both popularly and in the media, with 'aggro' ('bovver') and soccer hooliganism, thousands of terrace 'hard cases' made the trek to the local barbers. As Cohen and Robins have correctly pointed out, the skins did not create the football ends.[32] Football, more particularly the increasing coverage of violence at matches, gave them a highly visible public platform. What they contributed to the ends was an enhanced solidarity and, for a while, a common style. Furthermore, 'the skinhead movement' rallied many of the young working-class supporters who were already attending matches. It also attracted new recruits to bolster the developing *national* network of rival ends.

Skinheads and fighting at football

With the influx of the skins, 'gangs' began to take precedence over the game to a greater extent than had tended to be the case before. The distinctive aggressiveness of the skins, the degree of organization skinhead crews helped to bring to the football ends and the sense of unity that their style helped to give to young goal-terrace fans, all contributed to an intensification of the territorial preoccupations of rival factions. No greater disgrace, no greater loss of masculine pride could local fighting crews endure from the end of the 1960s onwards than to 'surrender' the home end to visiting fans. The popular goal-end terraces, already moving in that direction as a result of the interplay of official policies and relatively autonomous developments in popular culture and the working class, were increasingly transformed from that period onwards into 'territories' over the occupation of which rival supporters would do physical battle prior to and during the match.

Those charged with keeping order inside stadia were slow to appreciate the significance of the changes in match-day emphasis that were being brought about, at least in part, by the rise of the skins. Organized concerted ploys by away fans designed to violate the 'home turf', for example, often went unchecked, particularly in the provinces. Thus Leeds United 'took' Stoke City in January 1970, with the local police in disarray:

> Fanatical fans deliberately started the crowd sway at Stoke City's football ground which ended with 61 people being taken to hospital . . . 14 of them were detained, many with head injuries . . . Mr. Albert Henshall, Stoke Chairman, said, 'We could do nothing about it . . . The end where it happened is the popular one for our fanatical supporters. When they found their usual places taken by Leeds fans there was resentment. They were spitting at each other and shouting abuse.[33]

With the increasing frequency of such incidents, the Minister for Sport recommended that all grounds should be divided into manageable 'pens' in order to assist with crowd control. In October 1970 the FA advised all League clubs that grounds must meet new stringent standards, including the introduction of smaller self-contained enclosures.

The skinheads not only brought higher levels of solidarity and organization to the football ends and increased their sense of territorial identification and proprietorship. They also contributed to the spread of football hooliganism, not only to railway stations and the immediate vicinity of grounds, but also to city centres and beyond. In September 1969, for example, following their riotous return from a defeat at Derby, 500 Tottenham supporters were unceremoniously 'dumped' by British Rail 40 minutes before their train reached London. Undeterred, the North Londoners set to work on the Bedfordshire village of Flitwick, to destructive effect. Damage was widespread as villagers rushed away from a local function to protect their homes.[34] The repercussions of Flitwick in terms of the control of supporters travelling to and from football matches in England were considerable. However, the major significance of the Flitwick affair probably lay in its message for the general public; hooliganism was quite capable of moving into anyone's back garden.

Manchester United's 'Red Army'

In the late 1960s and early 1970s, 'bovver alerts' around the country continued to provide frequent headlines. Boots and even laces were confiscated at turnstiles as the term 'skinhead' began to become synonymous with 'football hooligan'. In March 1970 Chelsea fans, already to the fore in London, were assured by police in Coventry that they were 'the worst behaved supporters' that the local force had yet encountered.[35] The point was quickly impressed upon Manchester United fans. Following the Northern club's visit to Stamford Bridge a few weeks later, sixty-five fans (drawn from Chelsea as well as United) were charged with causing an affray near Ealbrook Common. This was one of the earliest publicized events in the rise of Manchester United fans – of the so-called 'Red Army' – to a position of supremacy among the country's football hooligans. Let us enquire into that process a little more closely.

As a result of its successes on the field, Manchester United had been able to mobilize nationwide support since at least the 1950s. In the late 1960s, however, its more troublesome followers earned from the press the name 'Red Army'. From that point onwards, attracted by the United legend, perhaps disillusioned by the impotence of their local ends and probably seduced by the excitement and feeling of collective strength which came from the identification with the dreaded 'Stretford Enders', young working-class fans from around the country started to augment United's disruptive following, particularly on away days.[36] Regional enmities, however, frequently intervened. Manchester-based United 'hard cases' were soon awaiting the arrival of 'Cockney Reds' at United's home games with the message that the 'Red Army's' formidable reputation was a matter for Manchester and *not* London concern.

By 1974 the *Daily Mirror* had placed United's 'Stretford Enders' at the top of its 'League of Violence', claiming that the Manchester club had the country's 'worst behaved fans' and that it was 'the team whose visit is most dreaded'.[37] This reputation was enhanced by their behaviour at Old Trafford. Manchester United's final game of the 1973–4 season was against local rivals Manchester City. Should United lose it, they would be relegated. With minutes of the match remaining and United in arrears, the Stretford End poured on to the pitch. Little violence was involved. The invasion was, it seems, a spontaneous collective gesture occasioned by a shared desire to halt the match, secure a replay and, hence, maximize the club's chances of avoiding relegation. In the event, the match was abandoned but the Football League ruled that the result should stand, hence sealing United's fate. More importantly for present purposes, however, the 1974 pitch invasion was central in leading Manchester United to erect a steel fence along the perimeter of the Stretford End, an act which had the unintended consequence of further enhancing both the solidarity of 'the Red Army' and their prestige in the eyes of ends elsewhere.

It had another unintended consequence, too. Earlier that season, following the first *televized* post-match 'ruck' – between Chelsea and Derby fans on the pitch at Derby County in August – Len Shipman, the President of the Football League, called for harsh punishments and declared "They are worse than hooligans. I can only describe them as wild animals.'[38] Such a designation began frequently to be used by the press from that time onwards. Far from being shamed into more orderly behaviour, however, the hard core of United's travelling crews seemed to revel in it. Moreover, they felt that their status as 'animals' was confirmed by the fact that they would henceforth have to watch, as it were, from inside a cage, a fact which led them to introduce the new chant 'We hate humans!'

Commenting on the fence, an *Observer* reporter wrote on 1 December 1974:

> The Stretford End ... is a kind of academy of violence, where promising young fans can study the arts of intimidation. This season the club installed a metal barrier between the fans and the ground. It resembles the sort of cage, formidable and expensive, that is put up by a zoo to contain the animals it needs but slightly fears. Its effect has been to make the Stretford terraces even more exclusive and to turn the occupants into an elite.

And a kind of elite they were! The hard core of the Stretford End drew recruits from far and wide as their members swarmed into the territories of opposing clubs. Robins and Cohen have described how the Red Army 'took' not only Arsenal's North Bank but also virtually the whole of that part of North London as early as the spring of 1972:

a thousand of their supporters marched from King's Cross Station
up the main road skirting the Monmouth estate to the stadium. On
the way they broke windows, smashed cars, threw rocks and
swore at passers-by. Scattered groups of local youths shouted
resistance – from a safe distance. At the end of the day the
Stretford end had not only 'taken' the North Bank, but the whole
of this part of north London.[39]

The height of 'the Red Army's' power to attract public
attention was probably reached in September 1974 when the
club – now in the Second Division – visited Cardiff. In fact
'the Cardiff affair' represented a watershed in the reporting of
football hooliganism because, previously, the game itself had
always merited at least equal news status prior to and on the
day of the match. As the Ninian Park meeting approached,
however, newspaper reports referring to 'Cardiff v United'
raised few questions about the forthcoming encounter *on the
field*. Only a week beforehand, Cardiff fans had provided a fair
share of the 125 arrests made at their match with Bristol City.
What the press and public were now awaiting was to see
whether the much-vaunted violence of the Stretford Enders
and their allies had finally met its match. The South Wales
police waited, too, their spokesmen announcing that 100 extra
officers had been drafted and predicting that 'the two groups
could be proud of their bad reputations and may try to fight it
out'.[40] As barricades were put up in the days before the match,
there were warnings that 500 'troublemakers' would be
making the trip to South Wales and that, 'to use their own
words, may try to see who rules'.[41]

On this occasion the massive police presence, together with
the preparations effected by the club, served to limit the scale
and seriousness of the confrontation between rival fans. That
was not so much the case, however, at the Manchester club's
match with West Ham at Upton Park in October 1975. When
Manchester fans arrived in London they found the East End in
a state of readiness for a siege. Staff on the underground had
decided to strike rather than ferry United supporters to the
ground. Hundreds of police and stewards were employed in
what was described as a 'massive security operation'.[42]
Despite these precautions, serious disturbances occurred in
and around the ground, 100 fans were reported to have been

injured, and the match was halted for several minutes as fighting fans and those seeking to protect themselves poured on to the field of play. Nevertheless, newspaper reports carried little hint of condemnation. Instead, the West Ham 'fighting crews' – which had, in fact, routed the visitors – were cast, alongside the police, in the role of 'avenging angels'. The *Sun*'s report of 27 October, for example, was jubilant. Under the headline 'The Day The Terrace Terrors Were Hunted Like Animals and *Hammered!*', (the *Sun*'s emphasis) its account of the scenes at Upton Park continued: 'Manchester United fans – the terrors of the terraces – were nursing their wounds yesterday after a savage hammering from their West Ham rivals. For once they were at the receiving end of a mass punch up. A United supporter said, "We were outnumbered and hunted like animals."'

Organization, planning and the rise of the superhooligans

Two years later in France, visiting United fans were accused of initiating disturbances that involved St Etienne supporters and riot police. Once again, the British game was widely reported to be 'in disgrace' but, according to the *Evening Standard*, so, too, were United's fighting gangs for they had been 'humiliated into surrender by a Dad's Army of peace-loving French fans'.[43] The Red Army's demise did not mean, however, that Britain's 'hooligan problem' was about to subside, for there were several other fan-groups eager to take their 'coveted' place at the top of the 'violence league'. Moreover, as the events at St Etienne showed very clearly, in that period, British, and more particularly English, fans were starting to export their hooligan activities to continental countries.[44]

Besides being exported abroad, from the mid-1970s onwards the behaviour of English football hooligans began to become less *ad hoc* and to involve a greater degree of planning. The first signs of this came through the production of leaflets urging fans to gather and fight at particular matches. In 1977, for example, Chelsea fans 'took' the previously impregnable St James' Park, Newcastle. Before the return fixture at Stamford

Bridge, thousands of photostated leaflets surfaced in the North East urging Geordie fans to make the trip to London to 'smash down the gates and kick the Cockneys all over the place'. The venture was necessitated, according to the leaflet's author, because, following the Chelsea success in the North, 'Geordies have become a joke for being soft'.[45] Newspaper headlines like 'Geordie Thugs of War'[46] and reports that Newcastle leaflets had found their way down to London added further fuel to the rivalry and resulted in a massive deployment of police in an effort to reduce the prospects of disturbances.

Revenge was also the motive for the printing of a Millwall leaflet in 1978. It was designed to rally dockland 'hard cases' for a meeting with West Ham. A Millwall fan, Ian Pratt, had died in September 1976 following a scuffle with West Ham rivals that led him to fall from a train. Millwall fans pledged their revenge and waited patiently for a match between their team and its East London neighbours. Their opportunity came in October 1978. In the weeks prior to what, for Millwall fans, was the 'needle' match with West Ham, a leaflet carrying a blurred photograph of Pratt circulated in pubs along the Old Kent Road, calling for revenge on 'the West Ham bastards' who had 'killed a Millwall fan'.[47]

The West Ham–Millwall match produced what, up until that time, was the most comprehensive and sophisticated show of force for dealing with spectators at an English Football League match. All told, more than 500 police officers took part. Those on foot included dog handlers. They were augmented by mounted policemen and assisted by aerial surveillance from a circling helicopter. In the event, we are told, 'the massive police presence stifled most of the fans' violent intentions'.[48] Nevertheless, seventy were arrested.

The greater levels of planning, organization, tactical sophistication and simple force of numbers that began to be employed by the police in combating football hooliganism in the late 1970s probably played an important part in producing, as a counter-development, the greater levels of planning, organization and tactical sophistication that began to be shown by groups of football hooligans around that time. In fact the football hooligans and the police are probably best conceptualized as being involved in a process of 'mutual' or 'co-production'. Hooligans throughout the 1970s and 1980s seemed to respond to controls and punishments, not by abandoning their commitment, but by devising strategies that enabled them to circumvent official controls and to fight with a minimum risk of being apprehended. For their part, the police and the authorities are equally committed to eradicating football hooliganism and, so great is their attachment to policies of punishment and control, that they respond to each innovation by the hooligans by producing harsher punishments and new, tighter and more comprehensive controls. And so the process goes on, in an ever-upwards spiral. It was probably in this way that what we have called the 'superhooligan' groups came into existence. West Ham's Inter City Firm can serve as an example. The members of West Ham United's self-styled Inter City Firm gave themselves this name because they do not travel to matches on football specials or in official supporters' club coaches but tend, instead, to use regular (Inter City) rail services. Alternatively, they travel by car or in hired vans. Such modes of travel maximize their chances of escaping official control and enable them to inject an element of surprise into their operations. Like many 'hard cases' since at least the early 1970s, the ICF eschew the forms of dress and the club emblems that are worn by many non-hooligan supporters and which still tend to be widely thought of as characteristic features of 'the hooligan style'. The ICF travel in this manner because one of their main objectives in attending matches is to fight and intimidate opposing fans, to 'take their ends', and establish territorial dominance over their 'turf'. Therefore, in order not to advertise themselves too soon, especially to the police, they avoid marks which would obviously identify them as supporters of their team.

The ICF have a hard core of about 150 members though they can call on the services of somewhere in the region of 400 for a 'needle' match. As we have said, they are one of a number of gangs who, in the late 1970s and early 1980s, began to bring a greater degree of organization and sophistication to the planning of football hooligan fighting and to the execution of the manoeuvres that are typically involved. Among the other comparable gangs are the Service Crew at Leeds, the Bushwackers and the Nutty Turn Out at Millwall, the Gooners at Arsenal, the Headhunters at Chelsea and the Baby Squad at Leicester. Similar, less well-publicized gangs have also attached themselves to clubs in Scotland. The ICF can again be used to illustrate the characteristic organization of such groups and the sorts of tactics they employ.

Members of the ICF tend to be in their late teens and twenties. They make use of young fans – 'the Under Fives' (they are, in fact, mainly fourteen and fifteen year olds) – in order to reconnoitre the numbers, locations and dispositions of opposing fans and the police. The ICF use complex strategies to avoid police controls and to infiltrate home territories on their visits to away grounds. Before matches away from home, they typically roam the streets and pubs of the local 'manor', seeking out local fans who can be identified as the opposition's equivalent to the ICF. At home matches the ICF try to attack and intimidate the members of visiting ends who show sufficient 'nerve' to visit West Ham. Often frustrated by the lack of opposition at Upton Park, the ICF will, on occasion, travel to other parts of London in the hope of engaging members of rival London ends on their own territories.

In 1985 the ICF and members of the Gooners Crew at Arsenal were involved in a number of violent incidents in clubs and discos as well as at football. In some of these incidents, clubs and tear gas were reported to have been used. The intensity of this rivalry may stem from an incident in 1982 when an Arsenal fan was stabbed to death, allegedly by a member of the ICF, at the Arsenal tube station. ICF 'calling cards', reading 'Congratulations, you have just met the ICF', were allegedly found at the scene of this incident.

Although it is doubtful whether the kind and degree of nihilism involved in acts of this kind is widespread, either in the ICF or any of the other 'superhooligan gangs', it is certainly the case that, correlatively with the emergence of such groups, football hooligan confrontations began, from the late 1970s, to grow more violent and to pose a threat to life itself more frequently than had previously been the case. In March 1979, for example, a petrol bomb was thrown in St James' Park, Newcastle, by an eighteen-year-old fan who was reported as having said in his defence that he 'wanted to put

Newcastle on the map'.[49] In January 1980 a Swansea fan was fatally stabbed to death outside Ninian Park, Cardiff, and in September 1983 a cache of petrol bombs was found before what turned into a riot involving Chelsea fans at Brighton. Two months later, groups of Chelsea fans on a train were themselves the victims of a petrol bomb attack by supporters of Leeds United.[50] To date, the culmination of this trend towards escalating violence involving English football hooligans has been, of course, the death of the thirty-nine mostly Italian fans at the Heysel Stadium in Brussels in May 1985.

Football hooliganism and the National Front

With the emergence of the superhooligans and the growing violence of at least the more serious football hooligan incidents, the belief began to gain ground that a conspiracy by far-right political groups was responsible for these trends. For example, serious violence at the FA Cup Quarter-Final match between Luton and Millwall in March 1985, which involved attacks on Asian shopkeepers as well as the police, was widely blamed on the National Front.[41] Members of right-wing groups were also allegedly involved in serious disturbances at Birmingham City in May of that year.[52] Similarly, following the Heysel tragedy, the Chairman of Liverpool FC spoke of how 'Six members of Chelsea National Front had boasted to him of their part in provoking the violence and said they seemed proud of their handiwork.'[53] According to the Popplewell Inquiry, a number of banners decorated with swastikas were recovered after the match. An NF contingent, it was reported, was also clearly seen in Blocks X and Y of the Heysel Stadium (those immediately adjacent to Block Z where the deaths occurred). Finally, a party of Londoners wearing Liverpool colours, tattooed with swastikas and the letters NF, and carrying Union Jacks, were observed leaving the main Brussels station.[54] Despite evidence of this kind, the Popplewell Committee reached the conclusion that 'there is little to connect (such groups) with organized violence' and that 'it is right that too much importance should not be attached to their activities'.[55] By and large we agree with Mr Justice Popplewell.

Let us look at some of the evidence that links extreme right-wing groups with football hooliganism. Faced with declining electoral support, the National Front and other similar far-right parties began in the late 1970s seeking to recruit disaffected lower-working-class youths from the football terraces. As far as we can ascertain, the clubs where they have been the most active to date are Chelsea, Leeds United, Millwall and West Ham. By the early 1980s *Bulldog*, 'the Paper of the Young National Front', was devoting a regular column to articles 'On the Football Front' and exhorting fans to 'join the fight for race and union'.[56] Around the same time, too, they began to become commercially active in a football context. For example, in a report published in October 1980, the *Daily Mail* revealed the existence outside Upton Park on match days of a trade in NF-doctored West Ham T-shirts which 'raised about £70 for party funds on a good day'.[57]

It would be pointless to carry on piling up evidence of this kind. There is no doubt about the involvement of the NF on the football terraces or about their influence on some hooligan groups. The lads and young men most frequently involved in football violence tend to have the sorts of life-experiences which make them susceptible to the ideologies of the racist right. This, of course, is what accounts for the interest shown in them by the NF (and by its splinter group, the BNP) as a promising source of recruits. Nor is there any doubt – although the Popplewell Committee were equivocal on this – about the frequent involvement of NF members in incidents of terrace violence. There are, however, doubts about the intensity and consistency of the support of some football hooligans for the fascist party. A nineteen-year-old West Ham fan interviewed in 1981, for example, claimed that much of the 'Sieg Heiling' is 'just good for a laugh . . . to wind the other side up'.[58] It has even been reported that, at an NF march in Lewisham, the ICF fought on behalf of the Socialist Workers' Party *against* the National Front.[59] Some members of the ICF involved were black.

The explanation of football hooliganism as resulting from an 'NF conspiracy' stands in marked contradiction to the depiction of football hooliganism as 'mindless violence'. It is as if people have to see the phenomenon either as completely chaotic and inexplicable mayhem or as totally orchestrated by 'sinister forces'. Alternatively, they may rely on the latter 'explanation' because they are unable to appreciate the fact that 'mindless' and 'moronic' football hooligans are quite capable of organizing their activities on their own. The point, of course, is that football hooliganism existed *before* the interest shown in it by the National Front. Moreover, whilst some superhooligans openly flout their membership (or perhaps simply their allegiance to and informal support for) the fascist party, others do not; that is, the organization and the tactical sophistication they display exist *independently* of the involvement of the National Front. It follows that football hooliganism requires a deeper explanation, one that probes to the roots both of football hooliganism as a social phenomenon and to what it is about football hooligans that makes them appeal to fascist groups. In Chapter 9 we shall address ourselves to that task.

CHAPTER 9

The social roots of aggressive masculinity

Introduction

So far in this study we have shown how spectator disorderliness has accompanied professional football in England since the game emerged in its modern form. However the frequency with which such disorderliness has been reported, its seriousness and the balance between different forms have varied considerably over time and regionally as well. Despite this, there have been some relatively constant features. One has been the display of aggressiveness by males. Another has been the strong, narrowly local identifications of the fans involved and the fact that, with the probable exception of referees and linesmen in the years before the First World War, both the initiators and the recipients of such aggressiveness have been, for the most part, working class. This immediately raises the question of what makes 'aggressive masculinity' a common and relatively persistent working-class social characteristic, especially among the less incorporated sections of the class. A related question concerns the strong and narrowly local identifications which also appear to be relatively common and persistent in sections of the working class. These identifications can lead football supporters to fight other fans who are socially like themselves simply because they come from somewhere else and support a different team. Alternatively, they can lead them to attack match officials and opposing players just because the latter are in a position, whether by fair means or foul, to prevent the side with which the fans identify from achieving victory.

184

We have already devoted considerable attention to these issues in passing, especially in Chapter 4. In the present chapter, however, we shall address them systematically and at length. We shall begin with a brief review of some of the literature on aggression. Then, at greater length, we shall undertake a critical examination of the principal sociological attempts to address the social roots of working-class male aggressiveness that are currently on offer. After that we shall present, in outline form, our own alternative model. As will be seen, this model is a synthesis based largely on a critical elaboration of aspects of Suttles' theories of 'ordered segmentation'[1] and 'the defended neighbourhood'.[2] It attempts to address the question of the comparative narrowness of working-class identifications and not just the social production in specific sections of the working class of a distinctive form of male aggressiveness. The chapter is also intended as a contribution to the theory of 'civilizing' processes.

The social composition of football crowds

We have shown how the available evidence suggests that, at the start of the modern game, football crowds tended to have a mixed social composition. As the nineteenth century drew to a close, however, perhaps partly as a consequence of the frequency with which crowd disorderliness was reported and perhaps, too, because, in a period of mounting class tension and conflict over amateurism and professionalism in sport, the game was becoming more and more publicly identified as professional and working class – both terms had similarly negative connotations for many upper- and middle-class people at that time – upper-class, middle-class and female attendance declined. 'Gentlemen' and 'ladies' who continued to attend now watched primarily from the stands, and the terraces became predominantly working-class male preserves.

This trend was reversed between the wars when, as far as we can tell because of the declining occurrence of crowd disorderliness and because of what we have described as the growing incorporation of the working class, there was a tendency for football to attract more 'respectable' men and women in growing numbers. The trend towards growing 'respectability' was by and large maintained between 1945 and 1950–1, the season in which attendance levels reached their peak. Since the mid-1950s, however, but particularly since the mid-1960s when football grounds began to be depicted in the media as places where disorders regularly took place, the game – although gates have continued generally to fall – has attracted increasing numbers of youths and young men from the 'rougher' sections of the working class. All the available evidence, however, suggests that 'respectable' working-class males continue to constitute the majority of the average crowd and that a not unsizeable number of lower-middle-class men attend the majority of matches.[3]

The social origins of the football hooligans

The available data on football hooligans, however, contrast markedly with survey data on crowd composition. They show a far higher concentration towards the bottom of the social scale. The Harrington Report, for example, concluded in 1968 that:

> the present evidence suggests that [football hooligans] are mainly from a working class background with the special problems inherent in large industrial cities and ports where violent and delinquent subcultures are known to exist. Some youths behave on the terraces in ways which are not unfamiliar to them in streets around their slum houses.[4]

More particularly, analysis of 497 convicted soccer hooligans by occupation showed a preponderance of labourers and unskilled workers (see Table 9.1)

Over a decade later Trivizas reached a similar conclusion. More particularly, on the basis of data about 520 offences committed in 'football crowd events' in the Metropolitan Police Area during the years 1974–6, he found that:

> more than two-thirds (68.1%) of those charged with football-related offences were manual workers, the majority being apprentices; 12% of football offences were committed by unemployed persons and 10% by schoolboys ... Only 8 football-related offences were committed by people in 'intermediate occupations'. 6 were committed by students, 3 by individuals in professional occupations, and 3 by members of the armed forces.

Table 9.1 Occupations of convicted soccer hooligans

Occupation	No.
School or apprentice	79
Unskilled/labourer	206
Semi-skilled	112
Skilled	50
Salesman/clerical	19
Professional and managerial	2
Not known or unemployed	29
Total	497

Source: J. A. Harrington, *Soccer Hooliganism*, John Wright, Bristol, 1968.

Interestingly in the light of popular ideas about the causes of football hooliganism, Trivizas also found that unemployed people were less frequently charged with offences such as 'using threatening or abusive or insulting words or behaviour' in the context of football than they were elsewhere.[5]

Harrison's impressionistic account of Cardiff City's 'committed rowdies' in 1974 paints a similar picture. He had them coming from 'Canton and Grangetown, rows of terraced houses with few open spaces, and from Llanrumney, a massive council estate with an appalling record of vandalism'.[6] Although Marsh et al. did not directly address the issue of class background, some of their informants did provide relevant comments. For example, one of them said 'If you live up on the Leys [a local council estate] then you have to fight or else people piss you about and think you're a bit soft or something.'[7] In fact, over half the large contingent of Oxford fans arrested during serious disturbances at the Coventry City–Oxford United FA Cup match in January 1981 came from the estate in question.[8] Evidence from Leicester supports this general picture. One council estate alone – we have called it 'the West Kingsley estate' – contributed eighty-seven, or 20.32 per cent, of the 428 local arrestees in the period 1976–80.[9]

Data such as these on persons arrested for football hooligan offences are, of course, not necessarily a reliable indicator of the occupational and social-class characteristics of football

Table 9.2   Occupations of West Ham United's Inter City Firm

2 Carpenters/joiners	1 Post Office worker	1 Insurance under-
1 Apprentice electri-	2 Labourers (British	writer
cian	Rail)	1 Bank manager
3 Electricians	4 Factory workers	4 Chefs
2 Bricklayers	1 Cigarette-factory	4 Plumbers
14 Bouncers	worker	6 Motor mechanics
1 Manager (clothing	1 Landscape gardener	6 Market traders
store)	8 Army personnel	2 Dockers
1 Cab driver	(incl. 1 sergeant)	2 Firemen
2 Painters/decorators	4 Lorry drivers	12 Ticket touts
1 Meat wholesaler	2 Solicitors' clerks	32 Unemployed
3 Clothes manufac-	2 Dustmen	1 Bus driver
turers	10 Rock musicians	1 Trainee publican
3 Publicans	2 Door-to-door	
	salesmen	

Total = 141

Source: Ian Stuttard of Thames Television.

hooligans generally.[10] Nevertheless, our data suggest that core football hooligans, even those who have managed to avoid arrest in the football context, tend to come from similar class backgrounds to those arrested for football-related offences; that is, they tend to come predominantly from around the bottom of the social scale. Take, for example, the occupations of 'the Kingsley lads', the football hooligans from the Leicester estate that we studied. In 1981 and 1982 the occupations of twenty-three leading members of this group were two drivers, one barman, one slaughterhouseman, three bouncers, one bookmaker's assistant, three factory workers (two in the hosiery trade and one in boots and shoes), one milkman, one apprentice printer, one apprentice electrician, one builder's labourer and eight unemployed.

Our most systematic and detailed data, however, are on the occupational and social class characteristics of the members of West Ham's Inter City Firm. As we saw in Chapter 8, the nucleus of the ICF numbers approximately 150, though for big games and/or when a major confrontation with opposing fans is anticipated this nucleus can swell to 350 or 400. Although we cannot be sure of their validity in all cases, we have

Table 9.3   Social class membership of West Ham's ICF
(Registrar General's classification)

Classification	Nos	%
1 Professional, etc.	0	0.0
2 Intermediate	8*	5.7
3 Skilled non-manual	2	
Skilled manual	34	24.1
4 Partly skilled	10	7.0
5 Unskilled	25**	17.7
Unemployed	32	22.7
Unclassifiable	30***	21.2
Total	141	

* Includes the bank manager, the insurance underwriter and the manager
  of the clothing store.
** Includes the 14 bouncers.
*** Includes the 10 rock musicians, all of whom were non-professional, the
  12 ticket touts, and the 8 members of the armed forces.

obtained data on the occupations of 141 members of the ICF.[11]
They are set forth in Table 9.2. In terms of the Registrar
General's classification scheme, the social class membership
of the ICF is as shown in Table 9.3.

We have thus, in all, data on 519 football hooligans who, at
the time of observation, were in employment. (This figure
excludes those from Trivizas' study because he gives percen-
tages but not numbers. For obvious reasons our figure also
excludes the numbers in Harrington's combined categories
'school or apprentice' and 'not known or unemployed'). Their
social class membership is set forth in Table 9.4. Thus the
overwhelming majority – 475 or 91.5 per cent of the employed
football hooligans on whom we have information work, or
worked, in manual occupations. Only a minority of these – 98
or 18.9 per cent – were skilled. The rest – 377 or 72.6 per cent
– were partly skilled or unskilled, and the unskilled category
provided the highest number – 245 or 47.2 per cent.
Furthermore, only a minority, albeit a large one, of the football
hooligans on whom we have information – thirty two (37.8
per cent) of the ICF and eight of 'the Kingsley lads' – were

Table 9.4   Social class membership of football hooligans
(Registrar General's classification)

Classification	Nos	%
1 Professional, etc.	2	0.4
2 Intermediate	13	2.5
3 Skilled non-manual	29	5.6
Skilled manual	98	18.9
4 Partly skilled	132	25.4
5 Unskilled	245	47.2
Total	519	100

unemployed at the time of the research. While there are, of course, regional variations in this regard, this contrasts with the idea, popular on the political left, that all or most football hooligans are unemployed. However, as we suggested earlier, this is not by any means to say that unemployment can be dismissed as a causal factor either in the genesis or perpetuation of football hooliganism.

These data also cast doubt on the idea that football hooliganism is a product, not of poverty and unemployment, but of affluence. Now, whilst the nucleus of the ICF contains a minority from higher up on the occupational scale, it is clear that the overwhelming majority, as is typical of football hooligans generally, come from the lower levels of the working class. Yet, according to one reporter recently, 'The image of the football hooligans coming from the most deprived inner-city areas is ... out of date. They are from upper working class, semi-affluent backgrounds.'[12] Such an idea is echoed in the Popplewell Report and buttressed by the disproportionate media attention given to the minority who come from such or even higher backgrounds.[13] It has presumably arisen partly because of the amounts of money that football hooligans are sometimes able to spend on their trips,[14] and partly because of the expensive clothes that some of them wear now that the 'casual' style has become the terrace norm among young fans. What this idea misses, however, is the fact that, because of its importance in their lives, young fans are willing to save for their football-related activities and for the 'casual' sweaters that, for them, are now increasingly essential accoutrements. Perhaps more importantly, it also misses the fact that many obtain funds from the 'hidden economy' whilst others get money from petty crime. It is instructive, for example, that in many cities on match days, clothes shops and sports shops are provided with a police guard. It is also instructive that twelve members of the ICF gave their occupations as ticket touts and that, although gainfully employed, some members of this group 'collect unemployment benefit, do the buying and selling of almost anything, and generally hustle'.[15]

But is it possible to get beneath the level of prejudice and shifting ideological fashions and to identify deeper, more recurrent causes of football hooliganism and the lifestyle that tends to be associated with it? In attempting to move in that direction let us first of all briefly examine some theories of aggression to which widespread credence has been given.

Theories of aggression

It is widely believed – by ethologists, sociobiologists and psychoanalysts, for example – that aggressiveness in humans, especially males, is an 'unlearned drive' or instinct and therefore universal. Others, principal among them experimental psychologists with a behaviourist orientation, see human aggression as a learned response and therefore as socially and historically variable.[16] We have neither the inclination nor the competence to become embroiled in this aspect of the age-old nature-versus-nurture controversy. However, it is perhaps in order to make a couple of general points. The first is that, while there is currently no direct evidence regarding the existence of an 'aggressive instinct' in human beings, aggressiveness is such a widespread human trait that it is clearly not inhibited by unlearned physiological mechanisms; that is, aggressiveness in humans may not be instinctively triggered nor is it, as is the case for example with wolves, instinctively controlled.[17] In broad terms we agree in this regard with Marsh et al. when they write that:

We do not wish to deny that the tendency to act aggressively may have a biological basis, that it [may] be related to some heritable feature, and explicable from the point of view of evolutionary advantage. But the social forms that the manifestations of the tendency take are very various and both historically conditioned and culturally determined.[18]

We wish to push this argument further. Whether or not an 'aggressive instinct' can be said to exist in humans, the fact of historical and cross-cultural variability in this regard implies unequivocally that human physiology not only permits but is partly dependent upon learned controls.[19] That is, the biology of human beings makes them dependent on a culture, and a central aspect of any culture consists of rules or norms concerning the expression and control of aggression. These rules or norms, however, are likely to vary, not only between different historical periods and different cultures, but between different classes in the same society. That is especially likely where class inequalities are great and where, consequently, members of the different classes live under widely differing circumstances.

Our second point is this. For people with a particular type of conscience and/or when there is a legitimating ideology (connected, for example, with a notion of occupational or national 'duty' or 'loyalty' to a community), certain forms of violence and aggressive behaviour can be positively sanctioned and enjoyable. There is no need to postulate an 'aggressive instinct' in order to account for such satisfactions. People are sometimes trained to behave aggressively and rewarded on that account; soldiers, policemen and professionals in certain sports are examples. (Some people are attracted to occupations of this kind because of the opportunities they allow for aggressiveness.) In such cases, apart from the prestige and financial rewards that can accrue, the pleasure and enjoyment derived from acting aggressively are, in part, a form of self-reward for 'a job well done', a kind of learned intrinsic 'job-satisfaction'. Moreover, fighting in its various forms – ranging from a battle in war or a campaign to catch a gang of criminals down to a closely-fought boxing or rugby match – can be exciting, and that, too, can be enjoyable. Such situations can 'get the adrenaline flowing' and, depending on the seriousness of the threat perceived as being posed, can serve as a pleasurable counter to normal routines, to the deadening effects of the 'emotional staleness' that is liable to result from continuous subjection to the constraints of occupational and other everyday activities.[20] The point, of course, is that, whilst little may be currently known about the genetic origins of aggressive behaviour or about the physiology of why some people find it enjoyable to behave in this way, there are clear occupational and other social differences in this regard. Apart from the occupational instances discussed above, there are also cases where no formal training in aggressiveness is involved. Instances of both these kinds are in many ways easier to observe and to investigate than the putative genetics of aggression. So let us look at some sociological attempts to explain aggressiveness, particularly the aggressiveness of working-class males.

Theories of male aggressiveness in the working class

It is not too difficult to explain why, under the majority of circumstances, human males tend to be more physically violent and aggressive than females. In Western and many other societies throughout history, males have performed military roles. They have also been expected to act as physical protectors of their families. Accordingly, they have tended to learn to behave more aggressively than females as part of their socialization. However, we are not so much interested in this context in the general aggressiveness of males as we are in the specific variants which, if our observations are sound, are to be found in particular sections of the working class. It is, therefore, on theories that are relevant in this connection that the following discussion is based.

As far as working-class male aggressiveness is concerned, two main theories seem to be currently on offer: the Marxist theory, which traces the roots of such aggressiveness to the constraints of manual work[21]; and the theory of 'the masculine identity crisis' which sees working-class male violence as 'a type of compulsive reaction-formation' to the socialization of males in 'predominantly female households'.[22] Since it appears to be more widely accepted, particularly in academic circles, we shall begin by outlining our critique of the Marxist explanation.

The Marxist theory

If our observations are correct, there is a specific 'aggressive masculine style' which, in Britain at least, nowadays tends to be characteristic mainly of males from particular sections of the lower working class. It is a variant of the overall masculinity norms found in advanced industrial societies and involves as a central feature a readier reliance on the open use of violence than is generally sanctioned by the dominant standards. In our view, whilst it cannot be said to be totally wrong, the Marxist explanation of this 'aggressive masculine style' is inadequate in a number of respects. In particular, its inadequacy derives from the fact that – in common with Marxist theories generally – it traces this social pattern solely or mainly to the 'material infrastructure', especially to the constraints and exigencies involved in performing manual labour. As a result, it ignores the part played, for example, by community structures and the relations between communities *relatively* independently of material or economic causation. It also arguably fails to cope adequately with the consequences of technical change. Our critique is best developed by dealing with this second aspect first.

It might be plausibly argued that, in pre-industrial and early industrial societies, the aggressiveness of males was – and continues to be in Third World societies today – rooted at least to some extent in the constraints and exigencies of manual labour. That is because, in societies of that type, manual work is (was) heavily reliant on muscular strength and capacity for physical endurance. However, with industrialization and the progressive mechanization of work, there has occurred a tendency for the amount of physical strength required to perform such occupations to decline. Increasingly, the ability to withstand long hours of monotony in performing routinized, repetitive, de-skilled and, in the sense that no great physical strength is demanded, 'de-masculinized' tasks has become the primary requirement for performing occupations of this type. Yet the evidence suggests that comparatively pronounced forms of 'aggressive masculinity' remain a central feature of at least lower-working-class culture. As we have seen, such forms of masculinity were probably characteristic of working-class males more generally in the late nineteenth and early twentieth centuries. That may have been the case because manual work was then less mechanized than today and was still reliant to a large extent on muscular strength. This suggests that what the continued stress on aggressive masculinity might be is a reaction against the progressive mechanization and 'de-masculinization' of work and, in that sense, expressive of an attempt to preserve an old cultural form in the face of changed conditions where it is less essential as far as work is concerned. However, if that were the case, one would expect the stress on male aggressiveness to be most pronounced at the higher levels of the working class and in those sections of the economy where the mechanization of production has proceeded farthest. That is, one would anticipate, to some degree at least, an inverse correlation between aggressive masculinity and the occupational need for physical strength. However, the reverse appears to be the case; that is, the evidence suggests that aggressiveness tends to be more firmly stressed by males who have little to offer in the market other than their relatively untrained physical capacities. In other words, the correlation appears to be direct. If that is so, it may be possible, even though aggressive masculinity cannot be said to derive in some direct and simple sense solely from the constraints and exigencies of manual labour, to argue that this particular occupational characteristic – as found in the building and construction trades, for example – is one of the constraints which help to produce and reinforce it. Even then, however, it is difficult to see how a form of masculinity which stresses ability to fight as a key source of identity can be explained in this manner; that is, as growing solely out of constraints located in the world of work. Different constraints, for example constraints connected with actual or perceived threats posed by males from other communities and/or with a tradition of frequent intra- and inter-community fighting would seem to offer greater explanatory purchase.

Aggressive masculinity could, of course, grow out of or be supported by work-related constraints under conditions where, as used, for example, to be the case in the docks, males had frequently to fight in order to obtain and keep their jobs. However, the generation of aggressive masculinity in lower-working-class communities does not seem to be tied to particular industries or systems of labour recruitment. It would seem, therefore, that there is not a necessary relationship between, for example, dockwork and/or casual labour and aggressive masculinity. Given that, reference can be fruitfully made in this connection to the relatively autonomous dynamics of community structures, intra- and inter-community relations, and the manner and degree of integration of communities into the wider society. We are thinking here particularly of the way in which the structure of lower-working-class communities leads regularly to the formation of fighting gangs of adolescent and young adult males. We shall elaborate on these structural characteristics in a moment. For the present, it is enough to stress that, by insisting that these intra- and inter-community dynamics are *relatively* autonomous, we are not claiming that they take place *independently* of economic considerations. All we are suggesting is that aspects of a community's economy, such as the fact that the majority of its members, if they are employed, work in manual occupations in an industry of a particular type, cannot be held *a priori* to determine every other aspect of its structure. These other aspects – its family and kinship patterns, the forms taken in it by relations between the sexes and the different age-groups, its overall organization, and the ways in and degrees to which it is integrated into the structure of society at large – even though they cannot be said to be independent of influence from the economic structure, are also of some significance in that regard.

The 'masculine identity crisis' theory

The theory of 'the masculine identity crisis' appears to us to be flawed as well. Thus, although it seems plausible to argue that socialization in a predominantly female household could, as a 'reaction-formation', lead to an exaggeration of masculine traits, there is nothing in such a household structure or pattern of socialization *per se* which can explain why an ability to fight should come to be regarded as a key attribute of masculinity, why fighting gangs of adolescent and young adult males should recurrently form in lower-working-class communities, or why such gangs should, for the most part, fight against others which are like themselves. Again, wider aspects of the structure of such communities and of their location in society overall appear to offer a more adequate explanation.

Our observations, furthermore, suggest that lower-working-class females tend to be more openly and physically aggressive than females higher up the social scale. Indeed, differences in this regard appear to us to be greater among females than males. However, the theory of the 'masculine identity crisis' cannot account for this. Moreover, even though many lower-class households appear to be 'female-centred' or 'matrifocal',[23] it could be held that a more salient structural characteristic in the determination of masculine aggressiveness is likely to be the degree of male dominance and the segregation of the sexes that lower-working-class communities tend to involve. As we shall argue later, this, coupled with a high degree of age-group segregation and the fact that lower-working-class children tend to be left to their own devices from an early age, is probably more crucial than socialization in predominantly female households in the genesis and reproduction of the pronounced forms of aggressive masculinity that tend to be characteristic of specific sections of the lower working class.

Some other theories

Other explanations of the aggressive masculinity of the lower working class appear to us to be similarly problematic. Brake, for example, contends that 'masculinism and violence' are characteristic of what he calls 'non-oppositional' working-class groups.[24] Such groups, he suggests, perceive society as run by lying and exploitative businessmen and politicians but fatalistically believe that they, themselves, are powerless to change things. 'This means,' he continues, 'that brutalized they often fall back on masculinism and violence as a form of self-reliance.' The weaknesses of this view are several. It is vague and fails to spell out the hypothesized connections between 'non-opposition' (a term which Brake presumably uses in the sense of 'non-political') and 'masculinism and violence'. Nor does it attempt to explain why, for example in terms of their structural location and the experiences it engenders, specific groups should be 'non-oppositional' and what it is about 'non-opposition' that is conducive to 'brutalization'. Above all, Brake fails to see that forms of what one might call 'non-political opposition' – towards the members of other groups at the same or a similar level in the stratification hierarchy – are central to the 'masculinism and violence' of the lower working class. These forms of 'opposition' between working-class groups are a recurrently generated, though slowly changing, structural feature of lower-working-class life and, through their expression in, for example, vandalism, gang fighting and football hooliganism, serve to bring such groups into manifest conflict with the established order, in that way providing them with a means for striking back at a society from which they feel excluded. This may be expressed through hooliganism and vandalism rather than through the framework of political parties and a coherent ideology, but it is a phenomenon of considerable political moment both in itself and in terms of the reactions it engenders.

Although he fails to make explicit its connections with the 'masculinism and violence' of the lower working class, Brake also refers to the symbolic importance of territory in working-class youth subcultures. Football hooliganism and similar forms of lower-working-class fighting are, he argues, conservative, ultimately reactionary transformations of working-class local pride caused by the decay of a district and its economy.[25] In his haste to draw out what he takes the political implications to be, however, he apparently does not conceive of the possibility that they may, at least in part, be generated by the structure of lower-working-class communities per se.

The view of Clarke et al. is similar to Brake's. The skinheads, they argue, resurrected an 'archetypal' and 'symbolic' form of working-class dress, and 'displaced' on to the football ground values to which most working-class adults no longer subscribe. In this, they were re-presenting 'a sense of territory and locality which the planners and speculators [were] rapidly destroying'. At the same time, they ' "declare[d]" as alive and well a game which was being commercialized, professionalized and spectacularized'.[26]

We do not wish to deny the effects which the activities of speculators and planners can have on working-class communities. The members of such communities are certainly less powerful than their middle- and upper-class counterparts to resist pressures from such sources. However, inherent in this kind of argument is a romanticization of the past of the working class which leads to a misrepresentation of both its past and present. Implicitly, at least, an ideal image of harmonious, coherent and stable working-class communities in the past is contrasted with a view of the present which sees such communities, entirely or almost entirely as a result of the activities of outside agents, as having been destroyed and become, internally, full of conflict and divided. In our view, this kind of analysis fails to provide an adequate picture of the changing balance between the polarities of conflict and cooperation, harmony and dissension, continuity and discontinuity as they are empirically observable in working-class communities. Although it lacks an historical dimension, the work of Gerald Suttles seems to provide the outlines of a more adequate approach to this 'Janus-headed' social phenomenon. We shall focus in this connection on Suttles' analysis of what he calls 'ordered segmentation' and 'defended neighbourhoods' and of how such a social configuration leads to the recurrent genesis of gangs. We shall start with a consideration of some of the ways in which 'ordered segmentation' tends to be manifested both in British lower-working-class communities and in a football context.

'Ordered segmentation' and football

Suttles' research in Chicago focused on communities whose overall pattern was one where 'age, sex, ethnic and territorial units are fitted together like building blocks to create a larger structure'.[27] He coined the term 'ordered segmentation' to capture two related features of the pattern of life in such communities: firstly, the fact that, while the segments that make up larger neighbourhoods are relatively independent of each other, the members of these segments nevertheless have a tendency regularly to combine in the event of opposition and conflict; and, secondly, the fact that these group alignments tend to build up according to a fixed sequence.[28] This pattern is similar in certain respects to what happens in 'segmental lineage systems'.[29] However, although there are clearly differences specific to societies at all these different stages – connected, for example, with types and degrees of effectiveness of state control – it is evidently as a general pattern not restricted solely to tribal and peasant societies. Robins and Cohen claim to have observed a similar pattern on a North London working-class estate.[30] And, significantly for present purposes, Harrison refers to what he calls 'the Bedouin syndrome' in the contemporary football context, namely the tendency for temporary *ad hoc* alliances to be built up between otherwise hostile fans.[31]

Our observations support the existence of such a pattern, both on working-class estates and in the football context. In Leicester, for example, intra-estate conflicts involving groups of adolescent and young adult males regularly give way to the requirements of defending the 'good name' of the estate as a whole against rival gangs that represent neighbouring estates. Thus, conflicts between groups of West Kingsley lads tend to be submerged in the event of conflict with their arch-rivals, lads from nearby Old Gardens. However, lads from these estates and others from Leicester and the surrounding area regularly stand side by side on the Filbert Street terraces and outside the Leicester City ground in the cause of 'home-end' solidarity in opposition to visiting fans. If the challenge is perceived in regional terms then, again, enemies may join forces. For example, Northern fans visiting London often complain about confrontations with combined 'fighting crews' from a number of metropolitan clubs. Euston Station used to be a favourite venue for encounters of this kind. Robins even refers to alliances between fans of smaller, neighbouring London clubs for purposes of confronting their large metropolitan rivals. QPR and Chelsea fans, and supporters of Orient and West Ham, are known to have formed such alliances.[32]

Southerners and Midlanders visiting the North, especially the larger Northern conurbations, also voice complaints about attacks by 'inter-end' alliances. Finally, at the international level, club and regional rivalries tend to be subordinated to the interests of defending England's national 'reputation'. Moreover, at each of these levels, particularly if opposing fans or the opposing gang are not present in sufficient numbers or if the challenge they offer is not perceived to be sufficient to unite otherwise rival groups in common opposition, lower-level rivalries sometimes re-emerge.

Having briefly established some of the ways in which it works both in working-class communities and in the football context, let us probe Suttles' analysis of 'ordered segmentation' in greater detail.

'Ordered segmentation' and the formation of 'street corner gangs'

According to Suttles, the dominant feature of a community characterized by 'ordered segmentation' is the 'single-sex peer group' or 'street corner gang'. Such groups, he argues, seem 'to develop quite logically out of a heavy emphasis on age-grading, avoidance between the sexes, territorial unity, and ethnic solidarity'.[33] However Suttles documents the regular occurrence in Chicago of conflict between gangs of the same ethnic group and recognizes elsewhere that ethnic differentiation and solidarity are contingent, rather than necessary factors in the formation of such groups.[34] In other words, age-grading – 'age-group segregation' is probably a better term[35] – segregation of the sexes and territorial identification appear to be the crucial *internal* social structural determinants. At this point we only wish to add that, whilst identification with a specific *locale* plays an important part both in the bonding of such groups and in the production of their characteristic values, they also tend to bond along kinship lines. Moreover, as is shown above all by their behaviour in the football context, their territorial identifications tend to be characterized by a degree of fluidity. Indeed, such fluidity seems to be implicit in their willingness to form temporary alliances on a variety of shifting levels, even to the extent, for example, that major ends can attract hooligan followers from different parts of the country. But let us look more closely into the ways in which such a social configuration leads to the recurrent formation of 'gangs'.

A strong degree of age-group segregation means that children in such communities tend to be sent into the streets to play, unsupervized by adults, at an early age. This tendency is exacerbated by a variety of domestic pressures. For its part, segregation of the sexes means that, by adolescence, there is a tendency for girls to be drawn into the home, although some form fairly aggressive gangs of their own or simply 'hang around' the lads where, again, their status tends to be subordinate. As a result of the interaction between these two aspects of such a social configuration, adolescent males are left to their own devices for long periods and tend to band into groups determined, on the one hand, by ties of kinship and close or common residence and, on the other, by the real or perceived threat posed by the parallel development of gangs in adjacent communities. Such groups also attract regular attention from the police, but this only tends to reinforce their solidarity. According to Suttles, lower-working-class communities of this type tend to be internally fragmented but achieve a degree of cohesion in the face of real or perceived threats from outside. An actual or rumoured gang fight engenders the highest degree of cohesion, he maintains, for such fights can mobilize the allegiance of males – sometimes adults as well as adolescents – throughout a community.[36]

In a later development of this analysis, Suttles introduced the concept of 'the defended neighbourhood', suggesting that the male adolescent street-groups that grow up in lower-working-class areas can be seen as in some ways analogous to 'vigilante groups' and that they arise out of 'the inadequacy of the formal institutions that have authorized responsibility for the protection of property and lives'.[37] This formulation neglects the extent to which these adolescent street groups see themselves, and are seen by others in their communities, as predatory; that is, the fact that they are attacking formations as well as formations which defend the 'home turf' against what are perceived to be external threats. Nevertheless, this is an interesting idea, in some ways consistent with Elias' theory of 'civilizing processes'. The latter lays stress on the part played in the development of more 'civilized' social standards, on the one hand by developing state control and, on the other, by a correlative shift in the balance between external controls and internalized controls in favour of the latter.[38] Accordingly one would expect, even in a complex, urban-industrial society to find gangs whose behaviour is characterized by a relatively high level of overt violence in communities where:

1 the state and its agencies have been unable to gain sufficient legitimation for, and have thus been unsuccessful in, their effort to exert effective control over street activities; and

2 the overall structure of the community and its manner and degree of integration into the wider society lead to the persistent generation of values and standards that are in some important ways divergent from those that are socially dominant.

Under such conditions, the local power of males who adhere to an aggressive masculine style will be reinforced and the gangs they form will continue to flourish. The coercive resort to 'saturation' policing may drive them off the streets for a while but such gangs will still be able to operate in situations where the police are not actually present. Under such conditions, members of lower-working-class communities who are striving for greater 'respectabilty' will have to contend with the aggressive street activities of 'rougher' elements and, in that way, the difficulties inherent in their attempt to live by different standards may be compounded.

Let us turn our attention now to some of the principal economic characteristics of lower-working-class communities and to the narrow local identifications that tend to be generated in such a context.

Lower working-class communities and the genesis of local identifications

Although he repeatedly lays stress on their poverty and its effects, Suttles fails to deal adequately with the ways in which lower-working-class communities are partly dependent for their structure on the character of the local economy and the ways in which this is articulated into wider economic interdependencies. Crucial in this regard is the degree to which a local economy is capable of providing sustained opportunities for unskilled and semi-skilled employment. Clearly, such opportunities and their attractiveness will vary over time. In general, however, only work within these occupational categories, together with the opportunities provided by informal 'street economies', is relevant as far as the personnel of lower-working-class communities are concerned. That is because their values tend to lead them to be hostile towards formal education. As Willis has shown, the masculine values of the street and the shop floor tend to be viewed as in some ways superior to those proffered by school.[39] Their life experiences and resultant personalities also militate against educational success. As a result, they tend to be perceived – and to perceive themselves – as employable only in jobs which require little formal education and/or training. This means that they tend to be low paid, are often employed only casually and are among the first to suffer when the rate of unemployment rises. There is also a tendency for some to work in the 'street economy' where 'street-smartness' and an ability 'to hustle' are at a premium. The poorest among them – which often includes those excluded from street networks – tend to be dependent financially on state benefits and/or petty crime.

Partly as a result of their employment – when they are in work – principally in jobs which require little formal education and training, the life-experiences of people from the lower working class tend, relative to those of people higher up the social scale, to have a degree of 'sameness' about them. Males, for example, tend to work in low-paid, insecure and monotonous jobs in which masculine traits are valued and in which they stand at or near the bottom, not only financially, but also in terms of the formal hierarchies of authority and prestige. As a result, they have a large number of experiences in common. If they are unemployed, they also have the common experience of having time on their hands which is generally spent hanging around the streets with their mates. In that way unemployment tends to extend and reinforce a pattern already inherent in the structure of a community based on 'ordered segmentation'. Other common experiences stem from the vagaries of having to live on a small, often irregular income, in small, frequently overcrowded, homes, and in poor, often physically decaying, neighbourhoods.

Yet another determinant of the 'experiential homogeneity' of the lower working class is their restricted interest in and opportunities for travel outside the local area When such travel does occur – as in the case of football trips – it tends to be a male-dominated group venture, if not exclusively male. Individuals who are more geographically mobile – for example, in connection with work in the building trade or membership of the armed forces – also tend to travel with and live among familiar masculine networks. In short, lower-working-class males who travel outside the local area take, as it were, their communities with them. This is both an expression of and tends to reinforce their opposition to 'outsiders'. In other words, lower-working-class communities tend for a number of reasons to be characterized by a low degree of 'cosmopolitanism'.

The strongest ties of members of the lower working class tend to be with others from their immediate locality. They also tend to have close ties with a wider range of kin than is generally characteristic of other social classes,[40] and there is a greater likelihood that several branches of a given kin group will live in the same locality; that is, their closest, emotionally most salient, links are to persons with whom they are familiar and are like themselves. In this sense one could say that they are linked to each other more strongly and exclusively than occurs in most other social classes by means of what Durkheim called 'bonds of similitude'.[41] Viewed as a whole, the communities where they live tend to be composed of aggregates of structurally similar groups; that is, they tend to be organized along what Blok called 'cellular' lines[42] and

Durkheim characterized as 'segmental organization'.[43] Given their narrow social horizons and close ties and identifications with one another, the members of any one 'segment' or 'cell' will tend to define as 'outsiders' and to be on hostile terms with the members of similar groups. In the case of segmentally-organized communities in a modern urban context, such 'outsiders' can come from a different local family or kin group, from a neighbouring street or estate, or from a different town or city. They can, of course, also come from a different racial or ethnic group.

It is, we believe, above all the relative narrowness of their experiences which works towards binding lower-working-class people to narrowly defined kin and neighbourhood groups. Apart from the 'street smartness' and the ability and willingness to fight of their adolescent and adult males, they have few power resources. This combination of narrowness of experience and relative lack of power tends to lead them to experience unfamiliar territories and people as potentially threatening. Usually it is only in the company of people with whom they are familiar and who are like themselves that it is possible for them to feel a relatively high degree of social assurance.[44] As a result, leisure activities conducted outside familiar territories are even more likely to be group activities than those conducted close to home. In a group context, however, particularly for adolescent and young adult males, trips away from 'the home turf' provide opportunities for excitement – a term which can embrace, inter alia for these groups, heavy drinking, the prospect of engaging in vandalism, petty crime, fighting with similar groups and the ever-present possibility of a brush with the authorities. Being part of a group augments their sense of power.[45] It also provides an opportunity to hit back at the established order and a context in which they can 'get their own back by taking the lid off . . . For a short, illusory moment, the outsiders are the masters; the downtrodden come out on top.'[46]

The positive feelings experienced by lower-working-class people in the company of neighbours and kin tend to be projected by some of them on to the territories where these feelings are generated, leading, however run-down and impoverished these neighbourhoods may appear to an observer, to a close and emotionally salient identification with the local territory *per se*. This identification is reinforced by the tendency of outsiders to define such people in terms of the community from which they come; that is, to tar all people who come from a particular estate with the same brush. Even though their perceptions are more communal and less individualistic, many lower-working-class people tend to perceive 'the local turf' as their own private property in much the same way as the members of higher classes perceive the houses which they own. We do not, of course, wish to argue that such feelings are experienced by *all* members of lower-working-class communities. Among other things, housing polices which dump 'problem families' on estates like West Kingsley contribute to feelings of alienation and lack of belonging, both among new residents and among older residents who are trying to maintain a more 'respectable' life-style.

This kind of territorial identification and sense of proprietorship tend to be extended with regular use to other public places such as the local football ground and the streets surrounding it. In fact, the local football ground, especially the 'home end' terraces, has come to be regarded by many adolescent and young adult males from the lower working class as a location which is both their own and where exciting experiences are a regular occurrence. As a result, they tend to see the entry of 'strangers' into 'their' territory, particularly of adolescent and young adult males whose intentions are, or are perceived to be, aggressive, as an 'invasion'. To an outside observer a gang fight over the invasion of a 'local turf' or 'football end' may seem like an indiscriminate mêlée involving the members of a completely undifferentiated mass but, in reality, whilst the homogeneity of their experiences tends to make them less individually differentiated than the majority of people higher up the social scale, the participants seek out for the most part only others who are like themselves[47] and are able to make finely graded distinctions in terms of local residence and kinship.

The 'bonds of similitude' which form the main basis of unity and opposition in these confrontations are also relatively fluid, in the sense that, as we suggested earlier, the members of otherwise hostile groups tend to unite in the face of a perceived or actual threat from a common outside enemy. Thus in the football context, as we have seen, groups from rival estates often unite in common defence of the 'end' they have appropriated and fight against similar groups from another town. Before or after a match they even frequently 'defend' the town as such, seeking out 'invaders' who have violated their wider territory. In this case they use as marks for distinguishing between 'friend' and 'foe' the insignia of identification with the visiting club. Alternatively, they distinguish strangers by their use of a non-local accent or because they have a dress style which, to the 'insiders', clearly reveals them as people from elsewhere.

'Aggressive masculinity' and the lower working class

So far in this analysis, we have focused principally on some of the ways in which members of the lower working class tend to develop narrow bonds of allegiance to community and kin, and how they form strong territorial identifications together with a sense of proprietorship over the 'local turf' and other areas which they appropriate, such as their 'football ends'. We can now consider the ways in which the structure of their communities tends to produce and reproduce 'aggressive masculinity' as a dominant characteristic.

To the extent that:

1 they have been less effectively incorporated and are, in that sense, less responsive to effective state or local control; and
2 their structures correspond to 'ordered segmentation';

lower-working-class communities will tend to generate norms or standards which, relative to those of groups higher in the social scale, are conducive to and tolerate a high level of open aggressiveness in social relations. Several aspects of the structure of such communities will tend to work in this direction. For example the comparative freedom from adult control experienced by lower-working-class children and adolescents, the fact that so much of their early socialization takes place on the street in the company mainly of their age peers, will mean that they tend to interact aggressively among themselves and to develop dominance hierarchies that are largely based on age and ability to 'handle oneself'. This pattern will be reinforced by the fact that, relative to the tendency of adults higher up the social scale, lower-working-class parents exert less pressure on their growing children to exercise strict and continuous self-control over aggressive behaviour.[48] Indeed, they often encourage aggressive traits more strongly than is done in other classes, particularly in their male children. To the extent that parents in the lower working class wish or are able to restrain their children in this or other regards, there is a greater tendency for them to resort to physical punishment.[49] Moreover, such children become more accustomed from an early age to seeing their parents and other adults, especially males, behave in an aggressive way. As a result they tend to grow up with a more positive attitude towards aggressive behaviour than their counterparts higher up the social scale and to be less inhibited about publicly taking part in and witnessing violent acts.

Also crucial to the formation of this pattern is the tendency towards male dominance and segregation of the sexes found in communities of this sort. The former has as one of its principal corollaries a comparatively high rate of male violence towards women. The latter means that the male members of such communities are not consistently subjected to 'softening' female pressure. Indeed, to the extent that some of the women in lower-working-class communities grow up to be relatively aggressive themselves and to value at least some of the macho characteristics of men, the aggressive propensities of the latter will be compounded. Further reinforcement is liable to come from the comparative frequency of feuds and vendettas between families, neighbourhoods and, above all, 'streetcorner gangs'.[50] In short, the 'rougher' sections of lower-working-class communities of the type we are describing appear to be characterized by feedback processes which encourage the resort to aggressive behaviour in many areas of social relations, especially on the part of males.

One of the effects of these processes is the conferral of prestige on males with a proven abilty to fight. Correlatively, there is a tendency for such males to enjoy fighting. For them and their peers who strive to emulate them, it is an important source of meaning, status and pleasurable emotional arousal. Correspondingly, there is a tendency for them to 'back down' less frequently than males from other areas and also on occasions actively to seek out fights and confrontations. Of course, males generally in our society are expected to defend themselves if attacked, but they are less likely than lower-working-class males to be the initiators in this regard. Lower-working-class males also tend to respond to characteristically different cues regarding what constitutes an insult or challenge. In fact, one of the central differences between the 'rougher' sections of the lower working class and their more 'respectable' counterparts in the upper, middle and working classes appears to be that, in the latter, violence in face-to-face relations tends to be normatively condemned whilst, in the former, there is a greater number of contexts in which the open expression of violence or aggression is tolerated or even positively sanctioned. A further difference is that there is a tendency in the 'respectable' classes for violence to be pushed behind the scenes. Moreover, when it does occur, there is a tendency in these classes for it to take, on balance, a more obviously 'instrumental' form and to lead to the arousal of feelings of remorse and guilt. By contrast, in the communities of the 'rougher' working class, violence tends to occur to a greater extent in public and to involve, on balance, more pronounced 'expressive' qualities, that is qualities more closely associated with the arousal of pleasurable feelings. Furthermore, whilst members of the more 'respectable' classes, especially 'respectable' males, are allowed – indeed expected – to behave aggressively in contexts that are defined as legitimate, such as formal sport, males from the 'rougher' sections of the working class tend either to regard formal sport as too regulated and 'tame'[51] or, when they do take part, they tend, on account of their overly physical, sometimes violent, approach, to fall foul of officials and opposing players.[52]

The identities of males from the 'rougher' sections of the working class thus tend to be based on what are, relative to the standards dominant in Britain today, openly aggressive forms of masculinity. Males of this kind also tend to have a high emotional investment in the reputations of their families, neighbourhoods and communities and, when they are into 'the football action', their 'ends' as aggressive and tough. This pattern is produced and reproduced, not only by the constituent *internal* elements of 'ordered segmentation' but also – and this is equally crucial – by some of the ways in which these communities are locked into the wider society. For example, males from the lower working class are typically denied status, meaning and gratification in the educational and occupational spheres, the major sources of identity, meaning and status available to men higher up the social scale. This denial comes about as a result of a combination of factors. For example, the majority of lower-working-class males, as we have seen, do not have – nor do they typically prize – the characteristics and values that make for educational and occupational success or for striving in these fields. At the same time, they tend to be systematically discriminated against in the worlds of school and work. This pattern results from deep-rooted cultural differences as well as from preju- dice and deliberate discrimination. It is also connected with the fact that the lower working class find themselves at the bottom of a hierarchical social structure which seems to require a relatively permanent and relatively impoverished 'underclass' as one of its constituent features.[53]

Because it is difficult for males from the 'rougher' sections of the lower working class to achieve meaning, gratification and status and to form satisfying identities in the formal sides of school and work, there is a greater tendency for them to rely for these purposes on forms of behaviour that include fighting, physical intimidation, heavy drinking and exploitative sexual relations. In fact, they tend to have many of the characteristics attributed by Adorno and his colleagues to 'the authoritarian personality'.[54] It is, of course, possible for these males to develop forms of relatively high self-esteem on the basis of local, and above all, peer group acknowledgment of their heavily masculine street credentials. It is also the case that such males are more liable than others to respond with physical aggression in situations which they construe to be seriously threatening to their self-esteem. However, openly violent behaviour, even on the part of males of this kind, tends to be confined to 'semi-institutionalized' settings such as those provided by local gang fights, football and weekend evenings with male peers 'downtown'. These are the prime and, in a locally specific sense, culturally approved sites for establishing satisfying male identities. Males who fight more indiscriminately - that is, almost regardless of the context, the odds, the likelihood of being arrested or of the other complex requirements of 'street smartness' - are liable to be labelled as 'nutters' by their peers. Thus, while males of the type we are discussing do tend to rely on physical intimidation and to fight more frequently than males from other groups, their fighting is generally limited for the most part to what are, again in a locally specific sense, culturally approved contexts and situations.

Some conceptual comments

It is important to stress that this has been a primarily *theoretical* chapter. As such, it has attempted via the construction of a general model to shed some light on the structural features of lower-working-class communities which lead to the recurrent generation within them of male adolescent gangs, an aggressive masculine style and relatively narrow bonds of identification. It does not attempt to take account of social changes or the nuances of 'lived experience'. It is also important to emphasize that it is not our contention that the values and attitudes which underpin the behaviour of lower-working-class males - their heavily masculine street styles, for example, and their exploitation of women - are in some sense entirely alien to the rest of British society. Far from it. Despite the slowly growing power of women, Britain remains a patriarchal society and a stress on masculinity and, correspondingly, on the subordinate role of women is a more or less common characteristic of *all* social classes. The display and celebration of extreme forms of masculinity and the sexual exploitation of females are also current themes in many current forms of popular culture, perhaps especially popular newspapers. The life experiences of the lower working class may produce more clear-cut distinctions between sex roles than is, for the most part, the case in other social classes. They may also lead to more extreme and more public displays of male aggressiveness. However, to the extent that our general culture and popular cultural forms continue to reflect and glorify such distinctions, they will help to reinforce lower-working-class males in their behaviour. They will also contribute to perpetuating the more muted, less publicly obvious, forms of such behaviour that tend to be characteristic of the males of other classes.

Following on from this, it is also important to stress that it is not our contention that youths and young men from the lower working class are the *only* football hooligans. Nor is it our contention that all adolescent and young adult males from the lower working class use football as a context for fighting. Some fight elsewhere and others hardly fight at all. Our point is, rather, that youths and young men from the 'rougher' sections of the working class seem on present evidence to be the most central and persistent offenders in the more serious forms of football hooliganism. However, the evidence also suggests that a sizeable proportion of football hooligans are skilled workers and that a small minority hold down middle-class jobs. This illustrates, among other things, the limitations of occupational status as a means of differentiating between 'rougher' and more 'respectable' lifestyles. It also shows that interest and involvement in a publicly-aggressive masculine style is not *solely* confined to the lower sections of the working class. Our suspicions regarding the minority of higher-class offenders is that at least some of them are likely to come from families which live in or close to 'rougher' areas or which have recently experienced mobility from such a *locale*. Others are liable to have turned to downtown networks and the 'football end', perhaps because of conflict with their parents or at school. Indeed, as unemployment bites ever deeper into lower-class areas, it is precisely these fans who are likely to be best able to keep up their hooligan activity.

Perhaps more importantly, at least some of the so-called 'soccer casuals' from 'better' backgrounds now identified so closely with football hooliganism in media accounts do not become regularly or seriously involved in the fighting. They may have been attracted on to the hooligan scene because of the glamourizing media attention devoted to the phenomenon or because of the recent growth of interest in expensive terrace styles. They may also find baiting the police and other fans, their involvement in football 'runs' and in match-day shoplifting forays exciting and rewarding. They may be racist and their activities in this and other respects might be in some ways connected to more widely prevalent ideologies and anxieties. They may even become match-day 'organizers' or 'planners'.[55] However they are not, typically, regular fighters. Nor are they in our experience typically involved in the fighting end of the more seriously violent incidents.

Clarification is also required of our use of the terms 'rough' and 'respectable' working class. By the former term we are referring principally to those sections of the working class which stand at or near the bottom of the overall social hierarchy and amongst whom openly aggressive interactions, particularly on the part of males, are a regularly observable fact of social life.[56] They can be distinguished from what are conventionally called the 'respectable' sections of the working class largely because members of the latter tend to identify more closely with society's dominant values, for example concerning the expression and control of aggression. In that sense, the 'rough' working class can be described as less fully 'incorporated' into the existing social order; that is, they are linked to other classes through the overall system of inter-dependencies of British society and exposed to dominant value influences, for example via their contacts with more 'respectable' people, authority figures and through the mass media and education. In that way, what might appear to be their distinctive values such as those surrounding 'aggressive masculinity' are really only variations on a stock of common themes.

The distinction between the 'rougher' and more 'respectable' sections of the working class is also largely, though not by any means entirely, coterminous with the internal economic stratification of the working class. Nevertheless, many poor people – the 'respectable poor' – adhere to 'respectable' values and are thus, to a degree, incorporated into the dominant value system. Some too – the 'abject poor' – are excluded or exclude themselves from the limited community networks of lower-working-class communities. Moreover, as the official figures on football hooliganism suggest, even though they tend to have higher and more regular incomes, some skilled workers adhere, at least in their non-work time, to some of the values of 'the roughs'. In that sense they can be said to be less incorporated than other comparable workers. Furthermore, members of the 'rough' working class occasionally make it economically, for example, via professional sport or even crime. For the most part, however, the 'rough' working class tend to stand towards the bottom of the social stratification hierarchy in terms of the cluster of attributes by which that hierarchy is determined.

Implicit in this discussion is the fact that the distinction between the 'rough' and 'respectable' working class should not be understood as referring to an absolute and clear-cut dichotomy. It refers, rather, to a continuum; that is, these different sections of the working class shade into each other and overlap. There are *degrees* of 'roughness' and *degrees* of 'respectability'. There is also movement up and down the scale, with some 'rough' individuals and families striving to obtain a reputation for greater 'respectability', and some who were formerly 'respectable' sliding down. Nor do these different sections of the working class always live in separate streets. They sometimes live cheek by jowl and affect one another mutually in a variety of ways. Moreover, most 'roughs' behave in certain situations with a degree of 'respectability' and, conversely, in some situations most if not all 'respectable' people are liable to engage in forms of behaviour more commonly associated with the 'roughs'.

Finally, it is not our contention that what we have described as some of the typical attributes and values of core football hooligans are entirely specific to the 'rougher' sections of the working class or solely generated by 'ordered segmentation'. Quite similar forms of masculinity are evident in the police and the armed services and perhaps in other occupational contexts such as some forms of professional sport.[57] In these contexts, however, recruits are inculcated into aggressive values by means of formal training, through their occupational experiences, and through their exposure to a heavily masculine occupational-culture. They are also subjected to a greater variety of formal controls. As far as the lower working class are concerned, aggressive masculinity is the byproduct of a social process that has meant that some sections of the working class are less incorporated than others. Correspondingly, they have tended to develop values that constitute distinctive variations on society's dominant value-themes.

CONCLUSION

Towards a developmental theory of football hooliganism

Introduction

What we have attempted to do in this book is to effect a synthesis of sociological, historical and psychological approaches to the study of football hooliganism. In that respect, what we have done constitutes a new departure. Such an approach may appear to some people to be overly ambitious but, by taking it, we have aimed at breaking down some of the barriers which divide sociology, history and psychology, to their mutual disadvantage. The social world is constituted by thinking, feeling and acting human beings. It cannot be properly understood independently either of its location in time and space or of the processes that occur in that connection. A largely arbitrary division of academic labour, however, in which sociological, historical and psychological specialists conduct their studies to a large degree independently of each other, is almost bound to produce distorted accounts of the social world. We have tried to avoid at least the major pitfalls one is liable to encounter in that regard.

It is inevitable in a wide-range study of this kind that we will have left a number of stones unturned. Fundamental to our view, however, is the belief that present-day problems such as football hooliganism cannot be adequately understood without reference, firstly, to the often violent past of British football and society and, secondly, to the processes of development that have brought us to the point at which we stand today. Some sociologists take a more short-term perspective. Others argue that historical methods are 'unscientific'. Some even deny the reality of social change.[1] Increasing numbers, however, are coming to the realization that social structures are dynamic, constituted by active and interdependent human beings who think and feel. Only by coming to grips with that is it possible to construct more object-adequate theories, theories which form a base on which others can build.

The present study is intended as a contribution towards the construction of a more object-adequate theory of football hooliganism. We have attempted to achieve this objective mainly by using aspects of Elias's theory of 'civilizing processes'. That is partly because Elias's theory is a pioneering attempt to construct the sort of sociological-historical-psychological synthesis that we ourselves have attempted. However, we have also used it because it is a theory based on the constant cross-fertilization of theory and research, and because it lays stress on both the thinking and feeling sides of interdependent men and women. Before going on to locate our study more explicitly in the context of the theory of 'civilizing processes', it will probably help the reader if first of all we draw out some contrasts between the 'Eliasian' approach as we have used it and what has probably constituted the dominant attempt in Britain in recent years to theorize the behaviour of working-class youth, the work of the Marxist 'subcultural school'.

'Subculturalist' theories of working-class youth

Critiques of the work of the Marxist subculturalists are now widely available, so we shall mention just two critical points.[2] The first is that there seems to be a strong undercurrent in the subcultural texts which insists that nearly all forms of working-class violence and stylistic adaptation constitute, in essence, forms of resistance to class-based inequality; that is, there is a strong tendency in much of this literature towards the 'ossification of subcultural adaptation' to the status of political struggles against 'the system'.[3] The second is that the subculturalists' approach seems to involve a considerable degree of historical amnesia; that is, it seems to propose that the aggressive parochialism of lower-working-class males is not only more or less politically aware but also a completely novel response to a recent historical conjuncture and that, prior to the late 1950s, working-class youth styles and collective violence among young working-class males were virtually unknown. A growing body of historical and sociological research, however, shows that this view is simply mistaken.[4] Indeed, youth styles and gang violence seem to have been persistent features of working-class life in the inter-war years and before. The subculturalist project, of course, is aimed at linking recent manifestations of working-class youth violence mainly to the contemporary 'crisis of capitalism'. Our own view is that recent socioeconomic and political develop ments have a considerable part to play in explaining the form and extent of present-day football hooliganism and other forms of youth violence. However, there are reasons for believing that some of its roots, for example the recurrent generation of an underclass, lie partly in the structural complexity of modern societies and not simply in the form taken by the ownership and control of the means of production. Moreover, the historical record suggests a far greater degree of continuity and persistence in the character and behaviour of sections of the working class than the subculturalists seem willing to allow.

In saying this we are not seeking to deny the elements of deliberate resistance that there are in the activities of football hooligans. These activities are, in some senses, ways of striking back at the 'posh cunts', the police and an overall society which discriminates against them. However, such resistance cannot be understood in terms of a simple, dichotomic and reductionist concept of class; that is, for core football hooligans, 'them' often includes more 'respectable' members of the working class as well as members of the middle and upper classes. Above all, the fact that their principal *direct* opponents in football and other confronta-tions are groups from the same class level as themselves points up the clear limitations of the 'hooliganism as resistance' thesis. As we said earlier, that fact *could* be accounted for in terms of the 'displacement of aggression', but it would, we think, be stretching credulity too far to 'read' such an expression of the disunity and relative weakness of the working class as simple, straightforward and undiluted 'resistance'. As we have tried throughout this book to show, although forms of resistance and hence of class awareness are involved in the sorts of lower-working-class behaviour we have been concerned with, these are mingled with other forms of behaviour that are produced by the structure and culture of the lower working class and by the fact that they are located at the bottom of the social scale. Such behaviour involves struggles for status and contains a greater expressive content than many radicals seem willing to allow. For many lower-working-class males in particular contexts, fighting, aggressive confrontations and vandalism involve not only character contests and the expression of frustration and resentment but also the arousal of pleasurable excitement.

It should be clear from our discussion in Chapter 9 that football hooligans and comparable groups are severely restrained in the formation of their personalities, their values and their actions by their restricted life experiences, their lack of comparative knowledge, and by constraints which lead to their interest and involvement in publicly aggressive forms of masculinity and 'street style'. It follows that hooligan activities have to be understood, at least in the first instance, in the hooligans' own terms; that is, as enjoyable, exciting and meaningful affairs. They also have to be understood as the product of values that are slowly changing but recurrently produced as part of a specific social configuration and not solely as reactions against the injustices of a class society conceived mainly in dichotomic terms. For example, gender relations, mediated though they are by other structural inequalities, seem to be at least as important in the production of aggressive masculinity as class relations *per se*. This is *not*, we hasten to add, a substitution of our own form of romanticism for that of the writers we are criticizing. Nor is it an argument for a simple relativism or some form of social reductionism designed to evade difficult moral questions. There *are* victims of football hooligans and comparable groups – women, blacks, Asians, working-class lads like themselves and those who are striving to be different, and, of course, more orderly football supporters. Moreover, to the extent that their activities and values help to keep them locked in poverty and at the bottom of the social scale – facts, of course, which cannot be understood independently of government policies and wider social pressures – the lads are victims of these activities and values themselves. We are not, then, proponents of some simple 'offender as victim' thesis, but neither, on the basis of our research, can we support the view that young males from the 'rougher' sections of the working class are faced with simple, free-floating moral choices which can be taken outside their limited and limiting experiences as people growing up and living in a poor working-class community in a society which regularly reproduces a relatively impoverished underclass as one of its constituent features. That, put simply, together with the limited opportunities for gaining status and enjoyment through what are regarded in the wider society as legitimate channels which such a situation entails, is the most fundamental reality underlying football hooliganism as we see it.

The theory of 'civilizing processes'

But let us take this analysis one step further and locate our results in the context of Elias's theory of 'civilizing processes'. The relevance of this theory to the present study may not be readily apparent. However, the struggles over football crowd behaviour in Britain during the past 100 years constitute a small-scale civilizing process in vivo. Morever, as we hope to show, because it focuses on long-term processes, avoids a simple dichotomic concept of class and pays equal attention to the rational and emotional sides of human beings, the theory of civilizing processes represents a basis on which a more adequate theoretical understanding of football hooliganism can begin to be constructed. It follows from the inherently changeable character of social structures, of course, that any such understanding will be developmental; that is, concerned with reflecting and explaining the structure and direction of social changes over time.

We shall attempt to go beyond Elias in this connection in three principal ways: firstly, by virtue of the fact that the working class forms our principal subject, whilst Elias has devoted comparatively little systematic and detailed attention to it; secondly, by drawing out some of the connections between the trajectory of the British 'civilizing process' over the past 100 years, that is the factual balance between 'civilizing' and 'de-civilizing' pressures that can be discerned in this connection, and what we have called the growing 'incorporation' of the working class; and thirdly, by 'unpacking' the somewhat undifferentiated concept of violence used by Elias, in particular by raising the complex issue of the changing balance between violence in its more 'instrumental' and more 'affective' or 'expressive' forms. Our first task, however, must be to provide a brief résumé of those aspects of Elias's theory that are directly relevant to the present study.

In a nutshell, what Elias has tried to show is that, in the societies of Western Europe between the Middle Ages and the twentieth century, a development towards 'higher' levels of civilization has occurred as the unplanned, yet structured, outcome of the interweaving of the intentional actions of countless more or less powerful interdependent groups and individuals over several generations. No value judgment is intended by this diagnosis. It is simply an attempt to come to grips with a process which can be demonstrably said to have occurred. Powerful elites standing at the nodal points of complex networks of interdependence, for example royal courts and large trading and manufacturing establishments, have so far been the principal standard-setting groups. Their social situation has entailed increasing pressure to exercise self-control and foresight; that is, basically on account of the increasingly complex requirements attached to their social positions and because they have found themselves more and more 'trapped' in a 'pincer movement' involving, on the one hand, the growing power of the state and, on the other, the growing power of lower social strata, they have been constrained to exercise greater self-restraint over their behaviour and feelings. According to Elias, of central importance to this process has been the following complex of interrelated long-term developments: economic growth; the lengthening of inter-dependency chains and the increasing 'monetization' of social relationships; state-formation, especially the formation of stable monopolies of force and taxation; and 'functional democratization', that is growing pressure on higher strata 'from below' as increasing interdependence leads to a growth in the power chances of lower social strata.[5] Conflict and violence have, throughout, been central to the unfolding of these processes. For example, 'elimination struggles' between contenders for the 'royal position' were crucial for the formation of the earliest tax and force monopolies, and 'functional democratization', to the extent that it is resisted by dominant groups, regularly leads, at least in the short-term, to increasing violence. Moreover, as is characteristic of social processes generally because of the part played in them by the learning of more or less knowledgeable and reflexive actors, none of these crucial developments should be mechanistically read as always and everywhere automatically producing identical results. One can speak of probabilities in that connection, but not of law-like certainties.[6]

Although Elias focused primarily on West European developments, or what he calls 'civilizing spurts', his theory of 'civilizing processes' is attuned to the occurrence of shorter- and longer-term 'counter-civilizing' developments, or 'de-civilizing spurts'. For example, he writes:

> this movement of society and civilization certainly does not follow a straight line. Within the overall movement there are repeatedly greater or lesser counter-movements in which the contrasts in society and the fluctuations in the behaviour of individuals, their affective outbreaks, increase again.[7]

One can add that the theory also implies a theory of 'de-civilization'; that is, it leads one, *ceteris paribus*, to anticipate that 'counter-civilizing' developments will occur in a society that experiences economic decline, a shortening of interdependency chains, diminishing state monopolies over force and taxation, and growing inequality in the balance of power between groups. Of course, since, as we have said, all social processes depend upon the learning of more or less knowledgeable and reflexive actors, any such change, however great its duration and extent, is unlikely to replicate in reverse the details and phasing of its counterpart.

For present purposes, this skeletal summary of some key aspects of Elias's theory must suffice. One aspect of the theory, however, does require further elaboration. Elias repeatedly stresses the significance of state-formation, the establishment of stable and effective force and tax monopolies by the state, a development that first began to come to full fruition in the 'absolute monarchies'. As Elias expresses it:

> Only with the formation of this kind of relatively stable monopolies do societies acquire those characteristics as a result of which the individuals forming them get attuned, from infancy, to a highly regulated and differentiated pattern of self-restraint; only in conjunction with these monopolies does this kind of self-restraint acquire a higher degree of automaticity, does it become, as it were, 'second nature'.
>
> When a monopoly of force is formed, pacified social spaces are created which are normally free from acts of violence. The pressures acting on individual people within them are of a different kind than previously. Forms of non-physical violence that had always existed, but hitherto had always been mingled or fused with physical force are now separated from the latter; they persist in a changed form internally within the more pacified societies. They are most visible so far as the standard thinking of our time is concerned as types of economic violence. In reality, however, there is a whole set of means whose monopolization can enable men as groups or as individuals to enforce their will upon others. The monopolization of the means of production, of 'economic' means, is only one of those which stand out in fuller relief when the means of physical violence become monopolized, when, in other words, in a more pacified state society the free use of physical force by those who are physically stronger is no longer possible.[8]

Thus, in a society with a relatively stable monopoly of physical force, people are largely protected from sudden attack, from the irruption of physical violence into their lives. At the same time, they are forced to suppress their own impulses to attack others physically.[9] Increasingly, parents demand this suppression of aggression in their children from an early age. As a result, fear, both of one's own aggressiveness and of a punitive response to it from powerful others, becomes internalized, a deep-rooted feature of the personality.

Under such conditions, social life becomes more regular and calculable. People learn from an early age to exercise greater rationality and foresight in steering their conduct through the complex networks of interdependency in which they find themselves enmeshed. Fear of social degradation, expressed through feelings of embarrassment or shame, comes increasingly to the fore in place of the fear of physical attack or of a sudden reversal of fortunes that is more common in a society without a stable monopoly of force. In a more 'civilized' society, people become more sensitive, among other things, towards committing or even witnessing violent acts. At the same time, official and many other forms of violence are pushed increasingly behind the scenes, and violent acts lead to the arousal of the anxieties and guilt-feelings which are typically deeply instilled in societies of this sort.

In a synthesizing statement, Elias outlines a fundamental precondition for the occurrence of a civilizing process. It is, he suggests, 'a rise in the standard of living and security', thus giving greater protection 'from the uncontrollable fears which erupt far more powerfully and frequently in societies with less stable monopolies of force'. 'The greater predictability of violence resulting from these more stable monopolies,' he maintains, is vitally important for the personality structure and behaviour of people in societies where they exist. Without them, the anxiety-inducing tensions and fears affecting our lives would grow stronger and 'reason', the 'relatively far-sighted and differentiated steering of our conduct, with its high degree of affect-control, would crumble or collapse'.[10]

The relevance for the present study of this excursus into the theory of civilizing processes may not, as we said earlier, be immediately clear. However, Elias's theory is, to our know-ledge, the most thoroughgoing attempt so far made to theorize, on the basis of a systematic body of time-series data, some of the principal relationships between violence, personality formation, and the development of social standards and social structures. It is, in other words, writ large, a study with fundamentally similar objectives to our own. Since, of course, it is concerned with social developments in several societies over several centuries, whilst we are concerned with social developments in a single society over about 100 years, it necessarily theorizes these relationships at a higher level of generality. That is, whilst providing a crucial theoretical guideline against which the specific developmental trajectories of particular European societies can be understood and offering fruitful leads towards the understanding of differences in this connection, it is fundamentally concerned with establishing the common line of development in Western Europe. Moreover, it is comparatively easy in a long-term study of the kind Elias has undertaken to determine whether chains of interdependence are lengthening or shortening, whether the power of the state is expanding or contracting, and whether or not functional democratization is occurring. When one focuses on a shorter time-span, it is more difficult to identify the prevalent tendencies of these complex configurations. Nevertheless, Elias's theory provides a crucial framework within which our own more specific analyses can be fruitfully understood. It is unlikely that Elias himself would entirely agree today with all of his early formulations. However, even in the early form of his theory from which we have quoted, it still provides a number of useful leads for understanding, not only the sociogenesis of the forms of aggressive masculinity which, we have argued, are centrally displayed in football hooligan encounters but also for understanding the public reactions to the behaviour that such encounters regularly evoke. Let us attempt to demonstrate how that is so and to spell out some of the modifications and developments of Elias's theory which are suggested by the small-scale study we have undertaken.

The 'civilizing process' and the lower working class

Although there are more or less considerable differences between them, the establishment of more stable monopolies of force within Western societies means that, in the longer term, life for the majority of people in these societies has become more stable and secure. Forms of cooperation take place at various levels in these societies but they are complexly interwoven with forms of intense competition. Prominent among these are occupational and economic competition, status struggles, competition between the sexes and between the different age groups. However, such forms of competition are forms in which the irruption of direct physical violence is relatively uncommon. Though, again, there are variations within and between societies in this regard, the social standards and personalities of people in more 'civilized' societies tend, in general, to reflect this. For such people, fear of social degradation, of downward social mobility or of loss of self-control are more ever-present realities than fear of physical attack. They may fear annihilation in an atomic war but, for most of them for most of the time, such a possibility is remote and does not deeply disturb them in their daily lives. They live in 'pacified social spaces' which are 'normally free from acts of violence'. In such societies, physical violence is normally 'confined to barracks' and, apart from the vicarious experience of violence via the mass media and sports (the demand for which appears partly to be generated by the degree to which violence has been factually suppressed), it breaks out only in extreme cases of war or social upheaval.[11]

In the present study we have used the term 'incorporation' to describe the constellation of developments which have served over the past century to integrate increasing sections of the working class into the mainstream of British society. However, despite the long-term spread of 'civilizing' pressures which have served to produce and are a product of increasing incorporation, we have also argued that, since at least the late nineteenth century, large sections of the British working class – although their standards and behaviour, too, have on balance, been transformed in a 'civilizing' direction – have remained less incorporated. In that connection they have had to contend with the regular irruption of specific forms of violence in their lives. Their economic circumstances, too, have been generally less secure. Growing affluence and increasing 'incorporation' may have had 'civilizing' effects on the majority of working-class people but what is today the less incorporated and relatively impoverished 'rougher' working-class minority, the social segment from which the football hooligans are principally recruited, is faced, from early in life, not only with economic insecurity but also with the regular irruption of violence from a variety of sources: when they are children, from their parents; as they grow up, from their peers in the street and at school; as adolescents, from gangs within their own and from neighbouring communities; as young adults, from prowling gangs on their nights 'downtown'; and on Saturdays, from invading 'fighting crews' who support a visiting football team. And, of course, in all these settings, because they tend to deviate in public from dominant standards and because they tend to respond aggressively when challenged, they are liable to experience rough handling by the police. There is also evidence that the police systematically discriminate against them in this regard[12]; that is, for them, the civil branch of society's 'monopoly of force' is not normally 'confined to barracks' to anything like the extent that is usually the case for members of the higher, more 'respectable' social strata. On the contrary, it is a regular and, as far as its specific manifestations are often concerned, in many ways unpredictable feature of their lives.

Not surprisingly, the fact that members of the 'rougher' sections of the contemporary working class grow up in a situation of severely limited power chances and live with a level of violence that is in excess of that which is usually experienced by groups higher up the social scale, has manifold consequences for their personality, their perception of other groups, their social standards and the structure of the communities they form.[13] As we saw in Chapter 9, many young males in 'rougher' working-class communities are constrained from early on to learn how to 'handle themselves'. Given the circumstances in which they live, a strict and prohibiting 'conscience' or 'super ego' with regard to engaging in and/or watching fights is liable to be unusual. Those who do develop greater sensitivity in these regards – perhaps because they are striving for educational success – tend to be labelled as 'divs' or 'swots' and to be regularly picked on by more aggressive males. The latter may not be conformists in terms of society's dominant standards but they are more conformist in terms of the standards that locally prevail. In lower-working-class communities, in short, the public expression of violence tends to be a more regular occurrence. Their members are constrained to adjust to this fact, not only at the level of their developing personalities as individuals but also, at the community level, in their standards and values. These, as we have seen, accord prestige to males who display loyalty and bravery in various forms of confrontation that, locally, are culturally approved. (Of course, disapprobation is accorded to 'nutters' who persistently seek out fights regardless of the odds.) Their involvement in and enjoyment of such confrontations are reinforced by the poverty of opportunities available to them in other spheres. Those which are available are often seen by them as unattractive.

It is largely because of the fact that their typical social situation and life experiences lead them to deviate in many ways from society's dominant norms, for example, to become involved in high-profile 'street' activities, various forms of petty crime and, of course, nowadays more prominently and regularly, football hooliganism, that some younger male members of lower-working-class communities frequently become involved in aggressive confrontations with the police. This tendency is reinforced to the degree that the civil branch of society's 'monopoly of force' has its own heavily masculine occupational subculture and recruits personnel with characteristics appropriate for performing 'hard' forms of policing. Moreover, to the extent that they are able to find work, males from the 'rougher' sections of the working class tend not to be employed or easily employable in occupations which might help to soften or dissipate their *macho* tendencies, for example because they demand for their performance 'a permanent effort of foresight and steady control of conduct'.[14] They live in a world of 'dense and extensive bonds of interdependence' but, in that context, they have fewer power resources than other groups. Far more than groups higher up the social scale, they are relatively 'passive objects of these interdependencies', being affected by distant events without being easily able to influence or even perceive them.[15] This situation is reinforced to the extent that such events – in the shape, for example, of economic downswings or government policies – help to maintain these groups in relative poverty with the restriction of life-chances that this entails. On account of their deviancy from dominant standards, prejudice and discrimination against them are also rife. In short, as a result of their overall social situation and the pattern of socialization that this typically engenders, males from the 'rougher' sections of the working class remain relatively unincorporated, and that means less subject to the sorts of 'civilizing' constraints and pressures which affect the members of higher classes.

'Ordered segmentation and "incorporation" in the civilizing process'

As we have seen, such aggressive tendencies do not derive simply from the manner in which 'rougher' working-class communities are integrated into the wider society. They also come from, and are reinforced by, specific features of the structure of lower-working-class communities *per se*. Following Suttles, we described this characteristic community structure by the term 'ordered segmentation', and attempted to show how such a pattern leads recurrently to the genesis of male adolescent fighting gangs and, correlatively, to an 'aggressive masculine style'. Also stemming from the same source and working in the same direction are the heavily male-dominated patterns of relations between the sexes in the communities of the lower working class. It is probably in general true to say that, to the extent that they are subjected to and internalize the values of a culture that is orientated towards child-rearing, women are constrained by the fact that they have the main responsibility in such a context for rearing children to be less violent in their social relations than men. However, in lower-working-class communities of the kind we are describing, females generally lack the power to be able to 'domesticate' their men, to exert much of a 'softening' or 'civilizing' influence upon them. Indeed, to the extent that females in lower-working-class communities prize at least some of the heavily masculine traits of males, the aggressive tendencies of the latter are liable to be reinforced.

Around the turn of the century, a much larger proportion of the British working class appears to have been less 'civilized' than tends nowadays to be the case. This was reflected, among other things, in the relatively high frequency with which violent incidents involving football spectators were reported. Between the wars, however, the incidence of reported violence by football spectators declined and remained low until the 1950s. We attributed this process to the growing incorporation of the working class as Britain gradually emerged as a more affluent, consumption-oriented mass society. Such developments were uneven and sometimes contradictory in their effects, producing intra-class as well as inter-class tensions and anxieties. Overall, however, they helped to produce broadly 'civilizing' tendencies for a complex of interrelated reasons. For those who experienced it, slowly growing affluence was conducive to improved life-chances, a greater degree of identification with groups higher up the social scale, and the gradual abandonment of many of the rough and ready ways of former times. An orientation towards greater material consumption was conducive to increased longer-term planning, the exercise of more foresight and the increasing deferral of immediate gratification. At the same time, growing numbers of working-class males became more integrated into the nuclear family and the home, and, in a context where the power of women was being slowly augmented, were thus more exposed to the domesticating, 'civilizing' influences of their wives. Working in the same direction were the spread of formal education and the formation of youth organizations of various kinds. And, to the extent that they joined and were active in them, membership of trades unions, political parties and other formal organizations would have exposed members of the working class to a further set of 'civilizing' constraints. The very act of joining would have been expressive of longer-term thinking and a degree of awareness of wider social interconnections. In that context, too, there would have been increasing social contact between the different classes, providing a further impetus for the twin processes of increasing incorporation and 'civilization'.

Although they were full of conflict, these processes were relatively non-violent, particularly after 1926 and the collapse of the General Strike. Up until that time, faced with the intransigence of dominant groups and the willingness of the latter to use the state's monopoly of violence to preserve the *status quo*, members of the working class had tended to express their slowly growing power to a considerable extent in violent terms. In this way the readiness, particularly of male members of the class, to behave more generally in violent ways tended to be reinforced. From that point on, however, as the labile balance of power at a societal level shifted back for a time even more decisively in favour of dominant groups, so more members of the working class were forced to adopt a more accommodative stance. In the circumstances which existed at that time, this facilitated the economic and political changes which enabled the foundations of the affluent, consumption-oriented mass society to be laid, hence permitting further incorporation. In that context, British society as a whole became more 'civilized', internally more pacified than had been the case before the First World War. As part of their increasing incorporation, larger sections of the working class were drawn under the umbrella of the monopoly of violence, slowly coming, since they now perceived themselves as having something to protect, to see the police more as necessary agents of social control rather than primarily as the representatives of an alien class.[16] In such a social setting they felt more able to pursue their aims and interests, even when these came into conflict with those of dominant groups, in a relatively peaceful manner. Fundamental to this process of inclusion was an emergent consensus shared between large sections of both the dominant and subordinate classes that violence, particularly but not solely at the level of intra-state relations – the 1930s were an era in which pacifist sentiments were prevalent in this country – was something to be used, if at all, as a means of last not first resort and in a calculated rather than impassioned way.

Processes of the kind we are describing never proceed without conflict. To the degree that they are accompanied by the use of force by ruling groups and do not involve, or are perceived as not involving, gains in the life-chances of the working class, they are likely to be met by widespread resistance. To the degree, however, that such processes involve more persuasive methods and are perceived by sections of the working class as yielding gains for them, they are more likely to be accepted, to result in the greater assimilation of the working class. As far as twentieth-century Britain is concerned, despite the occurrence of more short-term trends, forcible control and resistance appear to have been the dominant tendency up until the mid-1920s, increasing incorporation and assimilation of the working class the dominant tendency up until the late 1970s. The *overall* result appears to have been a degree of levelling and equalization of social standards, and the emergence of a more restrained and 'civilized' working class.

In attempting to analyze the last 100 years in the development of British society in these terms, we are not claiming that 'incorporation' and 'civilization' are, in some sense, 'good' or 'bad' things, either for the working class or British society as a whole. Rather, we are trying to come to grips with a complex set of processes that seem, on present evidence, factually to have occurred.[17] That is, independently of whether one wants to evaluate them in negative or positive terms, it seems clear that processes of incorporation and growing 'civilization' were among the most fundamental experiences of the British working class between the wars and in the immediate post-war years. More particularly, although, as we have seen, other developments such as technological change and the slowly growing power of women played a part as well, incorporation seems to have been the principal vehicle by means of which more restrained and orderly standards of conduct, standards that were initially developed by higher strata, percolated, with modifications, down the social scale.

It is also clear from what we have said so far that, as Elias sees it, processes of equalization and 'civilization' are closely interconnected. However, as far specifically as Britain is concerned, the occurrence of the 'civilizing process' has been limited because, since around the second half of the nineteenth century, the class structure appears to have grown more rigid in certain respects. Moreover, a very great degree of inequality still remains and, while there may be opportunities for short-range upward mobility, a number of impermeable barriers continue to exist. In fact, since the mid-1950s, these continuing inequalities and rigidities seem to have been one of the major sources of a simultaneous counter-trend. Since it is, in our view, central to an understanding of how the present-day phenomenon of football hooliganism arose and grew to 'social problem' status, let us elaborate on this rather complex notion.

Football hooliganism in the 'civilizing process'

At a time when sections of 'the establishment' were growing less confident in conjunction with Britain's waning power, when, partly in conjunction with full employment, the overall power of the working class was on the increase, and when social tensions and anxieties were growing about relations between the generations and between members of the 'host' and immigrant populations, the incidence of reported violence by soccer spectators began slowly to increase. Then from around the middle of the 1960s a major escalation started to occur. We attributed this increase partly to the growing power of the working class and partly to a shift in the balance of inter-generational power. However, we also attributed it partly to an 'advertizing' of the game as a context where fights and 'exciting' incidents regularly take place, a process which had the unintended consequence of making football attractive to 'rougher' working-class males who gain status and enjoyment from involvement in such affairs. That is, in the context of a society where the working class as a whole had, for some time, been becoming more incorporated, young males from the least incorporated minority were increasingly attracted to the game.

This occurred in a period – the 1960s – when 'liberal', more 'progressive' ideas and attitudes were in the ascendant and when a body of 'decriminalizing' legislation was beginning to be enacted.[18] In the sense that it involved a greater degree of identification with deviants and a willingness to embrace social and psychological causes in the explanation of their behaviour, this legislation and the ideas and attitudes that underlay it were, it seems reasonable to suggest, one manifestation of the 'civilizing process'.[19] However, another, simultaneous manifestation was the fact that members of the more 'respectable' classes, including the more 'respectable' sections of the working class, were growing more sensitive to violence and beginning to be less tolerant even of forms of behaviour that earlier generations would have been more likely to excuse as horseplay. This is not to deny that 'real' rates of delinquency were rising in that period. Nor is it to deny that this contributed importantly to the overall anxiety. The main point is that, in that situation, because young people are liable to behave in a high-spirited way, concern about 'the problem of youth' began to mount and this served to intensify public and official anxiety about football hooliganism as a 'social problem'. The increasingly disruptive behaviour of working-class males in a football context was thrown into even sharper relief by the fact that those in charge of the game were attempting in that period to broaden its appeal by moving away from the 'cloth cap' image. From the mid-1960s onwards, public and official anxieties were intensified still further as an emergent network of 'football end' rivalries developed its own, relatively autonomous momentum. Those involved in this network were enmeshed in a set of reciprocally aggressive relationships which demanded that home territories should be defended and meant that visits to rival football grounds were increasingly experienced by such young fans as dangerous and potentially exciting adventures. In short, starting in the mid-1960s, lower-working-class gang rivalries became, really for the first time in England, a regular part of the association football scene.

Simultaneously with the escalation of football hooliganism which started in the second half of the 1960s, 'liberal' and 'progressive' ideas and attitudes towards youth and deviance came under increasing attack, and the views of what one might call the 'law and order lobby' were in the ascendant. In such a situation, a range of punitive and preventive policies began to be introduced, policies based on simple, moralistic and sometimes simply wrong 'folk theories' or 'practical wisdom' about the genesis of football hooliganism and other similar problems, rather than research into who the football hooligans are and what leads them to behave as they do. In fact, for around twenty years now the authorities inside and outside football have been escalating the use of punitive and preventive measures in an attempt to solve the problem of football hooliganism, but with little success. Indeed, as we have seen, some of the measures they have introduced seem actually to have exacerbated the phenomenon, even helped to shape it. At best, they have displaced it. At the same time, with their cages and spiked fences, these measures have transformed the majority of football stadia in this country into fortress-like constructions. This, in itself, has contributed to the declining attractiveness of the game as a spectacle. There can be little doubt, however, that the phenomenon of football hooliganism per se has been of greater significance in this regard. Whilst it cannot, as we have said, be regarded as the sole or even the major cause of falling gates, it has undoubtedly been an important contributory factor. That is because the public display of violence and aggression in a football context is perceived, not only by members of the higher social classes but also by increasing numbers of more 'respectable' working-class people, as unacceptable.

'Instrumental' and 'expressive' violence

This discussion of incorporation, the 'civilizing process' and the usefulness of a developmental approach in extending the understanding of football hooliganism and comparable social problems should go some way towards explaining why we have been concerned to trace variations in the (reported) incidence of football hooliganism over time and why we have attempted to explain hooligan behaviour sociogenetically. It also shows more explicitly why we found the ahistorical anthropology of Marsh et al. and the, in many ways, speculative arguments of Taylor and Clarke unsatisfactory as explanations of why hooliganism occurs. Let us take the analysis one step further by 'unpacking' the concept of violence, and in particular by looking, firstly, at violence in its more 'instrumental' and 'expressive' forms, and, secondly, at some of the ways in which they interact. Given the space available to us here we cannot hope to do more than skate over the surface of this very complex problem.

Violence takes an 'instrumental' form when it is rationally and dispassionately chosen as a means for securing the achievement of a given goal. It is 'expressive' when it is engaged in as an emotionally satisfying and pleasurable end in itself or when it takes place under the impact of a powerful negative emotion such as frustration and/or anger. Examples of violence with a high instrumental content include the work of an emotionally detached professional assassin. Examples showing a high affective content include the use of torture for the pleasure such an activity can yield. In the former, violence is used in a calculated fashion as a means for achieving a medium- or longer-term goal. In the latter, means and ends are effectively fused. Either the emotional state itself, and not some more or less distant goal, is paramount, or this state is the immediate and involuntary consequence of an experience which is or is perceived to be threatening and unpleasant.

Some sociologists would call distinctions such as these 'ideal' types. However, we prefer to conceptualize them in terms of balances between interconnected polarities. That is, because human behaviour always involves a mixture between thinking and feeling, instrumental and expressive violence never occur in 'pure' or 'unmixed' forms but always veer, on balance, towards one pole or the other. Thus, an act of more or less instrumental violence can also be exciting and can yield feelings of satisfaction as a 'job well done'. Similarly, more or less expressive violence can be deliberately planned for and contrived. Let us tentatively apply these distinctions to the problem of football hooliganism.

We have argued that the life-experiences of males from the 'rougher' sections of the lower working class encourage what is, by dominant standards, a more frequent resort to violent and aggressive behaviour on their part. We have further argued that such behaviour is appealing to those involved for its affective qualities but that it also involves an appreciable level of instrumentality. Thus, while football hooligan confrontations are generally sought for the excitement they can generate, match-day targets are often carefully selected. Elements of instrumentality are also involved in the display of skill and adroitness in outwitting the police or outmanoeuvring rival fans. More importantly, fighting at the 'wrong' time, in the 'wrong' place and against the 'wrong' sort of fan can have disastrous consequences for the peer-group standing of those involved. As we have seen, 'nutter' status is generally reserved for those who fight more or less indiscriminately in these and other respects. In other words, although the affective experience in these confrontations is crucial, it is subtly blended with distinct elements of instrumentality.

Given the relatively high levels of affect involved in football hooligan fighting and the fact that it takes place in public, confrontations of this sort tend, to varying degrees, to offend the sensibilities of the majority of people. Largely for these reasons, too, members of the 'respectable' majority do not typically recognize the instrumentality involved in hooligan encounters. Instead, they tend to perceive violent incidents of this kind simply as chaotic, uncontrolled and threatening, and they condemn them on these grounds. They

are also liable to regard only violence of a more unambiguously instrumental kind – for example as used by the military
and the police – as legitimate. At the same time, their greater
sensitivity towards violence frequently leads them perceptually to magnify the seriousness of the violence they
encounter and to condemn it out of hand. The public
condemnation of football hooligan fighting and other comparable activities thus appears to be the censuring, by people
whose conscience and values lead them to experience such
behaviour as frightening and/or distasteful, of others whose
life-experiences are more liable to mean that such behaviour
can bolster their local status and that they experience
aggressive confrontations in public as exciting and even
pleasurable.

As we have seen, such censuring of football hooliganism
has played a part in leading the authorities to introduce more
punitive measures and stricter controls. These, in their turn,
far from eliminating the problem, have played a part in
increasing the use of rational planning by football hooligans;
that is, such measures and controls have contributed to the
emergence of increasingly instrumental forms of football
hooliganism. At the same time, however, the persistence of
hooligan behaviour in the face of escalating punishments and
controls, and the escalating violence of the more serious
football hooligan confrontations, have led rising numbers of
politicians, media personnel, 'celebrities', figures in the game
and members of the general public to call for the introduction
of flogging and other forms of physical punishment and
degradation as a remedial and/or deterrent device. That is, at a
time when the hooligans themselves are behaving in more
calculated ways to achieve their goals, the official and public
response to their behaviour is coming increasingly to take on a
highly charged, affective form. Unthinking retribution and
revenge, masked though they may be in the language of an
instrumental rhetoric, have begun increasingly to take precedence over measures dispassionately arrived at. This brief
discussion is not centrally concerned with highlighting the
need for new policy directions. Its intention is simply to point
to some of the complexities in the current situation and to
suggest that measures of a different sort will probably have to

be employed before it will be possible to break out of the 'mini'-cycle of violence that the present-day problem of football hooliganism represents.

The importance of research

But let us return to the subject of research and its importance. Among other things, we shall draw together in this connection the threads of what our analysis suggests regarding the part played by unemployment in the generation of football hooliganism.

The first thing worthy of note is that actually *doing* research ought not to open one up almost automatically to a charge of crude empiricism.[20] Nor should a critique of left-wing theories automatically expose one to the charge that one is, *ipso facto*, a supporter of or apologist for the political right. The social world is multi-dimensional and complex, and with their dichotomizing tendencies – you are either 'for us' or 'against us' – it cannot be adequately comprehended by simple political dogmas. Taylor's recent non-research-based assertions about the rise of a 'new, petit bourgeois hooligan' are sociologically interesting and appear to be supportable via an impressionistic survey of newspaper reports on the activities of 'soccer casuals', but, as we saw in Chapter 9, most of the available research-based evidence about English hooligans does not support this thesis. In fact, Taylor seems to lose faith in it himself when faced with the political dilemma of appearing to share the simplistic views of right-wingers on the connections between affluence and hooliganism.[21]

Our views on the part played by unemployment in the generation of aggressive masculinity and football hooliganism have already been made clear. All we wish to add is that its effects on the hooligan phenomenon appear in some ways contradictory. For example, it probably reduces its incidence by preventing fans from travelling and paying for entry to matches. At the same time, however, rising unemployment may have the effect of increasing hooliganism, for example by deferring, for some, the age of marriage, hence prolonging their active membership of hooligan groups.[22] Rising levels of unemployment also increase the use of the street as a forum for male activities, as well as providing for a potentially explosive rise in the frustration of even modest aspirations. Moreover, as the changing occupational structure continues to lead to the 'demasculinization' of work, an important site for the expression and reinforcement of heavily masculine characteristics is, in turn, disappearing. One possible consequence of changes of this kind might be a relative rise in the incidence of expressions of aggressive masculinity in other, non-work, contexts. However, the principal effect of unemployment in this regard is probably less direct and occurs via the part it plays in maintaining the relative poverty of the lower working class and, hence, in keeping substantial numbers of them locked into their 'rougher' milieu. Because their life-chances and life-experiences are more conducive to present-centred fatalism than to a pattern of deferred gratification, and because they tend to be more concerned with physical than intellectual attributes, they tend to be hostile to school, and even in some cases to reading and writing. In this, as in other regards, it is as if they were colluding with a system that depends on a disposable reserve of unskilled labour. They may fantasize about striking it rich; they may resent people who are more advantaged. Nevertheless, they generally think of themselves as performing only unskilled occupations. As a result of their lack of even basic educationally-required formal knowledge and skills – many of them, of course, have a sophisticated and highly intelligent knowledge of 'the street' and the activities that are prized there – if they do find employment they are among the first to be laid off when the rate of unemployment rises. As we have said, the direct effects of unemployment on football hooliganism appear to pull in contradictory directions, simultaneously reducing and increasing its incidence. Indirectly and in the longer term, however, it is conducive to football hooliganism and other forms of deviancy and conventional crime because it is symptomatic of the fact that most members of the lower working class are locked firmly at the bottom of the social scale. That, in its turn, serves to maintain their exposure to the constellation of internal and external constraints which, if our analysis is sound, are the principal agents at work in the production and reproduction of the heavily masculine, male-dominated 'rougher' subculture.

Summary

Summing up, it is our contention that the values expressed in contemporary hooligan encounters at football and elsewhere can be shown to be deeply rooted in the British past. It is not our contention that such behaviour and the reactions to it have been unchanging. Nor is it our contention that such behaviour can be understood without reference to regional variations, urban–rural differences and local traditions or 'to the specific political and economic conditions that structure features of lower working class life and thus mediate the life-experiences of that particular fraction of the working class'.[23]

Spectator disorders before the First World War seem to have primarily taken the form of attacks on match officials and players. At that stage, fights between rival fan-groups appear to have been rarer and less organized. And, although there was a body of middle-class opinion that decried the behaviour of football spectators as 'uncivilized', such behaviour was seen primarily as an evil necessarily attendant on an even greater one – professional sport. There was no deep or widespread, media-orchestrated moral panic over spectator misbehaviour and no pressure on the government to act.

Among the factors at work in shaping the specific character of the football hooligan phenomenon since the mid-1950s have been: social and economic policies of governments throughout the period, particularly as they have affected the material circumstances of the lower working class, the structural changes that have occurred within the 'rougher' and more 'respectable' sections of the working class and in the relationships between these sections; the rise of a specifically teenage leisure market and the various youth styles that have arisen, partly in connection with and partly independently of that fact; the increased ability and desire of young fans to travel to away matches, even abroad, on a regular basis; the ebb and flow of power relations between the sexes; the changing racial contours of British society; changes in the mass media, particularly the advent of television and the rise of a sensationalizing tabloid press; a media-orchestrated moral panic over football hooliganism and consequent pressure on the football authorities and the government to take remedial action; government and government-inspired attempts as a result of this pressure to curb hooligan behaviour; and, last but by no means least, the recent virtual collapse of the youth labour market. In our view, all these features – and they are all in some sense historically specific – have contributed more or less significantly to the forms, content and extent of football hooliganism since the 1950s. Where we differ from others who have written on this subject is over the extent to which any one of them can be afforded *central* causal status in the generation of football hooliganism, particularly football hooligan fighting. It has to be approached, in our view, as a socially produced form of behaviour that takes place as part of a *developing social configuration*. Moreover, we have argued that an adequate understanding of football hooliganism requires not only a short-term analysis of developments since the Second World War but, more crucially, a *longer-term, developmental* account, firstly of the manner in and degree to which heavily masculine values have been produced and reproduced in the working class over time and, secondly, of the varying extent to which the football context has formed an arena for the expression of such values.

We would be foolish to pretend that, in the current socioeconomic and sociopolitical climate, our recommendations for a more detached, research-based approach to football hooliganism and comparable social problems will be readily accepted by policymakers, the media or members of the general public. Indeed, the tensions and conflicts by which the British are currently beset, together with the anxieties aroused in that connection, appear to have been exacerbated by recent trends, trends that have been reflected in and reinforced by government policies. What we have in mind is not only the escalating violence associated with football hooliganism and the public response to it but also the fact that levels of crime and violence in Britain generally appear to be currently increasing.[24] The fear of violence and violent crime – of mugging, rape and attacks on old people – have been rising, too, fear which, despite its real basis, tends to be intensified and exaggerated by sensationalistic reporting.[25]

This is not the place for a full-scale analysis of these wider trends. It must be enough simply to say that they suggest the possibility that British society may, at present, be in the throes of a 'de-civilizing' process of greater or lesser magnitude and duration. The British are certainly experiencing an escalating 'cycle of violence' in a number of areas and spheres – in Northern Ireland, in industrial relations, in the inner cities and, of course, in conjunction with football. This, in its turn, brings us face to face with one of the major limitations in the current understanding of 'civilizing processes', namely the fact that we do not fully understand the periodicity and the 'ups and downs' of such processes, the conditions under which a society moves, on balance, in a 'civilizing' direction and the conditions under which a 'civilizing process' moves, as it were, on balance into 'reverse gear'.

We spoke earlier of the general conditions under which long-term 'reverse' developments in this regard are likely to occur. However, although it has experienced the loss of empire, Britain has not so far experienced *absolute* economic decline. Moreover, state-formation, the lengthening of inter-dependency chains and 'functional democratization' all appear to be developing in a direction which, if Elias's theory is correct, should be conducive to further 'civilization'. Perhaps what we are witnessing at present is nothing more than one of those short-term 'reverses' and increases in conflict and violence that have typically accompanied the European 'civilizing process' since the Middle Ages? Alternatively, perhaps we in Britain are currently at some kind of cross-roads where the interlacing decisions and actions of interde-pendent groups, a process in which the decisions and actions of those who are most powerful are likely to be of greatest moment, can push us, on balance, either in a 'civilizing' or 'de-civilizing' direction? In the present context, it is only possible for us to offer a few speculations regarding the complex issues that are raised in this connection.

In any society, problems are posed for its 'civilizing process' by the need to socialize and 'incorporate' each new generation. In complex industrial societies, especially given the pressures inherent in 'functional democratization', further problems are posed by the demands for integration of rising classes, immigrant groups and for finding new, non-patriarchal relationships between men and women. In complex industrial societies, too, intense competitive pressures are generated along with rising aspirations, and one of the preconditions for the continuing occurrence of a 'civilizing process' would appear to be a degree of flexibility on the part of dominant groups and a willingness to accommodate at least some of the demands of aspiring 'outsiders'. That appears to be the case whether one is talking of the members of an 'established' ruling class, of a 'host' society, of males or of adults.

The structure of British society, however, appears in many respects to be peculiarly rigid, and one of the fundamental sources of the 'de-civilizing' upsurge in violence and crime that Britain is currently experiencing appears to be the contradiction between the aspirations of increasing numbers of British people – the working class, women, blacks, people of Asian descent, the young – and an excessively rigid structure of class, gender, racial and age-group relations which prevents many of even the most modest of these aspirations from achieving a degree of fulfilment. It is important to add in this connection that the recent acceleration of this 'de-civilizing upsurge' cannot be isolated from wider sociopolitical trends which seem to be encouraging increasingly strident forms of acquisitive individualism as well as progressively 'hard line' and ultimately divisive approaches to what are complex and sensitive social problems. Under conditions of this kind, increasing incorporation of the majority at the real or apparent expense of those at the margins carries with it its own potential for raising levels of angry unrest and 'illegitimate' acquisitiveness among those who have been 'left behind'. It also has as one of its effects the strengthening among the incorporated of support for policies which have as their consequence the reinforcement, even the widening, of these divisions. It leads, in other words, to the effective protection of private and sectional interests at the expense of the 'public good'.

A society in which class, gender, racial and age-group inequalities have been eradicated is sociologically implausible. A central thrust of the findings reported in this book, however, would seem to be that, if problems such as football hooliganism are to be effectively tackled without doing further damage to the social fabric, the achievement of *greater* equality in all these spheres is necessary in contemporary Britain. Without it, the cycle of violence we have witnessed in recent years could well continue its uncontrolled growth, swelling to even more serious proportions. We do not pretend to be optimistic on this score. We hope, however, at the very least, that we will have persuaded the reader that football hooliganism is a complex and deeply-rooted social phenomenon. As such, it will not yield to blind rage or succumb to narrowly-focused strategies. If these types of response continue to hold sway, then the most practical advice we can offer to readers is that they had best reconcile themselves to a continuing life with hooliganism in football and elsewhere.

POSTSCRIPT

Heysel and after

We have been mainly concerned in this study with relatively persistent structures and long-term trends. Given this, we feel its main conclusions are likely to retain their relevance. In the spring and summer of 1985, however, a number of incidents occurred at football matches which were of such serious proportions that they came to represent something of a watershed in the post-war history of the game and its struggle against hooliganism. The ramifications of these incidents are liable to be felt in football for a considerable time and are thus deserving of this brief postscript.

In April and May 1985 massive crowd disturbances involving Leeds fans at Birmingham and Millwall fans at Luton provoked direct prime ministerial involvement in the hooliganism phenomenon. On the afternoon that Leeds fans were rioting in the Midlands, a wooden stand at Bradford was accidentally burned to the ground, killing fifty-five people. If the incidents at Birmingham and Leeds produced a new determination on the part of government to 'nail the hooligan' – and, at Luton, a revolutionary ban on visiting fans – the Bradford fire directed attention to the game's financial difficulties and the decrepit facilities at many grounds. The public response to the Bradford tragedy also revealed the enduring cultural significance of football in this country, even during a period of declining gates and apparently escalating hooligan excesses.

It was, however, the Heysel tragedy in May 1985 which

246

most clearly marked a new era in the struggle against English football's violent and disruptive followers. It also raised hooliganism more firmly to the status of an international political issue and highlighted both the incompetent administration of the game in Europe and the hooligan potential of continental as well as English fans.

For a while, in the face of the numbing shock which Heysel caused, the indefinite ban on English club sides from European competition which resulted, and the world-wide condemnation heaped upon the English, there was considerable unity among the principal actors in England on the need for radical action to stem hooliganism. Soon, however, cracks began to appear in this consensus. While FA officials continued to assert that there could be no return to Europe until the domesic game had 'put its house in order', a number of clubs immediately affected by the ban called unsuccessfully on the High Court to rule it unlawful. Amidst this damaging conflict over sectional interests and public responsibilities, Mrs Thatcher's 'war cabinet' on football hooliganism rolled imperiously into action. To date, the main results have been: control on the carriage, sale and consumption of alcohol; extensions on the use of closed-circuit television for purposes of surveillance and prosecution; changes in Public Order law aimed explicitly at football and providing exclusion orders for offenders; the use of undercover police to root out leaders of hooligan gangs; and pressure on the football authorities to secure the introduction of computerized membership schemes.

At the end of the 1985/86 season, publicity was given to estimates suggesting that a substantial reduction – in the region of 50 per cent – in arrests at football matches had taken place. At the same time, senior police officers spoke of a 'more responsible' attitude among spectators and of a general reduction in violence at football. These apparent developments were attributed partly to the determination of government and the football authorities to take 'tough' measures and partly to a growing realization among hooligan groups that their activities placed in jeopardy the very existence of the professional game. We say 'apparent developments' because such figures as were issued related mainly to arrests inside and nearby grounds whilst probably a majority of major incidents since the early 1970s have taken place outside and often at some distance from them. Measuring the national incidence of football violence poses complex methodological problems for precisely these sorts of reasons. Regional variations may also be important in this regard. Thus in 1986/87, while Merseyside police reported continuing lower levels of hooliganism and arrests post-Heysel, figures from the Metropolitan area suggest an increase, once again, towards pre-Heysel levels. Furthermore, serious incidents have continued to occur.

It would be surprising if none of the strategies implemented since 1985 had had any effects on levels and patterns of football hooliganism, e.g. by removing 'key' hooligans and 'organizers', inducing caution in others, or by helping further to displace hooligan activities from the terraces. (Hooliganism seems to have been increasing recently at cricket and boxing, and to have come to form a central ingredient of 'drinking holidays' abroad.) However it is also possible that such measures may have contributed simultaneously to the growing rationality and organization of football hooligans. They have certainly intensified the 'militarization' of match-day policing, a development which inconveniences orderly fans as much and sometimes more than it does their hooligan counterparts. Finally, any suggestion that the new measures might or might not be working in a fundamental senseand any hopes that their limited success might pave the way for a quick return to Europe – were placed in doubt in 1986 when fans of Manchester United and West Ham fought with knives and bottles on a ferry bound for Holland.

With the European Championships to be played in West Germany in 1988, and with spectator problems, perhaps particularly in the host country and the Netherlands, threatening to reach and, in some instances, even outstrip the levels experienced in England, the European authorities are currently devizing strategies designed to prevent or at least to minimize hooliganism involving fans from different countries. The post-Heysel backlash in Europe has produced much needed attention to stadium design and to the state of repair of some older European grounds. But the general pattern of policy making and implementation at the international level in this field is depressingly familiar to those who have watched anti-hooligan strategies develop in England over the last twenty years. Amidst the welter of recommendations contained in the *European Convention on Spectator Violence* of August 1985 for example, only a single paragraph is devoted to longer-term initiatives. To the extent that this document moves beyond calls for tighter and more comprehensive controls, moreover, there is an almost exclusive emphasis on the importance of changing attitudes via education rather than on the more fundamental issue of addressing the sorts of life circumstances and experiences which, if we are right, contribute centrally to the hooligan phenomenon. Despite the publicity given to them as anti-hooligan strategies many of the 'Football and Community' initiatives launched in England since Heysel necessarily suffer from the same limitations.

During the 1988 Championships, the image of the game as a whole and its capacity to bring nations together in friendly competition will come under close international scrutiny. English club sides are understandably desperate for a return to European competition, with or without their fans. But will a return mean a return, too, to the English-inspired violence of the 1970s and 1980s? Given present socio-economic trends in Britain and elsewhere, the spread and escalation of hooliganism abroad, and the increasing contact — by visit and post — between English and European football crews, it is a prospect about which it is difficult to be sanguine.

Leicester, May 1987

Notes and references

Introduction   Football hooliganism as a social phenomenon

1 See Norbert Elias, *What is Sociology?*, London, Hutchinson, 1978; *The Civilizing Process*, Oxford, Blackwell, 1978; and *State Formation and Civilization*, Oxford, Blackwell, 1982.
2 So, of course, are 'utopias', that is romanticized versions of the future.
3 *Public Disorder and Sporting Events*, Report of a Joint Sports Council/Social Science Research Council Panel, London, 1978, p.53.
4 *Ibid.*, p.17.
5 See Terence Morris, 'Deterring the hooligans', *New Society*, 30 May 1985, Vol.72, pp.326–7.
6 See Simon Jacobson, 'Chelsea Rule – Okay', *New Society*, 27 March, 1975, Vol.31, pp.780–3.
7 Norbert Elias, 'Problems of involvement and detachment', *British Journal of Sociology*, Vol.7, No.3, 1956, pp.226–52.

Chapter 1   Understanding football hooliganism: a critical review of some theories

1 Peter Marsh, Elizabeth Rosser and Rom Harré, *The Rules of Disorder*, London, Routledge & Kegan Paul, 1978.
2 Ian Taylor, 'Football mad: a speculative sociology of football hooliganism', in Eric Dunning (ed.), *The Sociology of Sport: a Collection of Readings*, London, Frank Cass, 1971, p.352–7; see also 'Soccer consciousness and soccer hooliganism', in Stanley

Cohen (ed.), *Images of Deviance*, Harmondsworth, Penguin, 1971, pp.134–64.

3 John Clarke, 'Football and working class fans: tradition and change', in Roger Ingham (ed.), *Football Hooliganism: the Wider Context*, London, Inter-Action Imprint, 1978, pp.37–60.

4 'Hooligan', Thames TV documentary, August 1985. (Directed by Ian Stuttard.) In January 1987 several leading members of the ICF – along with a number of Millwall fans – were arrested under what the police called Operation Full Time.

5 *The Times*, 14 November 1985. The quotation is an extract from Mr Tebbit's 1985 Disraeli Lecture.

6 Edward Grayson, 'We must beat the hooligan', *Sport and Recreation*, Vol.20, No.4, Autumn, 1979, p.28.

7 Marsh et al., 1978, *op. cit.*, p.28. See also pp.115ff.

8 *Ibid.*, pp.109–114.

9 *Ibid.*, p.127.

10 *Ibid*, p.129.

11 *Loc. cit.*

12 Konrad Lorenz, *On Aggression*, London, Methuen, 1967.

13 Marsh et al., 1978, *op. cit.*, p.110.

14 Peter Marsh, *Aggro: the Illusion of Violence*, London, Dent, 1979, p.12.

15 *Ibid.*, p.94.

16 *Ibid.*, p.142.

17 *Ibid*, p.143.

18 For a non-dichotomic discussion of the concept of 'social order', see Norbert Elias, *What is Sociology?*, London, Hutchinson, 1978, pp.75–6.

19 Marsh et al., 1978, *op. cit.*, p.88.

20 Taylor in Dunning (ed.), 1971, *op. cit.*, p.353.

21 *Ibid.*, p.361ff.

22 Taylor in Cohen (ed.), 1971, *op. cit.*

23 Taylor in Dunning (ed.), 1971, *op. cit.*, p.359.

24 Taylor in Cohen (ed.), 1971, *op. cit.*

25 Clarke in Ingham (ed.), 1978, *op. cit.*, p.55.

26 *Ibid.*, p.46ff.

27 *Ibid.*, p.51.

28 *Ibid.*, p.58.

29 Ian Taylor, 'On the sports violence question: soccer hooliganism revisited', in Jennifer Hargreaves (ed.), *Sport, Culture and Ideology*, London, Routledge & Kegan Paul, 1982, p.153. See also his 'Class, violence and sport: the case of soccer hooliganism in Britain', in Hart Cantelon and Richard Gruneau (eds), *Sport,*

Culture and the Modern State, Toronto, University of Toronto Press, 1982, pp.40–93.

30 Taylor, in Hargreaves (ed.), 1982, *op. cit.*, p.180 (our parentheses).

31. *Ibid.*, p. 189, note 8.

32 *Ibid.*, p.154.

33 *Loc. cit.*

34 *Ibid.*, p.155.

35 *Ibid.*, p.181.

36 *Loc. cit.*

37 *Ibid.*, p.182.

38 *Loc. cit.*

39 Taylor, in Cantelon and Gruneau (eds), 1982, p.48. (Taylor's italics).

40 Taylor, in Hargreaves (ed.), 1982, *op. cit.*, p.159.

41 *Ibid.*, p.186.

42 See Stuart Hall, Chas Critcher, Tony Jefferson, John Clarke, and Brian Roberts, *Policing the Crisis: Mugging, the State, and Law and Order*, London, Macmillan, 1978.

43 Taylor, in Hargreaves (ed.), 1982, *op. cit.*, pp.176–7.

44 Taylor, in Hargreaves (ed.), 1982, *op. cit.*, pp.177–8.

45 See Norbert Elias and Eric Dunning, 'Folk football in medieval and early modern Britain', in Dunning (ed.), *op. cit.*, pp.116–32.

46 John Hutchinson, 'Some aspects of football crowds before 1914', in *The Working Class and Leisure*, Proceedings of the Conference for the Study of Labour History, University of Sussex, paper no. 13, mimeo, 1975; and Wray Vamplew, 'Ungentlemanly conduct: the control of soccer crowd behaviour in England, 1888–1914', in T. C. Smart (ed.), *The Search for Wealth and Stability*, London, Macmillan, 1980.

Chapter 2　The football fever (1)

1 See Tony Mason, *Association Football and English Society*, Brighton, Harvester, 1980, and Geoffrey Green, *The History of the Football Association*, London, Naldrett, 1953, for analyses of the emergence of football as a professional sport.

2 See Eric Dunning, 'The development of modern football' in Dunning (ed.), 1971, *op. cit.*, p.148.

3 Mason, 1980, *op. cit.*, p.141.

4 *Ibid.*, pp.142–3.

5 Taylor in Dunning (ed.), 1971, *op. cit.*, p.357.

6 Mason, 1980, *op. cit.*, pp.42–3.

7 James Walvin, *The People's Game*, London, Allen Lane, 1975, p.53.
8 Hutchinson, 1975, *op. cit.*, p.10.
9 David Lockwood, *The Blackcoated Worker*, London, Allen & Unwin, 1958.
10 *The Scottish Football Annual*, 1880–1, p.18; quoted in Hutchinson, 1975, *op. cit.*, p.6
11 Anon., 'A football match', *All the Year Round*, 3rd series, Vol.3, Jan.–June, 1890), pp.393–4; quoted in Hutchinson, 1975, *loc. cit.*
12 Mason, 1980, *op. cit.*, p.148.
13 *Ibid.*, p.157.
14 Hutchinson, 1975, *op. cit.*, p.5.
15 Mason, 1980, *op. cit.*, pp.155–6; see also Hutchinson, 1975, *op. cit.*, p.8ff.
16 Mason, 1980, *op. cit.*, p.151.
17 *Loc. cit.*
18 *Loc. cit.*
19 *Ibid.*, pp.151–2.
20 *Ibid.*, p.152.
21 *Loc. cit.*
22 *Loc. cit.*
23 *Loc. cit.*
24 *Loc. cit.*
25 *Loc. cit.*
26 *Loc. cit.*
27 *Loc. cit.*
28 *Ibid.*, pp.152–3.
29 *Ibid.*, p.153.
30 W. M. McGregor, 'The crowd', in B. O. Corbett *et al.*, *Football*, London, 1907, p.19; quoted in Hutchinson, 1975, *op. cit.*, p.8.
31 Quoted in Mason, 1980, *op. cit.*, p.175.
32 *Ibid.*, pp.175–6.
33 *Pall Mall Gazette*, 23 March 1889; quoted in Mason, 1980, *op. cit.*, p.176.
34 *Nineteenth Century*, Vol.34, December, 1893; quoted in Mason, 1980, *op. cit.*, p.226.
35 Royal Commission on the Liquor Licensing Laws P.P. 1898, XXXVI, 26310, 26311; quoted in Mason, 1980, *loc. cit.*
36 F. E. Smith, 'The vogue of games: is it worth it?', *The New Fry's Magazine*, Vol.1, No.1, April 1911, p.3; quoted in Mason, 1980, *op. cit.*, pp.226–7.
37 Quoted in Mason, 1980, *op. cit.*, 236–7. 'Gavroche' was William Stewart, the first biographer of Keir Hardie.

38 *C. B. Fry's Magazine*, Vol.5, No.27, June, 1906, pp.196–8; quoted in Mason, 1980, *op. cit.*, p.177.
39 H. F. Abell, 'The football fever', *Macmillan's Magazine*, 89, 1903, p.280.
40 Charles Edwardes, 'The new football mania', *Nineteenth Century*, XXXVII, October, 1892, pp.622 and 627.
41 Ernest Ensor, 'The football madness', *Contemporary Review*, LXIV, November, 1898, p.758.
42 Abell, 1903, *op. cit.*, pp.278–9.
43 Leicester's daily paper, the *Leicester Mercury*, was called the *Leicester Daily Mercury* up until 1914.
44 Had we included incidents that were reported to the FA but not acted upon by them, the trend would, of course, have been different.

Chapter 3 'The football fever' (2)

1 *Leicester Daily Mercury*, 24 January 1899.
2 *Ibid.*, 25 January 1899.
3 *Birmingham Daily Mail*, 19 November 1889.
4 *Leicester Daily Mercury*, 20 January 1903.
5 *Ibid.*, 22 August 1903.
6 *Birmingham Gazette*, 9 January 1888.
7 *Athletic Journal*, 3 January 1888, p.9; quoted in Hutchinson, 1975, *op. cit.*, p.15.
8 *Birmingham Daily Mail*, 7 April 1890.
9 Brian Dobbs, *Edwardians at Play: Sport, 1890–1914*, London, Pelham, 1973, p.38.
10 J. A. H. Catton, *Wickets and Goals*, London, Chapman & Hall, 1926, p.225.
11 P. F. Young, *A History of British Football*, London, Stanley Paul, 1968, p.197.
12 *Leicester Daily Mercury*, 8 January 1900.
13 *Leicester Daily Mercury*, 20 December, 1898.
14 *Leicester Daily Mercury*, 31 March 1897.
15 Catton, 1926, *op. cit.*, p.216.
16 *Ibid.*, 4 December 1889.
17 *Leicester Daily Mercury*, 24 February 1890.
18 *Ibid.*, 30 September 1895.
19 *Birmingham Daily Post*, 19 October 1885.
20 *Birmingham Daily Mail*, 10 November 1890.
21 *Leicester Daily Mercury*, 27 December 1890.
22 *Birmingham Daily Post*, 17 January 1910.

23 *Birmingham Daily Mail*, 10 October 1888.

24 *Leicester Daily Mercury*, 19 January 1897.

25 Geoffrey Pearson, *Hooligan: A History of Respectable Fears*, London, Macmillan, 1983, p.40.

26 *Ibid.*, pp.94–6. The term 'Peaky Blinders' was, of course, a reference to the caps that they typically wore.

27 *Birmingham Daily Mail*, 30 December 1895.

28 *Birmingham Daily Mail*, 8 January 1900.

29 Hutchinson, 1975, *op. cit.*, p.14.

30 *Leicester Daily Mercury*, 19 April 1909.

31 *Glasgow Herald*, 19 April 1909; paraphrased in Hutchinson, 1975, *op. cit.*, p.14.

32 Minutes of the FA Emergency Committee, February 1913.

33 *Birmingham Daily Mail*, 13 October 1900.

34 *Birmingham Post*, 11 February 1902. The accidental death occurred, we are told, when a Derby supporter was pushed by the jostling crowd off the platform and under the wheels of an oncoming train.

35 *Birmingham Weekly Post*, 31 March 1894.

36 *Bygones Relating to Wales and the Border Counties*, Vol.VIII, 1889, p.88; quoted in Morris Marples, *A History of Football*, London, Secker & Warburg, 1954, p.173.

37 *Birmingham Daily Mail*, 24 March 1890.

38 *Leicester Daily Mercury*, 19 February 1896.

39 *The Times*, 27 April 1914.

Chapter 4   Football hooliganism and the working class before the First World War

1 Also relevant in this connection was the fact that, by this time, the authorities had only intervened to contain and control street life to a limited extent. Given that, and in the face of competing attractions, the comparatively inaccessible venue of football seems to have held no special appeal for those with disorderly intent. For some appreciation of the character of street hooliganism in Britain at the turn of the century, see E. G. Dunning, P. J. Murphy, W. H. T. Newburn and I. Waddington, 'Violent disorders in twentieth century Britain', in G. Gaskell and R. Benewick (eds), *The Crowd in Contemporary Britain*, Beverly Hills and London, Sage, 1987.

2 Pearson, 1983, *op. cit.*, p.40.

3 Peter Bailey, 'Will the real Bill Banks please stand up? Towards a role analysis of mid-Victorian working class respectability',

Journal of Social History, Vol.12, No.3, 1979, p.346.

4 *Ibid.*, p.342.

5 R. Baden-Powell, *Scouting for Boys*, London, Cox, 1908, p.40; quoted in Pearson, 1983, *op. cit.*, p.108.

6 Pearson, 1983, *op. cit.*, p.138.

7 On this issue, see, for example, Jerry White, *The Worst Street in North London: Campbell Bunk, Islington, Between the Wars*, London, Routledge & Kegan Paul, 1986.

8 Quoted in Pearson, *op. cit.*, p.57.

9 *Loc. cit.*

10 *Ibid.*

11 *Ibid.*

12 *Ibid.*

13 See Ann Dally, *Inventing Motherhood*, London, Burnett, 1982, esp. Chapters 1 and 2.

14 We are referring here to the sort of pattern described by Peter Wilmott and Michael Young in their *Family and Kinship in East London*, London, Routledge & Kegan Paul, 1957.

15 Pearson, 1983, *op. cit.*, p.59.

16 Stephen Humphries, *Hooligans or Rebels? An Oral History of Working Class Childhood and Youth, 1889–1939*, Oxford, Blackwell, 1981, p.178.

17 Quoted in Pearson, 1983, *op. cit.*, p.88.

18 *Loc. cit.*

Chapter 5   'An improving people?'

1 Green, 1953, *op. cit.*, pp.294–5.

2 *Ibid.*, p.301.

3 *Leicester Mercury*, 30 April 1923.

4 *Leicester Mercury*, 10 March 1937.

5 *Ibid.*, 23 January 1922. One can gain some idea from this letter of the sorts of social pressures that led growing numbers of grammar schools in this period to switch from soccer to rugby.

6 *Ibid.*, 7 January 1922. Photographs in the *Mercury* of crowds queuing to enter Cup-ties in this period often show substantial numbers of unescorted females.

7 *Ibid.*, 22 February 1925.

8 *Ibid.*, 7 March 1925.

9 *The Times*, 5 February 1926.

10 *Leicester Mercury*, 26 January 1929.

11 Minutes of the FA Emergency Committee, 7 October–8 December 1930.

12 *Ibid.*, 21 March–22 April 1922; 4 March–24 March 1924.

Chapter 6 'Incorporation' and English football crowds between the wars

1 Rex Pardoe, *The Battle of London: Arsenal versus Tottenham Hotspur*, London, Stacey, 1972, p.xii.

2 Pearson, 1983, *op. cit.*, p.30.

3 Anyone who doubts our evidence on this should read Bill Murray's excellent study of Celtic–Rangers rivalry, *The Old Firm: Sectarianism, Sport and Society in Scotland*, Edinburgh, John Donald, 1984.

4 *Ibid.*, p.173.

5 Tom Robertson, *Morton, 1874–1974: A Centenary History*, Greenock, Morton FC, 1974, pp.24–5.

6 *Ibid.*, p.145.

7 James E. Cronin, *Labour and Society in Britain*, London, Batsford, 1984.

8 Ted Gurr's study of long-term crime trends in London, Stockholm and Sydney reveals a remarkably similar pattern. See his *Rogues, Rebels and Reformers*, Beverly Hills and London, Sage, 1976, p.59.

9 Cronin, 1984, *op. cit.*, p.19.

10 There were, of course, power shifts in the opposite direction, too. For example, the privileges of many skilled workers were eroded during the war, a fact which played a part in the initial development of the shop stewards movement. As it grew in strength, however, this movement formed part of the overall shift of power chances towards the working class.

11 We say, 'on the whole' because the power chances of working-class males relative to working-class females would have been boosted as large numbers of women left the labour market.

12 Cronin, 1984, *op. cit.*, p.62.

13 *Ibid.*, p.42.

14 Derek H. Aldcroft, *The British Economy Between the Wars*, Deddington, Philip Allan, 1983, p.17.

15 *Ibid.*, p.18.

16 *Ibid.*, p.17.

17 *Ibid.*, p.19.

18 *Ibid.*, p.133.

19 *Ibid.*, p.144.

20 *Ibid.*, p.117.

21 *Ibid.*, p.116.

22 Cronin, 1984, *op. cit.*, p.87.

23 *Ibid.*, p.74.

24 *Ibid.*, p.87.

25 *Ibid.*, p.56.
26 *Ibid.*, p.63.
27 Aldcroft, 1983, *op. cit.*, p.117.
28 *Ibid.*, p.122.
29 *Ibid.*, p.124.
30 *Ibid.*, pp.124–6.
31 George Orwell, *The Road to Wigan Pier*; quoted in Aldcroft, 1983, *op. cit.*, p.132.

Chapter 7   'Soccer marches to war'

1 For a full analysis of these trends, see Sir Norman Chester, *The Football League: Report of the Committee of Enquiry into Structure and Finance*, Football League, Lytham St Annes, 1983.
2 Department of Education, *Report of the Committee on Football*, (The First 'Chester Report'), London, HMSO, 1968, p.97.
3 The distinction between the 'real' and the 'perceptual' dimensions of the problem, though perhaps helpful analytically, is, of course, a phoney one. That is because the perceptions of football hooligans by 'outsiders', that is people who are not directly involved, are no less real as part of the total phenomenon than the behaviour of football hooligans themselves.
4 *Leicester Mercury*, 15 May 1951.
5 *Ibid.*, 2 February 1955.
6 *The Times*, 5 March 1956.
7 *Ibid.*, 28 December 1957.
8 *Daily Express*, 13 November 1964.
9 *Ibid.*, 22 November 1964.
10 Murray, 1984, *op. cit.*, p.241, fn.5.
11 *Daily Herald*, 3 November 1963.
12 *News of the World*, 24 November 1963.
13 These words are from Tony Pullein, then Secretary of the NFFSC, quoted in the *Daily Mail*, 8 December 1964.
14 *The Times*, 28 December 1963.
15 *Daily Express*, 8 November 1965. The offenders were charged with public order offences and assaults. Two of those charged were over fifty and four over thirty.
16 *Daily Herald*, 8 January 1964.
17 *The Times*, 9 November 1964.
18 *Daily Mail*, 8 December 1964.
19 *The Times*, 9 November 1964.
20 *Daily Mail*, 8 December 1964.
21 For an analysis of this phenomenon see Stanley Cohen, *Folk Devils and Moral Panics*, London, Paladin, 1973.

22 See Stephen Wagg, *The Football World*, Brighton, Harvester Press, 1984, and Arthur Marwick, *British Society Since 1945*, Harmondsworth, Penguin, 1982, p.156.
23 *The Sunday Times*, 17 November 1963.
24 Stanley Cohen, 'Campaigning against vandalism', in C. Ward (ed.), *Vandalism*, London, Architectural Press, 1973, p.232.
25 *News of the World*, 24 November 1963.
26 The Liverpool team were verbally and physically abused by Italian supporters as well as by the Inter Milan players. The result of the match turned on a number of dubious refereeing decisions which favoured the home club. Allegations that the Italians had succeeded in bribing the referee were later given a degree of substantiation, but the European Football authorities seemed impotent or unwilling to bring the offenders to task.
27 *Daily Telegraph*, 9 October 1965.
28 *The Times*, 9 October 1965.
29 *Ibid.*, 11 October 1965.
30 In fact, no national newspaper appears to have picked up on the fighting which must have occurred following the game. It was not until the following September that the *Sun* reported on the injuries of a twenty-six-year-old Brentford fan who had been banned from the club's ground for using insulting behaviour. He reported that he had been beaten up by Millwall fans after the match in November 1965 and had spent six weeks in hospital. *Sun*, 27 September 1966.
31 Stanley Cohen, 1973, *loc. cit.*
32 See also Stuart Hall, 'The treatment of football hooliganism in the press', in Ingham (ed.), 1978, *op. cit.*, pp.15–36.
33 Reported in *The Times*, 31 October 1967.

Chapter 8   From the teds and the skins to the ICF

1 Cronin, 1984, *op. cit.*, p.147.
2 *Ibid.*, p.157.
3 *Ibid.*, p.146.
4 We are thinking, for example, of John Osborne's Jimmy Porter and Alan Sillitoe's Arthur Seaton.
5 This formulation is, of course, oversimplified in certain respects because, then as now, the power-chances of some working-class groups were being diminished in conjunction with technological change.
6 Cronin, 1984, *op. cit.*, p.166.
7 *Ibid.*, p.158.

8 For a discussion of this issue, see John Muncie, *The Trouble With Kids Today: Youth and Crime in Post-War Britain*, London, Hutchinson, 1984, esp. Ch.2, p.29ff.

9 Pearson, 1983, *op. cit.*, p.74ff.

10 *Leicester Mercury*, 4 June 1930.

11 T. R. Fyvel, *The Insecure Offenders: Rebellious Youth in the Welfare State*, Harmondsworth, Penguin, 1963, p.40.

12 Occupations were not usually given in newspaper accounts of teddy-boy trials. However, six teds convicted of disorderly conduct in Leicester in June 1959 all gave their occupations as 'labourers'. *Leicester Mercury*, 13 June 1959.

13 See Arthur Marwick, *British Society Since 1945*, Harmondsworth, Penguin, 1982, Chs 7–9; and Trevor Blackwell and Jeremy Seabrook, *A World Still to Win*, London, Faber & Faber, 1985.

14 Blackwell and Seabrook, 1985, *op. cit.*, p.86.

15 Marwick, 1982, *op. cit.*, p.127.

16 For a discussion of the effects of black youth styles on their white counterparts in Britain, see Dick Hebdige, *Subculture: the Meaning of Style*, London, Methuen, 1979.

17 *Daily Telegraph*, 29 March 1965.

18 David Robins and Phil Cohen, *Knuckle Sandwich*, Harmondsworth, Penguin, 1978, p.136.

19 *Guardian*, 3 October 1966.

20 *Daily Telegraph*, 21 November 1966.

21 *Sun*, 9 December 1966.

22 *The Times*, 5 September 1967.

23 *Sunday Telegraph*, 26 November 1967.

24 *The Times*, 26 September 1967.

25 See John Pearson, *The Profession of Violence*, London, Panther, 1973.

26 For a discussion of these options, see Phil Cohen, 'Sub-cultural conflict and working class community', *Working Papers in Cultural Studies*, No. 2, University of Birmingham Centre for Contemporary Cultural Studies, 1972.

27 J. Nuttall, *Bomb Culture*, London, Paladin, 1969, p.333.

28 See J. Clarke, 'Style' in S. Hall and T. Jefferson (eds), *Resistance Through Rituals*, London, Hutchinson, 1976, pp.180–1.

29 See, for example, G. Pearson, 1983, *op. cit.*; J. White, 1986, *op. cit.*; and Stephen Humphries, 1981, *op. cit.*

30 S. Daniel and P. Maguire, *The Paint House: Words from an East End Gang*, Harmondsworth, Penguin, 1972, p.21.

31 *Ibid.*, pp.21–2.

32 Robins and Cohen, 1978, *op. cit.*, p.139.

33 *The Times*, 12 February 1970.
34 *The Sunday Times*, 21 September 1969; *Daily Mail*, 27 September 1969.
35 *The Times* 2 March 1970.
36 This phenomenon is not confined to Manchester United. As the 1970s wore on, rising hooligan ends, like those at Leeds and Chelsea, began to draw in followers from a wide area around the country.
37 *Daily Mirror*, 6 May 1974.
38 Reported in the *Daily Telegraph*, 21 August 1973.
39 Robins and Cohen, 1978, *op. cit.*, p.151.
40 Reported in the *Guardian*, 28 August 1974.
41 These are the anxious words of the then Secretary of the Manchester United Supporters Club. They were reported in the *Daily Mail*, 29 August 1974.
42 The *London Evening News*, 25 October 1975.
43 The *London Evening Standard*, 15 September 1977.
44 For a discussion of the behaviour of English football fans abroad, see Williams *et al.*, *Hooligans Abroad*, London, Routledge & Kegan Paul, 1984.
45 Reported in the *Sun*, 17 March 1978.
46 *Loc. cit.*
47 Reported in the *London Evening Standard*, 5 October 1978.
48 *Stratford and Newham Express*, 14 October 1978.
49 *London Evening Standard*, 13 June 1980.
50 *Yorkshire Post*, 6 July 1984.
51 *Daily Mirror*, 15 March 1985.
52 See J. Williams, E. G. Dunning and P. J. Murphy, 'A Report on the Crowd Disturbances at the Match between Birmingham City and Leeds United, 11 May 1985', a submission to the Government Inquiry chaired by Mr Justice Popplewell.
53 *Committee of Inquiry into Crowd Safety and Control at Sports Grounds: Final Report* (the 'Popplewell Report'), London, HMSO, 1986, p.7.
54 *Loc. cit.*
55 *Loc. cit.*
56 *Football and the Fascists*, London, Centre for Contemporary Studies, mimeo, January, 1981.
57 *Daily Mail*, 27 October 1980.
58 Quoted in *The Sunday Times Magazine*, 20 September 1981, p.31.
59 This information came from Ian Stuttard during the making of the 'Hooligan' programme for Thames Television.

Chapter 9 The social roots of aggressive masculinity

1 Gerald Suttles, *The Social Order of the Slum: Ethnicity and Territory in the Inner City*, Chicago, University of Chicago Press, 1968.

2 Gerald Suttles, *The Social Construction of Communities*, Chicago, University of Chicago Press, 1972.

3 For a brief discussion of survey data on this issue see J. Williams, E. G. Dunning and P. J. Murphy, *All Sit Down: A Report on the Coventry City All-Seater Stadium, 1982/3*, University of Leicester, 1984, pp.58–66.

4 J. A. Harrington, *Soccer Hooliganism*, Bristol, John Wright, 1968, p.25.

5 Eugene Trivizas, 'Offences and offenders in football crowd disorders', *British Journal of Criminology*, Vol.20, No.3, July 1980, pp.281–3.

6 Paul Harrison, 'Soccer's tribal wars', *New Society*, 1974, Vol.29, p.602.

7 Marsh *et al.*, *op. cit.*, p.69.

8 *Oxford Mail*, 9 January 1981.

9 We are indebted to Inspector Stewart Callington of the Leicester Police for these data.

10 As the Harrington researchers pointed out in 1968, youths already known to the police or those with conspicuous dress or hair styles are more likely to be picked out. Moreover, core football hooligans are frequently skilled in evading detection and arrest (Harrington, 1968, *op. cit.*, p.11). More recently, several hundred man-hours of observation by plain-clothes officers were necessary under 'Operation Own-Goal' to arrest nine Chelsea hooligans.

11 There may well be occupational and other social differences between 'superhooligan' groups from different parts of the country, as a result, for example, of different local occupational structures and rates of unemployment. Generally speaking, however, we would expect the occupational profiles of, say, the Leeds Service Crew, the Huyton Baddies from Liverpool, and other comparable groups to be skewed, like the ICF, towards the bottom of the social scale.

12 Toby Young, *The Observer*, 2 June 1985.

13 *Committee of Inquiry into Crowd Safety and Control of Sports Grounds: Final Report*, HMSO, 1986, pp.55–6.

14 See the discussion in Williams *et al.*, 1984, *op. cit.*

15 'Hooligan', Thames TV, August 1985.

16 For an up-to-date summary of the literature on violence and

aggression, see Gerda Siann, *Accounting for Aggression: Perspectives on Aggression and Violence*, London, Allen & Unwin, 1985.

17 For an analysis of the instinctual control of aggression in non-human animals, see Konrad Lorenz, 1967, *op. cit.*.

18 Marsh *et al.*, 1978, *op. cit.*, p.28.

19 For a discussion of this issue, see Norbert Elias, 1978, *op. cit.*, esp. Chapter 4, p.104ff.

20 For a discussion of this issue see Norbert Elias and Eric Dunning, *Quest for Excitement: Sport and Leisure in the Civilizing Process*, Oxford, Blackwell, 1986.

21 See, e.g., John Clarke in Ingham (ed.), 1978, *op. cit.*, p.40; and Paul Willis, *Learning to Labour*, London, Saxon House, 1977, p.119ff.

22 See, e.g. Walter B. Miller, 'Lower class culture as a generating milieu of gang delinquency', *Journal of Social Issues*, Vol. 14, No. 13, 1958, p.9ff.

23 See, e.g. Michael Young and Peter Wilmott, 1957, *op. cit.*.

24 Mike Brake, *The Sociology of Youth and Youth Subcultures*, London, Routledge & Kegan Paul, 1980, p.83.

25 *Ibid.*, p.37.

26 John Clarke, Stuart Hall, Tony Jefferson and Brian Roberts, 'Subcultures, cultures and class', in Stuart Hall and Tony Jefferson (eds), 1975, *op. cit.*, p.40.

27 Suttles, 1968, *op. cit.*, p.10.

28 *Loc. cit.*

29 See, e.g., E. E. Evans-Pritchard, *The Nuer*, Oxford, Oxford University Press, 1940.

30 Robins and Cohen, 1978, *op. cit.*, p.73ff.

31 Harrison, 1974, *op. cit.*, p.604.

32 David Robins, *We Hate Humans*, Harmondsworth, Penguin, 1984, p.86.

33 Suttles, 1968, *op. cit.*, p.169.

34 See, e.g., *ibid.*, p.31–3. See also Suttles, 1972, *op. cit.*, pp.28–9.

35 That is because we are not dealing with a fully developed age-grading system of the type found, e.g., among African tribes such as the Kikuyu.

36 Suttles, 1968, *op. cit.*, pp.176, 181 and 194.

37 Suttles, 1972, *op. cit.*, p.225.

38 See Elias, 1978 (*The Civilizing Process*) and 1982, *op. cit.*

39 Willis, 1977, *op. cit.*

40 Aristocratic groupings, too, tend to maintain a wide range of kin-contacts.

41 Emile Durkheim, *The Division of Labour in Society*, Glencoe, Ill., Free Press, 1964.

42 Anton Blok, *The Mafia of a Sicilian Village, 1860–1960*, Oxford, Blackwell, 1974, p.93.
43 Durkheim, 1964, *op. cit.*
44 A similar point is made about Chicago 'gang boys' by J. F. Short and F. L. Strodbeck in their *Group Process and Gang Delinquency*, Chicago, Chicago University Press, 1965, p.128.
45 This point is made by the authors of the 'Joint Report'. See *Public Disorder and Sporting Events*, 1978, *op. cit.*, p.45.
46 Norbert Elias, 'Introduction', in Elias and Dunning, 1986, *op. cit.*, p.54ff.
47 For example, in the Thames TV programme 'Hooligan' (August, 1985), a member of the West Ham ICF says very clearly 'We only want to fight other thugs.'
48 One of the most systematic analyses of this issue is provided in B. M. Spinley, *The Deprived and the Privileged: Personality Development in English Society*, London, Routledge & Kegan Paul, 1953.
49 In the language of Basil Bernstein, there is a greater tendency for them to resort to 'positional' as opposed to 'personal' controls. See his *Class, Codes and Control: Vol. 1 Theoretical Studies Towards a Sociology of Language*, London, Routledge & Kegan Paul, 1971.
50 The fighting norms of males in these groups contain elements comparable to the 'vendetta' systems of Mediterranean and some other societies. That is, an individual who is slighted, attacked or challenged by the member of an outsider group often seeks revenge, not just by retaliation against that *particular* member but against *any* member of the outsider group. This is noted by Howard Parker in his *View from the Boys: a Sociology of Down-Town Adolescents*, Newton Abbot, David & Charles, 1974, p.143.
51 This is consistent with the observation of Paul Willis. See his *Profane Culture*, London, Routledge & Kegan Paul, 1978, p.29.
52 See also Howard Parker, 1974, *op. cit.*, p.35.
53 See, e.g., Herbert J. Gans, 'Urbanism and suburbanism as ways of life', in R. E. Pahl (ed.), *Readings in Urban Sociology*, Oxford, Pergamon, 1968, pp.95–118.
54 T. W. Adorno, E. Frenkel-Brunswick, D. J. Levinson and R. N. Sanford, *The Authoritarian Personality*, New York, Harper, 1950.
55 This was suggested to us by police officers involved in the 'Operation Own-Goal' initiative at Chelsea. Stylish young men from 'respectable' backgrounds seemed to be orchestrating hooligan assaults, but they rarely seemed to fight themselves. More generally, however, members of the London 'ends' seem more affluent than their counterparts in the provinces. There are,

of course, also middle- and upper-class forms of hooliganism, e.g. in rugby clubs. Generally speaking, however, these take place in private settings and, where vandalism occurs, the perpetrators are wealthy enough to pay for repairs and buy silence.

56 The studies by Parker and Willis are among the best documentations of the regular production and reproduction of aggressive masculinity in sections of the lower working class.

57 For a report on the *macho* tendencies of the Metropolitan Police, see D. J. Smith and J. Gray, *Police and People in London*, London, Policy Studies Institute, 1983. The feature of such occupations that appears to be principally responsible for the production and reproduction of these forms of masculine identity is the fact that, in them, ability to 'handle oneself' is an important occupational requirement. As far as professional sports are concerned, it is obviously an important requirement in boxing but it is also an important *desideratum* in soccer and rugby league.

Conclusion   Towards a developmental theory of football hooliganism

1 See, for example, the arguments by the philosopher K. R. Popper, in his *The Poverty of Historicism*, London, Routledge & Kegan Paul, 1957. For the denial by a sociologist of the reality of social change, see, e.g., Robert Nisbet (ed.), *Social Change*, Oxford, Blackwell, 1972, p.5. Pareto's theory of the 'circulation of elites', of course, constituted in effect such a denial; see, e.g., his *Treatise on General Sociology*, Dover, New York, 1963.

2 For example in Muncie, 1983, *op. cit.*, pp.124–33.

3 J. Young, 'Striking back against the empire', *Critical Social Policy*, Vol. 3, No. 2, 1984, p.135.

4 What does seem to be new about the modern period is the extent to which such styles become highly publicized and highly commercialized national phenomena. (As such they contrast markedly with the more localized styles of the period before the Second World War.)

5 A further important aspect of state-formation in Western Europe, according to Elias, has been the gradual break-up of private monopolies over the means of ruling and their transformation, increasingly, into public monopolies. In this way, the theory overcomes the apparent paradox posed by the fact this overall process has simultaneously involved trends towards monopolization and concentration, and the dispersion and equalization of power chances.

6 For a discussion of this issue, see Norbert Elias, 'The sciences:

towards a theory', in Richard Whitley (ed.), *Social Processes of Scientific Development*, London, Routledge & Kegan Paul, 1957.

7 Elias, 1982, *op. cit.*, p.253.

8 *Ibid.*, p.235.

9 *Ibid.*, p.236.

10 *Ibid.*, 326.

11 The phrase 'confined to barracks' is taken from Elias, *ibid.*, p.238. The routinized portrayal of 'real' and 'mimetic' violence by the media may, to an extent, reduce people's sensitivity on this score but this reduction goes hand in hand with a heightened sensitivity which leads to the condemnation as violent of acts which in earlier generations would probably have been accorded greater tolerance.

12 Thus Smith and Gray show how the Metropolitan Police regard members of the lower classes as 'slag' or 'rubbish'. See Smith and Gray, 1983, *op. cit.*, pp.162–5.

13 This does not mean, of course, that members of the 'rougher' working class are violent all the time and never cooperate or form warm relationships. Nor does it mean that more 'respectable' people are never violent. It is a *comparative* statement and implies nothing more than that there are observable class differences in these as in other regards.

14 Elias, 1982, *op. cit.*, p.249.

15 *Ibid.*, p.248.

16 See R. Reiner, *The Politics of the Police*, Brighton, Wheatsheaf, 1985, pp.40–1.

17 It is easy to see how negative value judgments could be placed on the sorts of developments we are describing. An affluent, consumption-oriented mass society, for example, is in some ways destructive from the standpoint of groups who favour the maintenance and development of 'high culture' and perhaps its spread to the working class. It is also sometimes argued, not unrealistically, that growing affluence has increased divisions in the working class, dissipating some of the more traditional solidarities of that class by producing a more acquisitive, self-centred ideology and lifestyle among the more prosperous sections of it. Incorporation, too, is anathema to many Marxists and others on the left who favour a revolutionary working class. It is, as they see it, evidence of 'false consciousness'.

18 In the 1960s this process culminated in the Children and Young Persons Act of 1969.

19 Part and parcel of this process has been the tendency for certain offenders, in particular youthful ones, to be increasingly re-defined as victims. However, this reclassification has by no means

necessarily improved the power chances of those subjected to it.

20 The point, of course, is to develop theoretically-grounded empirical work against the current of atheoretical empiricism which seems to be in evidence in some areas of sociology and criminology. See J. Young, 'The failure of criminology', in R. Matthews and J. Young, *Confronting Crime*, Beverly Hills and London, Sage, 1986, p.28.

21 Ian Taylor, 'Putting the boot into working class sport: British soccer after Bradford and Brussels', paper delivered to the Annual Conference of the North American Society for the Sociology of Sport, Boston, Mass., November, 1985.

22 Marriage, of course, is not universally a 'deterrent' in this regard. We know of several examples of married men who participate actively in football and other gangs.

23 Jennifer A. Hargreaves, 'Where's the virtue? Where's the grace? A discussion of the social production of gender relations in and through sport', *Theory, Culture and Society*, Vol. 3, No. 1., 1986, p.114.

24 See, for example, *Personal Violence*, Home Office Research Study 89, HMSO, 1986. The report shows that, 'comparing 1974 with 1984, 3,000 more of the most serious offences of personal violence were recorded, half of that increase being attributable to the rise in armed robbery', p.4.

25 As J. Lea and J. Young, *What's to be Done About Law and Order?*, Harmondsworth, Penguin, 1984, pp.36–49, show, crime is sensationalized and distorted by the media but it also affects certain groups disproportionately. Thus, for residents in inner city areas fears about the likelihood of being a victim of crime are more rational and realistic then similar fears expressed in other, low-risk areas.

Index

Abell, H. F., 42–4, 55, 254n
Abrams, M., 160
adolescence, 160
Adorno, T. W., 211, 264n
affective violence, 222
affluence, affluent society, 24,
   121, 126–8, 146, 155, 158ff,
   190, 227, 230, 231, 232, 239
age-grading, 201
age-group segregation, 197, 201,
   202
aggression: enjoyment of, 192,
   193, 209ff, 220, 228, 229, 234,
   236ff; theories of, 191ff
aggressive masculinity, 80ff, 129,
   184ff, 197, 203, 208ff, 220, 240
aggressive masculine style, 194ff,
   212, 213, 214, 230
aggro, 19–21, 29, 30
Aldcroft, D. H., 125, 257n
Almond, H. H., 40
amateur ethos, 42, 44
arrest rates, 247
attacks: on match officials, 7,
   59–61, 75, 108, 112; on
   players, 7, 61–4, 75; on police,
   89, 108
authoritarian personality, 211
authoritarian populism, 28

Baby Squad, 180
Baden-Powell, R., 83, 84, 256n

Bailey, P., 81, 82, 255n
balance of power: between
   classes, 121ff, 158ff, 230ff;
   between the sexes, 88, 128,
   129, 147
barracking, 96, 97
Bedouin syndrome, 200
Bernstein, B., 264n
Blackwell, T., 260n
Blok, A., 205, 264n
bonds of similitude, 205, 207
Booth, C., 83, 84
bourgeoisification, 24, 25, 74
brake clubs, 115, 116
Brake, M., 197, 198, 263n
Bridgeton Billy Boys, 116
British National Party, 182
Bushwackers, 179

calling cards, 180
casual style, 190, 191
Catton, J. A. H., 254n
cellular organization, 205
Chelsea Headhunters, 17, 180
Chester Committee, 135
Chester, N., 258n
civilizing process(es), 85, 129,
   185, 203, 218, 221ff, 243, 244,
   265n
Clarke, J., 13, 18, 21, 23, 24–30,
   53, 57, 74, 75, 170, 198, 236,
   251n, 252n, 260n, 263n

class conflict, 39, 121–4
Cohen, P., 166, 169, 172, 175, 200, 260n, 261n, 263n
Cohen, S., 258n, 259n
control, over working-class communities, 89, 90, 203, 208ff
crime, 88, 96, 191, 204, 206, 214, 215, 229, 240, 242, 244
Cronin, J. E., 122, 123, 124, 126, 159, 257n
crowd break-throughs, 57–9
crowd control, 101ff
crowd encroachments, 101–5

Dally, A., 256n
dangerous class, 82ff, 162
Daniel, S., 171, 260n
de-civilization, 223, 243, 244
de-civilizing pressures, 222
declining attendances, 4, 24, 132, 133, 146, 154
decomposition: of working-class neighbourhoods, 27, 28; of working-class sport, 27, 28
defended neighbourhoods, 185, 199, 202, 203
democratization, 43, 82, 83
detour via detachment, 11
developmental approach, 1, 221, 236, 242
disorders, outside grounds, 68–73
Dobbs, B., 254n
dress of football fans, 3, 12
drinking, 13–15, 40ff, 70, 71, 105–7
Dunning, E., 252n, 255n, 261n, 262n
Durkheim, E., 205, 206, 261n, 263n, 264n

economic developments, 158ff
economic growth, 124–6, 222
economic stratification, of the working class, 214
Edwardes, C., 42, 43, 44, 55, 254n

Elias, N., 1, 11, 81, 203, 218, 221–6, 243, 250n, 251n, 252n, 263n, 264n, 265n, 266n
elimination struggles, 223
emotional arousal, in fights, 210, 226
Ensor, E., 42, 43, 44, 55, 254n
ethology, ethologists, 19–21
Evans-Pritchard, E. E., 263n
expressive violence, 210, 222, 236–9

FA Cup, 32–4
female attendance, 37, 38, 56, 77, 78, 99ff
fighting between fan groups, 6, 7, 8, 16, 67–8, 75, 76, 111, 112, 113ff, 143, 149ff, 167ff, 172ff, 260n
fighting crews, 157, 227
figurational-developmental approach, 1, 221, 242
folk antecedents, of modern football, 30
Football Association, 32, 45, 48, 49, 69, 71, 72
football, as a family game, 56, 78
football crowds, size and social composition of, 33ff, 117ff, 185, 186
football ends, 6, 145, 157, 164–7
football hooligans: social origins of, 78ff, 186–91; status-hierarchy of, 153, 155
football hooliganism: academic explanations, 13ff; in the civilizing process, 233ff; as a form of behaviour, 5ff, 14ff; organization and planning, 5, 177–81, 214, 248; policies regarding, 4, 5, 157; popular explanations, 13ff; press coverage, 8ff, 151ff; rules governing, 19–22; and social class, 154, 186ff; as a social problem, 17, 23, 141ff, 148ff, 233ff

Football League, 32, 39, 45, 91, 132, 133
force monopoly, 224, 226ff
Frenkel-Brunswick, E., 264n
functional democratization, 222, 223, 226, 243
Fyvel, T. R., 260n

gangs, 79, 80, 88–90, 116, 161, 162, 165, 172ff, 196, 199, 200–3, 230
Gans, H. J., 264n
gender relations, 220
Gilbert, E., 160
Gooners, 179, 180
Gorst, J., 85
Gray, J., 265n, 266n
Grayson, E., 18, 251n
Green, G., 91, 252n, 256n
Gurr, T., 257n

Hall, S., 252n, 259n, 263n
Hargreaves, J. A., 251n, 267n
Harré, R., 13, 23 (see also, Marsh, P.)
Harrington, J. A., 186, 262n
Harrington Report, 186
Harrison, P., 187, 200, 262n, 263n
Heysel tragedy, 11, 181, 246–9
hippies, 170
historical approach, 1ff
historical methods, 45ff, 217, 218
human aggression, 20, 21, 191ff
Humphries, S., 89, 256n, 260n
Hutchinson, J., 30, 35, 36, 50, 53, 57, 65, 252n, 253n, 254n

incorporation, 92, 120ff, 154, 162, 185, 208, 214, 215, 216, 222, 227, 229, 230ff, 236
industrial relations, 121–4
instrumental violence, 210, 222, 236–9
Inter City Firm, 13, 17, 179, 180, 182, 188–91
internationalization, 24, 25, 74

Jackson, N. L., 40
Jacobson, S., 250n
Jefferson, T., 252n, 263n

Lang Report, 4, 5
law and order lobby, 235
Lea, J., 267n
lengthening of interdependency chains, 222
levels of causation, 14ff
Levinson, D. J., 264n
local Derbies, 16, 20, 75, 90
Lockwood, D., 253n
Lorenz, K., 251n, 263n
lower working class: 195ff, 204ff, 212ff; in the civilizing process, 226ff; economic characteristics, 196, 204ff; experience of violence, 227, 228; experiential homogeneity, 205–7; females, 197, 209

macho concept of masculinity, 88–90
Macmillan, H., 158
male dominance, 87, 881, 197, 209, 230
masculinization, of the terraces, 78
McGregor, W., 39, 40, 253n
Maguire, P., 171, 260n
Marsh, P., 13, 18, 19–23, 29, 187, 191, 192, 236, 250n, 251n, 269n
Marxist subcultural school, 218–21
Marxist theory of male aggressiveness, 193, 194–6
Marwick, A., 259n, 260n
masculine identity crisis, 193, 196, 197
masculine occupational subculture, of police, 229, 265n
masculinity norms, 14, 15
Mason, T., 34–9, 252n, 253n
maximum wage, abolition of, 24, 147

Mears, J., 145
media treatment of football
 hooliganism, football crowds,
 8ff, 21, 29, 76–8, 92, 97, 103,
 104, 105, 107, 108, 109, 110,
 134, 135, 137, 144, 146, 156Iff,
 176, 186
metonymic violence, 19, 22
middle-class hooligans, 265n
military rhetoric, 134, 152, 155
Miller, W. B., 263n
missile throwing, 6, 15, 22, 59,
 60, 110–12, 115, 136, 137, 144
mods, 135, 157, 169, 170
monetization, 222
moral panic(s), 10, 77, 78, 134,
 135, 141, 146, 151, 241
Morris, T., 250n
Muncie, J., 260n, 265n
Murphy, P. J., 255n, 261n, 262n
Murray, B., 114, 115, 257n

National Front, 9, 181–3
Newburn, W. H. T., 255n
Nisbet, R., 265n
Nuttall, J., 260n
nutter(s), 212
Nutty Turn Out, 179

occupational structure, 87, 88,
 126ff, 240
Operation Full Time, 251n
Operation Own Goal, 262n, 264n
ordered segmentation, 185, 199ff,
 208ff, 230ff
Orwell, G., 127, 258n

Pardoe, R., 111, 257n
Pareto, V., 265n
Parker, H.; 264n, 265n
participatory democracy, 25, 30
patriarchy, 83, 212
Pearson, G., 64, 84, 87, 88, 112,
 254n, 256n, 257n, 260n
permissiveness, permissive
 society, 13, 16–19
pitch invasions, 6, 24, 26, 74, 91,
 92, 101–5, 174, 175 (see also,

crowd breakthroughs,
 encroachments)
police, and the lower working-
 class, 228, 229
policing, of football matches, 5,
 20, 23, 58, 68, 71, 77, 102, 103,
 104, 105, 138, 176, 178, 179,
 248
Popper, K. R., 265n
Popplewell Inquiry, 181, 182,
 190, 261n
Powellism, 171
power resources, of lower
 working-class, 206
professionalization, 25, 26, 32,
 39ff, 75
proletarianization, of the
 terraces, 78
punishments and controls, 4, 5,
 178, 179, 235, 238

'real' violence, 19
Red Army (Manchester United),
 173–7
Reiner, R., 266n
resistance, 25, 120, 218–20, 232
ritual aggression, aggressive
 action, 19–21
ritualized aggression, theory of,
 19–23
Roberts, B., 252n, 263n
Robertson, T., 257n
Robins, D., 166, 172, 175, 200,
 260n, 261n, 263n
rockers, 138, 157, 169
Rosser, E., 13, 23 (see also,
 Marsh, P.)
Rugby Union, 39, 77, 118

Sanford, R. N., 264n
Scottish fans, 113–17, 143
Seabrook, J., 260n
segmental organization, 206
segregation and penning, 4, 5, 6,
 23, 145, 167–9
self-fulfilling prophecy, of media
 representations, 10

sensationalized reporting, 11, 134, 151ff
Service Crew, 179
sexual segregation, 87, 197, 201, 202, 209, 212
Shipman, L., 175
Short, J. F., 264n
Siann, G., 263n
skinheads, 17, 27, 157, 169–73, 198, 199
Smith, D. J., 265n, 266n
Smith, F. E., 41, 253n
soccer casuals, 213
soccer consciousness, 24, 25
sociogenesis, sociogenetic approach, 1, 236
solidarity, of goal-terrace fans, 5
songs and chants, 3, 7, 8, 12, 153, 164, 165
spectacularization, 25, 26, 75
Spinley, B. M., 264n
Sports Council – SSRC Report, 3, 250n
state-formation, state-control, 203, 222, 224ff
street economies, 127, 129, 204
street life, 85ff
street smartness, 204, 206, 212
street corner gangs, 201–3, 230
strikes, 121–4
Strodbeck, F. L., 264n
structural properties, of stratified societies, 22
Stuttard, I., 188, 251n, 261n
superhooligans, 17, 157, 177–81
suppression of aggression, 224
Suttles, G., 185, 199ff, 230, 262n, 263n
swearing, 44, 55–7, 74, 77, 97
symbolic demasculinization, 8
symbolic violence, 19

tax monopoly, 224
Taylor, I., 13, 18, 21, 23, 24–30, 34, 53, 74, 75, 236, 239, 250n, 251n, 252n, 267n
Tebbit, N., 18, 251n

teddy boys, 138, 139, 140, 141, 157, 161–4
territorial identifications, 201, 204ff
Thatcher, M., 247
Thatcherism, 28
Thorne, G., 42
train-wrecking, 109, 110, 139, 140, 142, 164
triggers, of hooligan incidents, 14, 15
Trivizas, E., 186, 187, 262n

underclass, 27, 211, 219, 221
unemployment, 13, 16–19, 27, 28, 123, 124–6, 187, 190, 204, 205, 213, 239, 240
upper-class hooliganism, 265n

Vamplew, W., 30, 50, 53, 252n
vandalism, 64–7, 109
violence, on the field of play, 13–16

Waddington, I., 255n
Wagg, S., 259n
Walvin, J., 34, 253n
White, J., 256n, 260n
Williams, J., 261n, 262n
Willis, P., 204, 263n, 264n, 265n
Wilmott, P., 263n
work experiences, of lower working-class, 204, 205
working class: 27, 28, 30, 34ff, 39, 40, 55, 78ff, 120ff, 133, 146, 157ff, 184; male aggressiveness, 88–90, 193ff; rough-respectable division, 28, 36, 81, 83, 84, 85, 128, 154, 155, 156, 163, 203, 210, 211, 212–16, 221, 227ff; violence, structural sources of, 82ff
World Cup Finals (1966), 17, 133, 148–51, 155

Young, J., 265n, 267n
Young, M., 263n
Young, P. F., 254n

Young, T. F., 86, 262n
youth, 3, 25, 26, 29, 85ff, 138, 141, 143, 145, 155, 159–61, 163, 198, 218–21, 234, 235